西方社会与文化丛书

美国社会与文化

American Society and Culture

主　编　李冰雯

副主编　周　爽　袁　燕

西北工业大学出版社

【内容简介】 本书是为了帮助大学生掌握美国社会与文化的基础知识，拓展大学生人文知识的深度和广度，促进学生综合素质的提高而编写的。更重要的是为了激发和增强其英语语言学习的兴趣，提高英语水平。全书介绍了美国的地理环境、民族特点、种族关系、历史发展、政治制度、宗教信仰，教育制度，生活习惯，饮食娱乐，节日民俗，新闻媒介，文学艺术等，适合非英语专业本科生阅读。

图书在版编目(CIP)数据

美国社会与文化：英文/李冰雯主编. —西安：西北工业大学出版社，2012.3
(西方社会与文化丛书)
ISBN 978-7-5612-3326-9

Ⅰ.①美… Ⅱ.①李… Ⅲ.①英语—语言读物②美国—概况
Ⅳ.①H319.4:K

中国版本图书馆CIP数据核字(2012)第038609号

出版发行：西北工业大学出版社
通信地址：西安市友谊西路127号　　**邮编**：710072
电　　话：(029)88493844　88491757
网　　址：www.nwpup.com
印 刷 者：陕西向阳印务有限公司
开　　本：727 mm×960 mm　1/16
印　　张：18.125
字　　数：385千字
版　　次：2012年3月第1版　　2012年3月第1次印刷
定　　价：35.00元

前　言

当今世界，经济全球化、科技一体化、文化多元化、信息网络化的发展趋势加快，世界各国之间的竞争日趋激烈，这对我国的专业人才提出了新的挑战，对人才培养和教材建设提出了新的更高的要求。如何培养具有国际视野和创新能力的人才，是国家、社会和高校教师共同关注的问题，也是教材编撰者和教材出版者关心和重视的问题。

本书是为了帮助大学生掌握美国社会与文化的基础知识，拓展大学生人文知识的深度和广度，促进学生综合素质的提高而编写的。更重要的是为了激发和增强其英语语言学习的兴趣，提高英语水平。

本书针对非英语专业本科生编写，不仅介绍了美国的地理环境、民族特点、种族关系、历史发展、政治制度、宗教信仰、教育制度、生活习惯、饮食娱乐、节日民俗、新闻媒介、美国文学等，还在每个单元后设计了若干培养学生思辨能力的讨论题目。后续还将编写《英国社会与文化》等，形成系列教材。

本书编者具有在美国学习和生活的经历，因此，在编写过程中除参考大量书籍与网络资料外，也将在美国的所闻所感融汇其中。同时，为了增强教材的趣味性和时代感，还附有大量辅助阅读材料，使得社会与文化的方方面面生动地展示出来，也为学生接触地道的英语提供了条件。不过这也不可避免地出现了材料中语言较难或篇章较长的现象，因此辅助材料由学生根据情况选择阅读，或教师指导阅读。

在编写本书的过程中，我们受到了很多研究美国的学者们的启发，感谢不尽。尤其要感谢网络百科全书的大量有价值的资料。

鉴于水平有限，编写时间仓促，书中尚有许多不足之处，恳请读者指正。

编　者

2012 年 1 月

目　录

Chapter 1 Panoramic View

1.1 Overview

The United States of America (commonly referred to as the United States, the US, the USA, or America) is a federal constitutional republic comprising fifty states and a federal district. The country is situated mostly in central North America, where its forty-eight contiguous(相连的)states and Washington, D. C., the capital district, lie between the Pacific and Atlantic Oceans, bordered by Canada to the north and Mexico to the south. The state of Alaska is in the northwest of the continent, with Canada to its east and Russia to the west across the Bering Strait. The state of Hawaii is an archipelago(群岛)in the mid-Pacific. The country also possesses several territories, or insular(岛屿的)areas, in the Caribbean(加勒比海) and Pacific.

At 3.79 million square miles (9.83 million km^2) and with about 308 million people, the United States is the third or fourth largest country by total area, and the third largest by land area and population. The United States is one of the world's most ethnically diverse and multicultural nations, the product of large-scale immigration from many countries. The US economy is the largest national economy in the world, with an estimated 2008 gross domestic product (GDP) of US $14.4 trillion (a quarter of nominal global GDP and a fifth of global GDP at purchasing power parity). It is a leading economic, political, and cultural force in the world.

Indigenous(土著的) peoples, probably of Asian descent, have inhabited what is now the mainland United States for many thousands of years. This Native American population was greatly reduced by disease and warfare after European contact. The United States was founded by thirteen British colonies located along the Atlantic seaboard. On July 4, 1776, they issued the Declaration of Independence, which proclaimed their right to self-determination and their establishment of a cooperative union. The rebellious states defeated Great Britain in the American Revolutionary War, the first successful colonial war of independence. The Philadelphia Convention adopted the current United States Constitution on September 17, 1787; its ratification(批准) the following year made the states part of a single republic with a strong central government. The Bill of Rights, comprising ten constitutional amendments guaranteeing many fundamental civil rights and freedoms, was ratified in 1791.

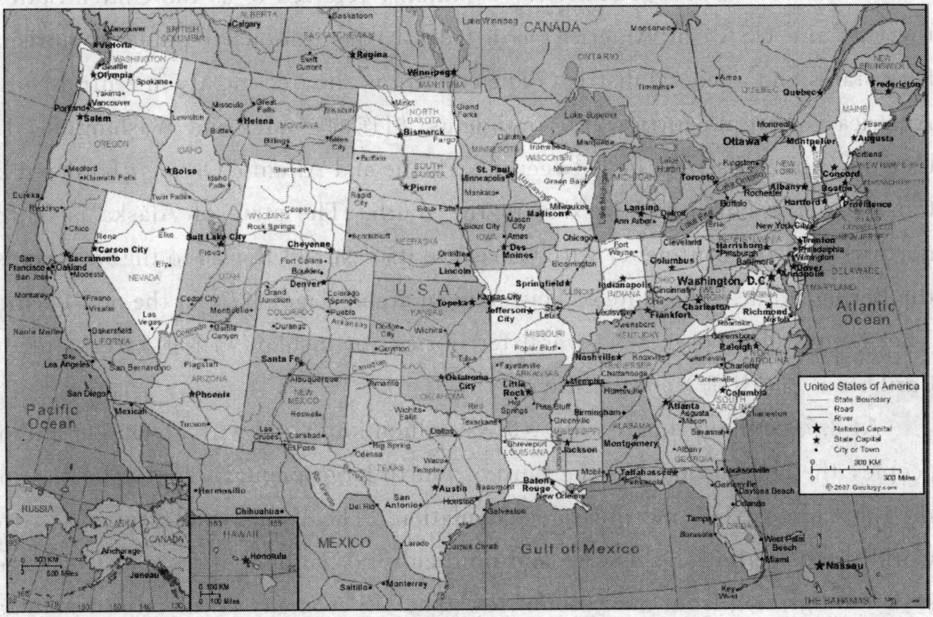

Map of the United States

In the 19th century, the United States acquired land from France, Spain, the United Kingdom, Mexico, and Russia, and annexed(并吞) the Republic of Texas and the Republic of Hawaii. Disputes between the agrarian South and industrial North over states' rights and the expansion of the institution of slavery provoked the American Civil War of the 1860s. The North's victory prevented a permanent split of the country and led to the end of legal slavery in the United States. By the 1870s, the national economy was the world's largest. The

Spanish—American War and World War I confirmed the country's status as a military power. It emerged from World War Ⅱ as the first country with nuclear weapons and a permanent member of the United Nations Security Council. The end of the Cold War and the dissolution of the Soviet Union left the United States as the sole superpower. The country accounts for two-fifths of global military spending and is a leading economic, political, and cultural force in the world.

American Culture

The development of the culture of the United States of America — History, Holidays, Sports, Religion, Cuisine(烹饪), Literature, Poetry, Music, Dance, Visual Arts, Cinema, and Architecture — has been marked by a tension between two strong sources of inspiration: European ideals, especially British, and domestic originality.

American culture encompasses traditions, ideals, customs, beliefs, values, arts, and innovations developed both domestically and imported via colonization and immigration. Prevalent ideas and ideals from the European continent such as Democracy, various forms of Monotheism(一神论), and Civil liberties are present as well as those which evolved domestically such as important National holidays, uniquely American sports, proud military tradition, innovations in the arts and entertainment, and a strong sense of national pride among the population as a whole.

It includes both conservative and liberal elements, military and scientific competitiveness, political structures, risk taking and free expression, materialist and moral elements.

It also includes elements which evolved from Native Americans, and other ethnic subcultures; most prominently the culture of former African-American slaves and different cultures fromLatin America. Many cultural elements, especially popular culture have been exported across the globe through modern mass media, but a few of the cultural elements have remained rather exclusive to North America.

1.2 Geography of the United States

Physiographic(地形的)Divisions

The eastern United States has a varied topography(地形学). A broad, flat coastal plain lines the Atlantic and Gulf shores from the Texas-Mexico border to New York City, and includes the Florida peninsula. Areas further inland feature rolling hills and temperate forests. The Appalachian Mountains form a line of low mountains separating the eastern seaboard from the Great Lakes and the Mississippi Basin. The five Great Lakes are located in the north-central portion of the country, four of them forming part of the border with Canada. The southeast United States contain subtropical forests and, near the gulf coast, mangrove(红树林) wetlands, especially in Florida. West of the Appalachians(阿巴拉契亚山脉[北美洲]) lies the Mississippi River basin and two large eastern tributaries, the Ohio River and the Tennessee River. The Ohio and Tennessee Valleys and the Midwest consist largely of rolling hills and productive farmland, stretching south to the Gulf Coast.

The Great Plains lie west of the Mississippi River and east of the Rocky Mountains. A large portion of the country's agricultural products are grown in the Great Plains. Before their general conversion to farmland, the Great Plains were noted for their extensive grasslands, from tallgrass prairie(草原) in the eastern plains to shortgrass steppe(大草原)in the western High Plains. Elevation rises gradually from less than a few hundred feet near the Mississippi River to more than a mile high in the High Plains. The generally low relief(地貌) of the plains is broken in several places, most notably in the Ozark and Ouachita(美国中南部沃希托山脉)Mountains, which form the US Interior Highlands, the only major mountainous region between the Rocky Mountains and the Appalachian Mountains. The Great Plains come to an abrupt end at the Rocky Mountains. The Rocky Mountains form a large portion of the Western US, entering from Canada and stretching nearly to Mexico. The Rocky Mountains generally contain fairly mild slopes and low peaks compared to many of the other great mountain ranges, with a few exceptions (such as the Teton Mountains in Wyoming and the Sawatch Range in Colorado). In addition, instead of being one generally continuous and solid mountain range, it is broken up into a number of smaller, intermittent mountain ranges, forming a large series of basins and valleys.

West of the Rocky Mountains lies the Intermontane Plateaus (also known as the Intermountain West), a large, arid desert lying between the Rockies and the Cascades and Sierra Nevada(内华达山脉) ranges. The large southern portion, known as the Great Basin, consists of salt flats, drainage basins, and many small north-south mountain ranges. The Southwest is predominantly a low-lying desert region. A portion known as the Colorado Plateau, centered around the Four Corners region, is considered to have some of the most spectacular scenery in the world. It is accentuated in such national parks as Grand Canyon, Arches, and Bryce Canyon, among others.

The Intermontane Plateaus come to an end at the Cascade Range and the Sierra Nevada. The Cascades consist of largely intermittent, volcanic mountains rising prominently from the surrounding landscape. The Sierra Nevada, further south, is a high, rugged, and dense mountain range. It contains the highest point in the contiguous 48 states, Mount Whitney (14,505 ft; 4,421 m). These areas contain some spectacular scenery as well, as evidenced by such national parks as Yosemite and Mount Rainier. West of the Cascades and Sierra Nevada is a series of valleys, such as the Central Valley in California and the Willamette Valley in Oregon. Along the coast is a series of low mountain ranges known as the Pacific Coast Ranges. Much of the Pacific Northwest coast is inhabited by some of the densest vegetation outside of the Tropics, and also the tallest trees in the world (the Redwoods).

Alaska contains some of the most dramatic and untapped scenery in the country. Tall, prominent mountain ranges rise up sharply from broad, flat tundra(苔原)plains. On the islands off the south and southwest coast are many volcanoes. Hawaii, far to the south of Alaska in the Pacific Ocean, is a chain of tropical, volcanic islands, popular as a tourist destination for many from East Asia and the mainland United States.

The geography of the United States varies across their immense area. Within the continental US, eight distinct physiographic divisions exist, though each is composed of several smaller physiographic subdivisions. These major divisions are:

• Laurentian Upland—part of the Canadian Shield that extends into the northern United States Great Lakes area.

• Atlantic Plain—the coastal regions of the eastern and southern parts includes the continental shelf, the Atlantic Coast and the Gulf Coast.

• Appalachian Highlands—lying on the eastern side of the United States, it includes the Appalachian Mountains, the Watchung Mountains, the Adirondacks and New England province originally containing the Great Eastern Forest.

• Interior Plains—part of the interior contentintal United States, it includes much of what is called the Great Plains.

• Interior Highlands—also part of the interior contentintal United States, this division includes the Ozark Plateau.

• Rocky Mountain System—one branch of the Cordilleran system lying far inland in the western states.

• Intermontane Plateaus—also divided into the Columbia Plateau, the Colorado Plateau and the Basin and Range Province, it is a system of plateaus, basins, ranges and gorges between the Rocky and Pacific Mountain Systems. It is the setting for the Grand Canyon, the Great Basin and Death Valley.

• Pacific Mountain System—the coastal mountain ranges and features in the west coast of the United States.

1.3 Climate & Environment

Climate of the United States

The United States includes a wide variety of climate types due to its large size, range of geographic features, and noncontiguous arrangement. In the contiguous United States to the east of the 100th meridian(子午线), the climate ranges from humid continental in the north to humid subtropical in the south. The southern tip of Florida is tropical. The Great Plains west of the 100th meridian are semi-arid. Much of the Rocky Mountains, the Sierra Nevada, and the Cascade Range are alpine(高山气候). The climate is arid in the Great Basin, desert in the Southwest, Mediterranean(地中海气候) in coastal California, and oceanic in coastal Oregon and Washington. The state of Alaska—on the northwestern corner of the North American continent—is largely subarctic, with an oceanic climate in its southern edge and a polar climate in the north. The archipelago state of Hawaii, in the middle of the Pacific Ocean, is tropical.

Extreme weather is not uncommon—the states bordering the Gulf of Mexico are prone to hurricanes, and tornadoes(龙卷风) regularly occur in the area of the Midwest referred to as Tornado Alley. The United States has more tornadoes than the rest of the world combined

Environment of the United States

Biota

With habitats ranging from tropical to Arctic, US plant life is very diverse. The country has more than 17,000 identified native species of flora(植物群), including 5,000 in California (home to the tallest, the most massive, and the oldest trees in the world). More than 400 mammal, 700 bird, 500 reptile(爬行类) and amphibian(两栖), and 90,000 insect species have been documented. Wetlands such as the Florida Everglades are the base for much of this diversity. The country's ecosystems include thousands of nonnative exotic species that often harm indigenous plant and animal communities.

Many plant and animal species became extinct soon after first human settlement, including the North American megafauna(巨型动物); others have become nearly extinct since European settlement, among them the American Bison(野牛) and California Condor(秃鹫).

Environmental Law and Conservation

In 1872, the world's first national park was established at Yellowstone. Another fifty-seven national parks and hundreds of other federally managed parks and forests have since been formed. Wilderness areas have been established around the country to ensure long-term protection of pristine habitats.

Altogether, the US government regulates 1,020,779 square miles (2,643,807 km^2), 28.8% of the country's total land area. Protected parks and forestland constitute most of this. As of March 2004, approximately 16% of public land under Bureau of Land Management administration was being leased for commercial oil and natural gas drilling; public land is also leased for mining and cattle ranching.

1.4 American Dream

The American Dream is a national ethos(民族精神)of the United States of America in which democratic ideals are perceived as a promise of prosperity for its people. In the American Dream, first expressed by James Truslow Adams in 1931, citizens of every rank feel that they can achieve a "better, richer, and happier life". The idea of the American Dream is rooted in the second sentence of the Declaration of Independence which states that "all men are created equal" and that they have "certain inalienable Rights" including "Life, Liberty and the pursuit of Happiness".

The "American Dream" has been credited with helping to build a cohesive American experience but has also been blamed for overinflated expectations. The presence of the American Dream has not historically helped the majority of minority race and lower class American citizens to gain a greater degree of social equality and influence. Instead, the American wealth structure has often been observed to sustain class differences in which well-positioned groups continue to be advantaged.

In common parlance, the term American Dream is often used as a synonym for home ownership since homes have historically been seen as status symbols separating the middle classes and the poor. This usage, though, while common, is generally considered a very specific use of a more general term.

Since the early 19th century, the United States has regarded and promoted itself as a beacon of liberty and prosperity achieved through a combination of the philosophical and ethical principles propounded by its founders and implemented in their most perfect form. In tandem with this is its natural wealth and bounty within the New World.

The meaning of the 'American Dream' has evolved over the course of American history. While historically traced to the New World mystique — the availability of land and the continuing American expansion—the ethos today simply indicates the ability, through participation in the resonant society and culture of the United States, to bring prosperity to oneself.

America has been viewed as a land in which one's prospects in life are defined by one's talents and energy rather than by one's family wealth or political connections.

According to the dream, this includes the opportunity for one's children to grow up and receive an American education and its consequent career opportunities. It is the opportunity to make individual choices without the restrictions of class, caste, religion, race, or ethnic group.

According to researcher Tommi Uschanov, "american dream" actually characterizes better European societies in which people who born to lower social classes are—according to statistical data—more likely to reach upper social classes during their lives than in the United States.

Historian and writer James Truslow Adams coined the phrase "American Dream" in his 1931 book Epic of America:

> "The American Dream is that dream of a land in which life should be better and richer and fuller for everyone, with opportunity for each according to ability or achievement. It is a difficult dream for the European upper classes to interpret adequately, and too many of us ourselves have grown weary and mistrustful of it. It is not a dream of motor cars and high wages merely, but a dream of social order in which each man and each woman shall be able to attain to the fullest stature of which they are innately capable, and be recognized by others for what they are, regardless of the fortuitous (偶然的) circumstances of birth or position."

In recent years, the concept of the American Dream as a national ideal has been studied by various organizations. The conclusions of these studies indicate that during the 1990s to the 2000s, a period of remarkable wealth for the US, an increasing number of people confess to having lost faith in the American Dream.

Questions

1. Three primary characteristics of the American landscape are its insulation from Europe and Asia (by the Atlantic and Pacific oceans), its expanse and variety of resources, and its natural network of waterways. How have these physical features encouraged national integration of the country?

2. Describe the geography of three or four regions in the United States.

3. Why is tornado a unique American climate phenomenon?

4. Discuss the importance of Mississippi River and Rocky Mountains?

5. How do you think of "American Dream"?

Supplementary Reading 1

The Gift of Tongues

By Michael Erard

What makes some people learn language after language?

Babel No More: The Search for the World's Most Extraordinary Language Learners

CARDINAL MEZZOFANTI of Bologna was a secular saint. Though he never performed the kind of miracle needed to be officially canonised, his power was close to unearthly. Mezzofanti was said to speak 72 languages. Or 50. Or to have fully mastered 30. No one was certain of the true figure, but it was a lot. Visitors flocked from all corners of Europe to test him and came away stunned. He could switch between languages with ease. Two condemned prisoners were due to be executed, but no one knew their language to hear their confession. Mezzofanti learned it in a night, heard their sins the next morning and saved them from hell.

Or so the legend goes. In "Babel No More", Michael Erard has written the first serious book about the people who master vast numbers of languages—or claim to. A journalist with some linguistics training, Mr. Erard is not a hyperpolyglot himself (he speaks some Spanish and Chinese), but he approaches his topic with both wonder and a healthy dash of scepticism.

Mezzofanti, for example, was a high-ranking clergyman born in 1774. In most of his interactions, he would have been the one to pick the topic of conversation, and he could rely on the same formulae he had used many times. He lived in an age when "knowing" a language more often meant reading and translating rather than speaking fluently with natives. Nonetheless, Mezzofanti clearly had speaking talent; his English accent was so good as to be almost too correct, an Irish observer noted.

To find out whether anyone could really learn so many languages, Mr. Erard set out to find modern Mezzofantis. The people he meets are certainly interesting. One man with a mental age of nine has a vast memory for foreign words and the use of grammatical endings, but he cannot seem to break free of English word-order. Ken Hale, who was a linguist at the Massachusetts Institute of Technology and died in 2001, was said to have learned 50 languages, including notoriously difficult Finnish while on a flight to Helsinki. Professional linguists still swear by his talent. But he insisted he spoke only three (English, Spanish and Warlpiri—from Australia's Northern Territory) and could merely "talk in" others.

Mr. Erard says that true hyperpolyglottery begins at about 11 languages, and that while legends abound, tried and tested exemplars are few. Ziad Fazah, raised in Lebanon and now living in Brazil, once held the Guinness world record for 58 languages. But when surprised on a Chilean television show by native speakers, he utterly flubbed questions in Finnish, Mandarin, Farsi and Russian (including "What day is it today?" in Russian), a failure that lives in infamy on YouTube. Perhaps he was a fraud; perhaps he simply had a miserable day. Hyperpolyglots must warm up or "prime" their weaker languages, with a few hours' or days' practice, to use them comfortably. Switching quickly between more than around six or seven is near-impossible even for the most gifted.

Does that mean they don't really know them? Is instant availability of native-like competence the only standard for "knowing" a language? How should partly knowing a tongue be tallied? What if you can only read in it? Mr. Erard repeatedly peppers his text with such questions, feeling his way through his story as a thoughtful observer, rather than banging about like an academic with a theory to defend or a pitchman with a technique to sell.

Hyperpolyglots are more likely to be introverted than extroverted, which may come as a surprise to some. Hale's son always said that, in his father's case, languages were a cloak for a shy man. Another, Alexander Arguelles, has learned dozens of languages only to read them, saying "It's rare that you have an interesting conversation in English. Why do I think it would be any better in another language?" Emil Krebs, an early-20th-century German diplomat who was also credited with knowing dozens of languages, was boorish in all of them. He once refused to speak to his wife for several months because she told him to put on a winter coat.

Different hypotheses may explain part of the language-learner's gift. Some hyperpolyglots seem near-autistic. In support, Mr Erard points to the theory of Simon Baron-Cohen, of Cambridge University, that autists have an "extreme male brain" that seeks to master systems. Another hypothesis is the "Geschwind-Galaburda" cluster of traits. Supposedly resulting from abnormal antenatal exposure to hormones, this cluster includes maleness, homosexuality, left-handedness, poor visual-spatial skills, immune disorders, and perhaps also language-learning talent. Brain areas are also keyed to certain skills. The left Heschl's gyrus is bigger than average in professional phoneticians. People who learn new vocabulary quickly show more activity in the hippocampus. Krebs's brain, preserved in slices at a laboratory in Düsseldorf, shows various unusual features.

The discovery of the FOXP2 brain gene, a mutation of which can cause language loss, was met with considerable excitement when it was announced over a decade ago. But the reality is that many parts of the brain work together to produce speech and no single gene, region of the brain or theory can explain successful language-learning. In the end Mr Erard is happy simply to meet interesting characters, tell fascinating tales and round up the research without trying to judge which is the best work.

At the end of his story, however, he finds a surprise in Mezzofanti's archive: flashcards. Stacks of them, in Georgian, Hungarian, Arabic, Algonquin and nine other tongues. The world's most celebrated hyperpolyglot relied on the same tools given to first-year language-learners today. The conclusion? Hyperpolyglots may begin with talent, but they aren't geniuses. They simply enjoy tasks that are drudgery to normal people. The talent and enjoyment drive a virtuous cycle that pushes them to feats others simply shake their heads at, admiration mixed with no small amount of incomprehension.

*http://www.economist.com/node/*21542170

Supplementary Reading 2

Harder for Americans to Rise from Lower Rungs

By Jasondeparle

WASHINGTON — Benjamin Franklin did it. Henry Ford did it. And American life is built on the faith that others can do it, too: rise from humble origins to economic heights. "Movin' on up", George Jefferson-style, is not only a sitcom song but a civil religion.

But many researchers have reached a conclusion that turns conventional wisdom on its head: Americans enjoy less economic mobility than their peers in Canada and much of Western Europe. The mobility gap has been widely discussed in academic circles, but a sour season of mass unemployment and street protests has moved the discussion toward center stage.

Former Senator Rick Santorum of Pennsylvania, a Republican candidate for president, warned this fall that movement "up into the middle income is actually greater, the mobility in Europe, than it is in America." National Review, a conservative thought leader, wrote that "most Western European and English-speaking nations have higher rates of mobility." Even Representative Paul D. Ryan, a Wisconsin Republican who argues that overall mobility remains high, recently wrote that "mobility from the very bottom up" is "where the United States lags behind."

Liberal commentators have long emphasized class, but the attention on the right is largely new.

"It's becoming conventional wisdom that the US does not have as much mobility as most other advanced countries," said Isabel V. Sawhill, an economist at the Brookings Institution. "I don't think you'll find too many people who will argue with that."

One reason for the mobility gap may be the depth of American poverty, which leaves poor children starting especially far behind. Another may be the unusually large premiums that American employers pay for college degrees. Since children generally follow their parents' educational trajectory, that premium increases the importance of family background and stymies people with less schooling.

At least five large studies in recent years have found the United States to be less mobile than comparable nations. A project led by Markus Jantti, an economist at a Swedish university, found that 42 percent of American men raised in the bottom fifth of incomes stay there as adults. That shows a level of persistent disadvantage much higher than in Denmark (25 percent) and Britain (30 percent) — a country famous for its class constraints.

Meanwhile, just 8 percent of American men at the bottom rose to the top fifth. That compares with 12 percent of the British and 14 percent of the Danes.

Despite frequent references to the United States as a classless society, about 62 percent of Americans (male and female) raised in the top fifth of incomes stay in the top two-fifths, according to research by the Economic Mobility Project of the Pew Charitable Trusts. Similarly, 65 percent born in the bottom fifth stay in the bottom two-fifths.

By emphasizing the influence of family background, the studies not only challenge American identity but speak to the debate about inequality. While liberals often complain that the United States has unusually large income gaps, many conservatives have argued that the system is fair because mobility is especially high, too: everyone can climb the ladder. Now the evidence suggests that America is not only less equal, but also less mobile.

John Bridgeland, a former aide to President George W. Bush who helped start Opportunity Nation, an effort to seek policy solutions, said he was "shocked" by the international comparisons. "Republicans will not feel compelled to talk about income inequality," Mr. Bridgeland said. "But they will feel a need to talk about a lack of mobility — a lack of access to the American Dream."

While Europe differs from the United States in culture and demographics, a more telling comparison may be with Canada, a neighbor with significant ethnic diversity. Miles Corak, an economist at the University of Ottawa, found that just 16 percent of Canadian men raised in the bottom tenth of incomes stayed there as adults, compared with 22 percent of Americans. Similarly, 26 percent of American men raised at the top tenth stayed there, but just 18 percent of Canadians.

"Family background plays more of a role in the US than in most comparable countries," Professor Corak said in an interview.

Skeptics caution that the studies measure "relative mobility" — how likely children are to move from their parents' place in the income distribution. That is different from asking whether they have more money. Most Americans have higher incomes than their parents because the country has grown richer.

Some conservatives say this measure, called absolute mobility, is a better gauge of opportunity. A Pewstudy found that 81 percent of Americans have higher incomes than their parents (after accounting for family size). There is no comparable data on other countries.

Since they require two generations of data, the studies also omit immigrants, whose upward movement has long been considered an American strength. "If America is so poor in economic mobility, maybe someone should tell all these people who still want to come to the US," said Stuart M. Butler, an analyst at the Heritage Foundation.

The income compression in rival countries may also make them seem more mobile. Reihan Salam, a writer for The Daily and National Review Online, has calculated that a Danish family can move from the 10th percentile to the 90th percentile with \$45,000 of additional earnings, while an American family would need an additional \$93,000.

Even by measures of relative mobility, Middle America remains fluid. About 36 percent of Americans raised in the middle fifth move up as adults, while 23 percent stay on the same rung and 41 percent move down, according to Pew research. The "stickiness" appears at the top and bottom, as affluent families transmit their advantages and poor families stay trapped.

While Americans have boasted of casting off class since Poor Richard's Almanac, until recently there has been little data.

Pioneering work in the early 1980s by Gary S. Becker, a Nobel laureate in economics, found only a mild relationship between fathers' earnings and those of their sons. But when better data became available a decade later, another prominent economist, Gary Solon, found the bond twice as strong. Most researchers now estimate the "elasticity" of father-son earnings at 0.5, which means if one man earns \$100,000 more than another, his sons would earn \$50,000 more on average than the sons of the poorer man.

In 2006 Professor Corak reviewed more than 50 studies of nine countries. He ranked Canada, Norway, Finland and Denmark as the most mobile, with the United States and Britain roughly tied at the other extreme. Sweden, Germany, and France were scattered across the middle.

The causes of America's mobility problem are a topic of dispute — starting with the debates over poverty. The United States maintains a thinner safety net than other rich countries, leaving more children vulnerable to debilitating hardships.

Poor Americans are also more likely than foreign peers to grow up with single mothers. That places them at an elevated risk of experiencing poverty and related problems, a point frequently made by Mr. Santorum, who surged into contention in the Iowa caucuses. The United States also has uniquely high incarceration rates, and a longer history of racial stratification than its peers.

"The bottom fifth in the US looks very different from the bottom fifth in other countries," said Scott Winship, a researcher at the Brookings Institution, who wrote the article for National Review. "Poor Americans have to work their way up from a lower floor."

A second distinguishing American trait is the pay tilt toward educated workers. While in theory that could help poor children rise — good learners can become high earners — more often it favors the children of the educated and affluent, who have access to better schools and arrive in them more prepared to learn.

"Upper-income families can invest more in their children's education and they may have a better understanding of what it takes to get a good education," said Eric Wanner, president of the Russell Sage Foundation, which gives grants to social scientists.

The United States is also less unionized than many of its peers, which may lower wages among the least skilled, and has public health problems, like obesity and diabetes, which can limit education and employment.

Perhaps another brake on American mobility is the sheer magnitude of the gaps between rich and the rest — the theme of the Occupy Wall Street protests, which emphasize the power of the privileged to protect their interests. Countries with less equality generally have less mobility.

Mr. Salam recently wrote that relative mobility "is overrated as a social policy goal" compared with raising incomes across the board. Parents naturally try to help their children, and a completely mobile society would mean complete insecurity: anyone could tumble any time.

But he finds the stagnation at the bottom alarming and warns that it will worsen. Most of the studies end with people born before 1970, while wage gaps, single motherhood and incarceration increased later. Until more recent data arrives, he said, "we don't know the half of it."

http://www.nytimes.com/2012/01/05/us/harder-for-americans-to-rise-from-lower-rungs.html? scp=2&sq=American%20dream&st=cse

Chapter 2 A Nation of Immigration

American immigration (emigration to the United States of America) refers to the movement of non-residents to the United States. Immigration has been a major source of population growth and cultural change throughout much of American history. The economic, social, and political aspects of immigration have caused controversy regarding ethnicity, religion, economic benefits, job growth, settlement patterns, environmental impact, impact on upward social mobility, levels of criminality, nationalities, political loyalties, moral values, and work habits. As of 2006, the United States accepts more legal immigrants as permanent residents than any other country in the world. In 2006, the number of immigrants totaled 37.5 million.

A record 1,046,539 persons were naturalized as US citizens in 2008. The leading countries of birth of the new citizens were Mexico, India and the Philippines.

The Statue of Liberty was a common sight to many immigrants who entered the United States through Ellis Island

While an influx of new residents from different cultures presents some challenges, "the United States has always been energized by its immigrant populations..." At the 1998 commencement address at Portland State University, US president Bill Clinton voiced support for immigrants, including immigrants from Asia and Latin America when he said that "America has constantly drawn strength and spirit from wave after wave of immigrants ... They have proved to be the most restless, the most adventurous, the most innovative, the most industrious of people."

Given the distance of North America from Eurasia and the difficulty of travel before commercial airlines, most historical US immigration was risky. Passenger aircraft have facilitated travel to the United States since the 1960s, but migration remains difficult, expensive and dangerous for those who cross the United States-Mexico border illegally.

History

American immigration history can be viewed in four epochs: the colonial period, the mid-nineteenth century, the turn of the twentieth, and post-1965. Each epoch brought distinct national groups—and races and ethnicities—to the United States. The mid-nineteenth century saw mainly an influx from northern Europe; the early twentieth-century mainly from Southern and Eastern Europe; post-1965 mostly from Latin America and Asia. From 1836 to 1914, over 30 million Europeans migrated to the United States.

Immigration 15,000 BC - AD 1,500

The first humans in North America are believed to have migrated from northeast Asia, via the Beringia land bridge available during the most recent glaciation. The land bridge was closed when the ice melted about 10,000 years ago. The group of people locked into the Americas at that time developed into most of the various indigenous peoples of the Americas. The Inuit (因纽特人) migration occurred separately and later.

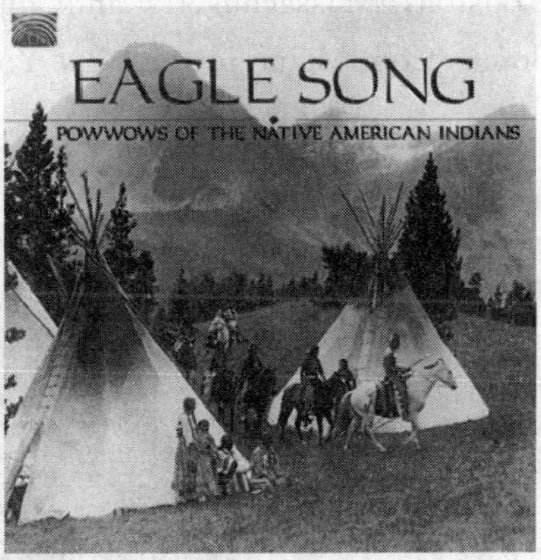

Tepee: Indians' tent made of animal skins and wooden poles

2.1 The Colonial Period

Immigration AD 1500 – 1600

European immigration to the current territory of the US started a few decades after Columbus' discovery in 1492 and was mainly composed of Spaniards.

Immigration AD 1600 – 1790

The first successful English colony in the present-day United States was established as a barely successful business enterprise, after much loss of life, in 1607 in Jamestown, Virginia. Once tobacco was found to be a profitable crop, many plantations were established along the Chesapeake Bay and along the southern rivers and coast.

English Pilgrims (清教徒) established a small settlement near Plymouth, Massachusetts in 1620; much larger numbers of English Puritans (清教徒) came to Boston, Massachusetts and adjacent areas from about 1629 – 1640. The colonies from Maine to the New York border were the New England colonies.

The *Mayflower* transported Pilgrims to the New World in 1620

The Dutch established settlements along the Hudson River in New York starting about 1626. Starting in about 1680 Pennsylvania was settled by Quakers (教友会教徒) and other English, German Protestant(新教徒) sects settling initially around Philadelphia and the Delaware River valley. The earlier colony of New Sweden had settled parts of the lower Delaware River, with immigrants of Swedes, Finns and others. Along with New York, New Jersey and Baltimore, Maryland this is normally considered the core of the middle colonies.

The fourth main colonial center of settlement is the western frontier in the western parts of Pennsylvania and the South which was settled in the early 1700s to late 1700s by mostly Scots-Irish, Scots and others mostly from northern England border lands. Between 250,000 and 400,000 Scots-Irish migrated to America in the 18th century. The Scotch-Irish soon became the dominant culture of the Appalachians from Pennsylvania to Georgia. Areas where people reported 'American' ancestry were the places where, historically, Scottish and Scots-Irish Protestants settled in America: in the interior of the South, and the Appalachian region. It is believed the number of Scottish Americans could be in the region of 20 million and Scots-Irish Americans at 27 million.

The mostly agricultural Southern English colonies initially had very high death rates for new settlers from malaria, yellow fever and other diseases as well as Indian wars. Despite this, a steady flow of new settlers, mostly from central England and the London area, kept the population growing. The large plantations were mostly owned by friends (mostly minor aristocrats) of the British-appointed governors (Sir William Berkeley initially). Many settlers arrived as indentured(契约的) servants who had to work off their passage with five to seven years of work for room and board, clothing etc. only. The wages they earned went to pay for their passage. The same deal was initially offered to some black slaves, but gradually the term of servitude became accepted in the South as life for them. After their terms of indentures, many of the Europeans settled small farms on the frontier or started small businesses in the towns. The Southern colonies were about 55% British, 38% Black and roughly 7% second or third generation German. By 1780, nearly all Blacks were native born with only sporadic additions of new slaves being brought in.

Over half of all European migrants to Colonial America arrived as indentured servants. Around 60,000 convicts were transported to the British colonies in North America in the 18th century.

The colonial western frontier was mainly settled from about 1717－1775 by mostly Presbyterian(长老会的) settlers from northern England border lands, Scotland, and Northern Ireland, fleeing bad times and persecution in those areas. After the American Revolution these same areas in Britain were the first to resume significant immigration. Most initially landed in family groups in Philadelphia or Baltimore but soon migrated to the western frontier where land was cheaper and restrictions less onerous.

2.2 The Old Immigration

Immigration 1790 to 1849

From 1831－1840, immigration increased greatly, to 599,000 total, as 207,000 Irish —even before the Irish Potato Famine (1845－1849)—started to emigrate in large numbers as Britain eased travel restrictions. 152,000 Germans, 76,000 British, and 46,000 French formed the next largest immigrant groups in that decade. From 1841 to 1850, immigration exploded to 1,713,000 total immigrants as at least 781,000 Irish, with the famine of 1845－1849 driving them, fled their homeland to escape poverty and death. Bad potato crops and failed revolutions struck the heart of Europe in 1848, contributing to the decade's total of 435,000 Germans, 267,000 British and 77,000 French immigrants. Bad times in Europe drove people out; land, relatives, freedom, opportunity and jobs in America lured them in.

In 1849, the California Gold Rush spurred significant immigration from Mexico, South America, China, Australia, and Europe. The Gold Rush also caused a mass migration within the US, resulting in California's admittance to the union on September 9, 1850 with a population of about 90,000.

The Mid-nineteenth Century

Immigration 1850 – 1930

Between 1850 and 1930, about 5 million Germans emigrated to the United States with a peak in the years between 1881 and 1885, when a million Germans left Germany and settled mostly in the Midwest. Between 1820 and 1930, 3.5 million British and 4.5 million Irish entered America. Before the 1840s most Irish immigrants were Irish or Scots-Irish Presbyterians. After 1840, Catholics arrived in large numbers, in part because of the famines of the 1840s. Mortality rates of 30% aboard the coffin ships were common.

The 1910s marked the high point of Italian immigration to the United States. Over two million Italians immigrated in those years, with a total of 5.3 million between 1820 and 1980. About a third returned to Italy, after working an average of five years in the US.

About 1.5 million Swedes and Norwegians immigrated to the United States within this period, due to opportunity in America and poverty and religious oppression in united Sweden-Norway. This accounted for around 20% of the total population of the kingdom at that time. They settled mainly in the Midwest, especially Minnesota and the Dakotas. Danes had comparably low immigration rates due to a better economy; after 1900 many Danish immigrants were Mormon converts who moved to Utah.

Over two million Eastern Europeans, mainly Catholics and Jews, immigrated between 1880 and 1924. People of Polish ancestry are the largest Eastern European ancestry group in the United States.

In 1882 Congress passed the Chinese Exclusion Act. The Dillingham Commission was instituted by the United States Congress in 1907 to investigate the effects of immigration on the country. The Commission's analysis of American immigration during the previous three decades led it to conclude that the major source of immigration had shifted from northern and western Europeans to southern and eastern Europeans.

From 1880 to 1924, around two million Jews moved to the United States, mostly seeking better opportunity in America and fleeing the pogroms(大屠杀)of the Russian Empire. After 1933 Jews who tried to flee Nazi Germany were often denied access to the United States.

2.3 New Immigration

The Turn of the Twentieth

New immigration was a term from the late 1880s that came from the influx of immigrants from southern and eastern Europe (areas that previously didn't have large numbers of immigrants) into the United States. Some Americans feared the new arrivals. This raised the issue of whether the US was still a "melting pot", or if it had just become a "dumping ground", and many Americans subsequently became unhappy with this development.

Americans' preference of old immigration rather than new immigration reflected a sudden rise in conservatism. Immigration, although always being a part of American culture, swelled during the 19th century, coinciding with the rise of urban America. Before the "flood" which occurred in the 1870s was a period called "old" immigration. Old immigrants were mostly from Western Europe, especially Britain, Germany, Ireland and Scandinavia. Since most of them, with the exception of the Irish, had Anglo-Saxon or Protestant backgrounds, they were quickly incorporated into American society, welcomed into the "asylum of liberty". However, beginning in 1870, "new" immigration began, with large numbers of people arriving from eastern and southern Europe as well as Asia, Russia, and Japan. They were predominantly Jewish and Catholic(天主教徒), which sparked tensions.

The unfortunate circumstances that the new immigrants arrived in made their image even worse. They came to the new urban America, where disease, overcrowding and crime festered. As a result, relations became openly hostile, with many Americans becoming anti-immigrant, fearing the customs, religion, and poverty of the new immigrants, considering them less desirable than old immigrants. In reality, this perceived difference did not exist; the new immigrants, although seeming different, brought the same sort of values as old ones did. Statistically, they did not commit any more crime or contribute to any more of the misfortunes as any previous immigrant generation.

New immigrants arriving on Ellis island in 1902

By the 1920s, the United States had relatively large populations of many European immigrants spread out over 150 years who had joined the original British descendants majority in America. The foreign born population in the US has never exceeded 15% since before 1675 and has never been a land of immigrant majorities since then. Americans of European ancestry have always been and remain in the majority.

Congress passed the Emergency Quota Act in 1921, followed by the Immigration Act of 1924, which was aimed at further restricting the Southern and Eastern Europeans who had begun to enter the country in large numbers beginning in the 1890s. Most of the European refugees (principally Jews) fleeing the Nazis and World War Ⅱ were barred from coming to the United States.

In 1924, quotas were set for European immigrants so that no more than 2% of the 1890 immigrant stocks were allowed into America. In addition, Congress passed a literacy act in 1917 to curb the influx of low-skilled immigrants from entering the country.

Immigration restrictions laws passed in the 1920s tried to achieve four goals: reduce drastically the number of unskilled immigrants; favor uniting of families by giving preferences to relatives; keeping the ethnic distribution stable by allocating quotas to various ethnic groups; with no quotas initially set for Mexico and Latin America because of the ongoing Mexican Revolution. In 1900, when the US population was 76 million, there were about 500,000 Hispanics.

The Mexican Revolution of 1911 - 1929 killed an estimated one million Mexicans and drove at least a million refugees temporarily into the US Many returned in the 1920s or 1930s. The recorded immigration was 219,000 from 1910 - 1920 and 459,000 from 1920 to 1930. Because of the porous border and the poor or non-existent records from this time period, the real numbers are undoubtedly higher. This recorded number of Mexican immigrants drops to only 23,000 from the decade of 1930 to 1940. Indeed 100,000s returned during the Great Depression either voluntarily or with some US persuasion.

Mulberry Street, along which Manhattan's Little Italy is centered. Lower East Side, circa 1900.

Issue of "Whiteness"

The issue of "whiteness" arose after 1790 when the US congress began to restrict naturalization to "white persons". While the requirements for naturalization changed over time, they still existed in one form or another until 1952. Between 1790 and 1952 there were a reported 52 cases that were brought before various courts arguing whether one was "white". These cases not only forced the courts to define what a "white persons" was, but also explain why someone was white.

The courts offered many different explanations as to who was "white". Over time two methods developed to help determine a persons "whiteness"; common knowledge and scientific evidence. Common knowledge was described as popular, widely held conceptions of race and racial divisions. Scientific evidence, on the other hand, dealt with the naturalistic studies of humankind. These rationales both arose out of the court case In re Ah Yup decided in 1878 by the federal district of California.

By 1909 changes in immigration demographics and scientific definitions created a schism(分裂)between common and scientific knowledge. The court opted for common knowledge because "scientific manipulation" it believed had ignored racial differences by including under Caucasian "far more [people] than the unscientific mind suspects" even some persons the Court described as ranging "in color ... from brown to black". This shift from scientific knowledge to common knowledge demonstrated that race depended on social demarcations (分工).

2.4 Most Recent Immigration

Immigration 1930 – 2000

Immigration patterns of the 1930s were dominated by the Great Depression, which hit the US hard and lasted over ten years there. More people left the US than arrived in some years in the 1930s.

Tydings-McDuffie Act

In 1934, the Tydings-McDuffie Act, which provided for independence of the Philippines on July 4, 1946, stripped Filipinos of their status as US nationals. Until 1965, national origin quotas in the immigration law strictly limited immigration from the Philippines. In 1965, after revision of the immigration law, significant Filipino immigration began, totaling 1,728,000 by 2004.

Jewish Refugees

In 1938, the immigration that never happened is one of the great tragedies of the 20th century as shown in the Evian Conference of 1938. The immigration of the oppressed from Nazi Germany and Adolf Hitler's policies was limited to only a small fraction of those who wanted to leave Germany. Due in part to anti-Semitism(反犹太), isolationism, the Depression and xenophobia(仇外), the immigration policy of the Roosevelt Administration made it very difficult for refugees to obtain entry visas.

Postwar Immigration

In 1945, the War Brides Act allowed foreign-born wives of US citizens who had served in the US armed forces to immigrate to the United States. In 1946, The War Brides Act was extended to include fiancés of American soldiers who were also allowed to immigrate to the United States.

At the end of World War Ⅱ, "regular" immigration almost immediately increased under the official national origins quota system as refugees from war torn Europe started immigrating to the US. After the war, there were jobs for nearly everyone who wanted one, including immigrants, while most women employed during the war went back into the home. From 1941 to 1950, 1,035,000 people immigrated to the US, including 226,000 from Germany, 139,000 from the UK, 171,000 from Canada, 60,000 from Mexico and 57,000 from Italy.

The Displaced Persons (DP) Act of 1948 finally allowed displaced people of World War Ⅱ to start immigrating. Some 200,000 Europeans and 17,000 orphans displaced by World War Ⅱ were initially allowed to immigrate to the United States outside of immigration quotas.

1950s

In 1950, the Korean War left a war ravaged Korea behind. There was little US immigration because of the national origin quotas in the immigration law. In 1965, after revision of the immigration law, significant Korean immigration began, totaling 848,000 by 2004.

In 1954, Operation Wetback forced the return of thousands of illegal immigrants to Mexico. Between 1944 and 1954, "the decade of the wetback", the number of illegal immigrants coming from Mexico increased by 6, 000 percent. It is estimated that, in 1954, before Operation Wetback got under way, more than a million workers had crossed the Rio Grande illegally.

The failed 1956 Hungarian Revolution, before being crushed by the Soviets, forged a temporary hole in the Iron Curtain that allowed a burst of refugees to escape, bringing in 245,000 new Hungarian families to the US by 1960. In the decade of 1950 to 1960, the US had 2,515,000 new immigrants with 477,000 arriving from Germany, 185,000 from Italy, 52,000 new arrivals from Holland, 203,000 from the UK, 46,000 from Japan, 300,000 from Mexico, and 377,000 from Canada.

After the Cuban revolution of 1959, led by Fidel Castro, refugees flowed in from Cuba. An estimated 409, 000 new families had emigrated to the US by 1970.

Hart-Cellar Act

The Immigration and Nationality Act Amendments of 1965 (the Hart-Cellar Act), passed by a Democratic controlled Congress, abolished the system of national-origin quotas. Over 28, 000, 000 have legally immigrated since 1965 under its provisions. Prior to 1965, the US was taking in around 178,000 legal immigrants annually.

The Immigration and Nationality Act Amendments of 1965 removed quotas on large segments of the immigration flow and legal immigration to the US surged. The number of legal immigrants rose from about 2. 5 million in the 1950s to 4. 5 million in the 1970s to 7. 3 million in the 1980s to about 10 million in the 1990s. In 2006, legal immigrants to the United States number approximately 1,000,000 legal immigrants per year of which about 600,000 are Change of Status immigrants who already are in the US Legal immigrants to the United States are at their highest level ever at over 35, 000, 000. Net illegal immigration also soared from about 130,000 per year in the 1970s, to 300,000+ per year in the 1980s to over 500,000 per year in the 1990s to over 700,000 per year in the 2000s. Total illegal immigration may be as high as 1, 500, 000 per year with a net of at least 700,000 more illegal immigrants arriving each year to join the 12,000,000 to 20,000,000 that are already here.

Because of the wide use of family preferences put into immigration law, immigration from then on was mostly "Chain migration" where recent immigrants who were already here sponsored their relatives. Instead of a "national origins system", what the US now has in terms of family-based immigration is an "immigrant origins system" (not as an operation of law) where ever increasing numbers of the recent immigrants sponsor ever increasing numbers of their relatives. However, in employment-based immigration, the "national origins system" still operates. Such a system disfavors countries with large populations such as China. In addition, due to historical immigration policies and laws, most of the citizens of the US are still descended from Europe. The result was that most of legal immigrants now come from Asia and Latin America, and not Europe. Total immigration for the decade totaled 3,321,000 immigrants including about 200,000 each from Germany, Italy and the UK, 400,000 from Canada and 453,000 from Mexico.

The US withdrawal from South Vietnam and the subsequent armed Communist takeover of South Vietnam, Laos, and Cambodia in 1975 brought a new wave of refugees, many of whom spent years in Asian camps waiting to get into the US By 1990, 543,000 Vietnamese family members were settled in the US and 863,000 by 2000. Significant Filipino immigration started with 501,000 family members in 1980, 913,000 in 1990 and 1,222,000 by 2000. South Korean immigration started in 1980 with 290,000 family members in 1980, 568,000 in 1990 and 701,000 in 2000. In 2000, turmoil and war in Central America brought 692,000 family members from the Dominican Republic and 765,000 from El Salvador by 2000. Cuban Americans also continued to grow, with 608,000 family members in 1980, 737,000 in 1990 and 952,000 in 2000.

1980s

In 1986, the Immigration Reform and Control Act (IRCA) was passed, creating for the first time, in theory at least, penalties for employers who hired illegal immigrants. IRCA, as proposed in Congress, was projected to give amnesty to about 1,000,000 undocumented workers. In practice, amnesty for about 3,000,000 immigrants already in the United States was granted. Most were from Mexico. Legal Mexican immigrant family numbers were 2,198,000 in 1980, 4,289,000 in 1990 (includes IRCA) and 7,841,000 in 2000. Adding in another 12,000,000 illegals of which about 80% are thought to be Mexicans would bring the Mexican family total to over 16,000,000—about 16% of the Mexican population.

21st Century

Two new large immigrant groups showed up in 2000: the Chinese with 1,391,000 family members; India with 1,003,000 family members. Both groups were well represented with high levels of expertise and education.

2.5 Contemporary Immigration

Demography(人口统计学)

Current immigration rates are moderate, even though America admitted more legal immigrants from 1991 to 2000 (between 10 - 11 million) than in any previous decade. In the most recent decade, the 10 million legal immigrants that settled in the US represent an annual growth of only about one-third of 1% (as the US population grew from 249 million to 281 million). By comparison, the highest previous decade was 1901-1910 when 8.8 million people arrived increasing the total US population by 1 percent per year as the US population grew from 76 to 92 million during that decade. Specifically, "nearly 15% of Americans were foreign-born in 1910, while in 1999, only about 10% were foreign-born."

"The racial and ethnic identity of the United States is—once again—being remade. The 2000 Census counts some 28 million first generation immigrants among us. This is the highest number in history—often pointed out by anti-immigration lobbyists—but it is not the highest percentage of the foreign-born in relation to the overall population. In 1907, that ratio was 14 percent; today it is

10 percent."

Legal immigration to the US increased from 250,000 in the 1930s, 2.5 million in the 1950s, 4.5 million in the 1970s, and 7.3 million in the 1980s to about 10 million in the 1990s. Since 2000, legal immigrants to the United States number approximately 1,000,000 per year, of whom about 600,000 are Change of Status immigrants who already are in the US Legal immigrants to the United States now are at their highest level ever at over 37,000,000 legal immigrants. Illegal immigration may be as high as 1,500,000 per year with a net of at least 700,000 illegal immigrants arriving each year to join the 12,000,000 to 20,000,000 that are already there. (Pew Hispanic Data Estimates) Immigration led to a 57.4% increase in foreign born population from 1990 to 2000.

While immigration has increased drastically over the last century, the foreign born share of the population was still higher in 1900 (about 20%) than it is today (about 10%). A number of factors may be attributed to the decrease in the representation of foreign born residents in the United States. Most significant has been the change in the composition of immigrants. Prior to 1890, 82% of immigrants came from north and western Europe. From 1891 to 1920, that number dropped to 25%, with a rise in immigrants from East, Central, and South Europe summing up to 64%. Animosity(憎恨)towards these different and foreign immigrants rose in the United States, resulting in much legislation to limit immigration.

Contemporary immigrants settle predominantly in seven states: California, New York, Florida, Texas, Pennsylvania, New Jersey and Illinois. These are all high foreign-born population states, together comprising about 44% of the US population as a whole. The combined total immigrant population of these seven states is much higher than what would be proportional, with 70% of the total foreign-born population as of 2000. Of those who immigrated between 2000 and 2005, 58% were from Latin America.

Bureau figures show that the US population grew by 2.8 million between July 1, 2004, and July 1, 2005. Hispanics accounted for 1.3 million of that increase. If current birth rate and immigration rates were to remain unchanged for another 70 to 80 years, the US population would double to nearly 600 million. The Census Bureau's estimates actually go as high as predicting that there will be one billion Americans in 2100, compared with one million people in 1700 and 5.2 million in 1800. Census statistics also show that 45% of children under age 5 are from a racial or ethnic minority.

In 2006, a total of 1,266,264 immigrants became legal permanent residents of the United States, up from 601,516 in 1987, 849,807 in 2000, and 1,122,373 in 2005. The top twelve migrant-sending countries in 2006, by country of birth, were Mexico (173,753), People's Republic of China (87,345), Philippines (74,607), India (61,369), Cuba (45,614), Colombia (43,151), Dominican Republic (38,069), El Salvador (31,783), Vietnam (30,695), Jamaica (24,976), South Korea (24,386), Guatemala (24,146), Other countries—606,370. In fiscal year 2006, 202 refugees from Iraq were allowed to resettle in the United States. Muslim immigration to the US is rising and in 2005 alone more people from Muslim countries became legal permanent US residents — nearly 96,000 — than in any year in the previous two decades.

Asylum(避难)for Refugees

In contrast to economic migrants, who generally do not gain legal admission, refugees, as defined by international law, can gain legal status through a process of seeking and receiving asylum, either by being designated a refugee while abroad or by physically entering the United States and requesting asylee status thereafter. A specified number of legally defined refugees, who either apply for asylum overseas or after arriving in the US, are admitted annually. Refugees compose about one-tenth of the total annual immigration to the United States, though some large refugee populations are very prominent.

Since World War Ⅱ, more refugees have found homes in the US than any other nation and more than 2 million refugees have arrived in the US since 1980. Of the top ten countries accepting resettled refugees in 2006, the United States accepted more than twice as much as the next nine countries combined. For example, Japan accepted just 16 refugees in 1999, while the United States took in 85,010 for resettlement, according to the United Nations High Commissioner for Refugees (UNHCR).

The US will accept 70,000 refugees in fiscal year 2007, and President Bush stated that his eventual goal is a program that resettles 90,000 refugees in the United States each year. In 2006, the State Department officially re-opened the Vietnamese resettlement program. In recent years, the main refugee sending-region has been Africa (Somalia, Liberia, Sudan, Ethiopia). A July 22, 2007 article notes that in the past nine months only 133 of the planned 7000 Iraqi refugees were allowed into the United States. The ceiling for refugee resettlement for fiscal year 2008 is 80,000 refugees. The United States expects to admit a minimum of 17,000 Iraqi refugees in fiscal year 2009.

In 1991 - 1992, Bhutan expelled roughly 100,000 ethnic Nepalis, most of whom have been living in seven refugee camps in eastern Nepal ever since. At present, the United States is working towards resettling more than 60,000 of these refugees in the US as third country settlement programme.

Illegal Immigration

Illegal immigration has recently resurfaced as a major political issue. Various bills are in the United States Congress either to provide for legalization and amnesty of those present in the country illegally, or to crack down on employers that hire undocumented workers and build a wall along the Mexican border.

The illegal immigrant population of the United States is estimated to be between 7 and 20 million. The majority of the illegal immigrants are from Mexico.

The US Census Bureau estimated that 8.7 million illegal immigrants were living in the United States in 2000.

Interpretive Perspectives

The American Dream is the belief that through hard work and determination, any United States immigrant can achieve a better life, usually in terms of financial prosperity and enhanced personal freedom of choice. This Dream has been a major factor in attracting immigrants to the United States. According to historians, the rapid economic and industrial expansion of the US is not simply a function of being a resource rich, hard working, and inventive country, but the belief that anybody could get a share of the country's wealth if he or she was willing to work hard. Many have also argued that the basis of the American greatness is how the country began without a rigid class structure at a time when other countries in Africa, Europe, China, India and Latin America had much more stratified social structures.

Legal Perspectives

Hiroshi Motomura, University of North Carolina law professor and nationally recognized expert on citizenship and immigration, has identified three approaches America has taken to the legal status of immigrants (considering only legal immigrants) in his book *Americans in Waiting: The Lost Story of Immigration and Citizenship in the United States*. The first, dominant in the 19th century, treated immigrants as in transition—that is, as prospective citizens. As soon as people declared their intention to become citizens, and before the five year wait was over, they received multiple low cost benefits, including eligibility for free homesteads (in the Homestead Act of 1869), and in many states the right to vote. The goal was to make America attractive so large numbers of farmers and skilled craftsmen would settle new lands. By the 1880s, a second approach took over, treating newcomers as "immigrants by contract". An implicit deal existed whereby immigrants who were literate and could earn their own living were permitted in restricted numbers (with the exception of Asians). Once in the United States, they would have somewhat limited legal rights, but were not allowed to vote until they became citizens, and would not be eligible for the New Deal government benefits available in the 1930s. The third more recent policy is "immigration by affiliation", Motomura argues, whereby the treatment in part depends on how deeply rooted people have become in America. An immigrant who applies for citizenship as soon as permitted, has a long history of working in the United States, and has significant family ties (such as American-born children), is more deeply affiliated and can expect better treatment.

Questions:

1. What were the factors which forced the early European immigrants to move to the new land?

2. Some describe the US as "melting pot" "salad bowl" or "pizza", how do you understand these metaphors?

3. Please introduce the Immigration and Nationality Act Amendments of 1965 and its influence on later immigration.

4. Introduce the contemporary immigration of the US.

5. Describe the immigrants in the historical context and point out their distinctive features in national origins and religious beliefs. They were respectively "the early immigrants" "the old immigrants" "the new immigrants" and "the most recent immigrants".

Supplementary Reading 1

Maternity Tourists in San Gabriel

By Bonnie Erbe

This is the kind of story that can change one's view on immigration. I'm not herewith criticizing individual immigrants. They are, for the most part like any other people — good, honest, hard workers seeking economic freedom.

I am talking however about revisiting the phenomenon of today's mass immigration prompted not by a desire for amnesty or to escape political repression or certain death based on one's political beliefs, but simply on the basis of trying to partake in America's largesse.

The New York Times and many online news organizations this week reported the shutdown of a San Gabriel, Calif., group of townhouse that for months were the homes to so-called maternity tourists. Who are they, you ask?

In the San Gabriel case, they were well-off women from China who had paid tens of thousands of dollars to deliver their babies in the United States.

By order of so-called birthright citizenship, the US delivery of those infants makes them automatic American citizens. Local officials shut down the homes, sending the 10 mothers who had been living there with their babies to nearby motels.

According to the Times, "These were not women living in squalor. It was a well taken care of place and clean, but there were a lot of women and babies," said Clayton Anderson, a city inspector who shut down the house on March 9. "I have never seen anything like this before. We really couldn't determine the exact number of people living there."

Let's all agree the number of maternity tourism births is relatively low. But it's emblematic, nonetheless, of some troubling trends in US immigration.

Particularly at a time when debate over so-called birthright citizenship is roiling some sectors of the country, the San Gabriel episode proves those opposed to birthright citizenship are hardly on the loony fringe.

If, as in the case of these well-to-do Chinese mothers, women are entering the country for the sole purpose of delivering a baby with US citizenship, what has caused our immigration policy to go so awry as to provoke this type of bizarre, expensive and one could even argue dangerous behavior?

The sad answer, I believe, is money. There's little left among today's immigrants of patriotism or nation-building or even a mere desire to be free.

The motivation for many of them is a two-car garage, a house in the suburbs, tons of Christmas presents for the kids and a desire for the consumer-driven American lifestyle. And that is a sad commentary on today's immigrant and mass immigration.

Center for Immigration Studies' Executive Director Mark Krikorian wrote a book in 2008 called, "The New Case Against Immigration, Both Legal and Illegal."

The Center's website describes the central thesis of the book as follows: "what's different today is not the immigrants, but us. Today's immigrants are very similar to those of a century ago, but they are coming to a very different America — one where changes in the economy, society, and government create fundamentally different incentives for newcomers."

In the first great wave of immigration (roughly post Civil War until 1920 or so) people were driven from their homelands by massive famines or severe political repression.

They came to America to work hard and make a new start. US government largesse was almost non-existent. Remember, there was no welfare and the public school system was just starting to sprout.

The Department of Education was launched in 1867 to help struggling states start and keep alive publicly funded schools and at that point, some poor states had few, if any, public schools. Free health care was unheard of, as was Medicaid.

The maternity tourism story proves that people are emigrating for all kinds of reasons but few of them are the right reasons. And that's reason enough to re-examine immigration policy right there.

*http://www.koreatimes.co.kr/www/news/opinon/*2011/04/137_84302.*html*

Supplementary Reading 2

New Faces of Childhood

Census Shows Hispanic and Asian Children Surging as Whites, Blacks Shrink.

America's child population grew more far diverse over the past decade as a decline in the ranks of white children was offset by surging growth of Asians and Hispanics.

All told in 2010, the Census Bureau counted 74.2 million people under age 18, up 1.9 million from 2000.

The number of non-Hispanic whites fell in 46 states and 86 of the 100 largest metropolitan areas. In 10 states, white children are now a minority among their peers, including six that tipped between 2000 and 2010. Others will follow soon: In 23 states, minorities make up more than 40% of the child population.

The number of black and Native American children declined as well, but by a far smaller degree than whites, according to an analysis of 2010 Census data to be released Wednesday by the Brookings Institution, a left-leaning think tank in Washington. The Census Bureau released the first results of its once-a-decade head count of US residents, regardless of citizenship, late last year; over subsequent months, Census released state and local data.

The report reflects a transformation under way in the country's racial and ethnic makeup.

"It's a new melting pot in the United States," said William Frey, a demographer at Brookings who wrote the report. "This is the beginning of how our country will look."

The data show the extent to which the US has become dependent on minorities—Hispanics in particular—for the next generation of Americans. From 2000 to 2010, almost half of states saw a decline in the number of children.

Without Hispanics, America's under-18 population would have declined between 2000 and 2010. And in places that did see an increase, Hispanics accounted for most of the growth. In Texas, the state with the largest population gain over the decade, Hispanics accounted for 95% of the growth among the population under age 18.

Most Hispanic children have parents of Mexican origin. The origins of the Asian children are fairly evenly split, with five countries—China, India, the Philippines, Vietnam and Korea—accounting for about 80%, according to Jeffrey Passel, senior demographer at the Pew Hispanic Center.

The Asian population is concentrated along the West coast and in metropolitan areas while Latinos live in rural and urban areas across 50 states, according to Kenneth Johnson, senior demographer at the Carsey Institute at the University of New Hampshire.

From 2000 to 2010, Hispanics and Asians were the driving force behind growth in the under-18 population. The number of non-Hispanic white children fell by 4.3 million over the decade. Children in two other longstanding US minority groups, blacks and Native Americans, also saw small decreases. Meantime, the number of Hispanic and Asian children grew by 5.5 million, with 4.8 million of those Hispanic.

Part of the decline in white children is a result of an increase in mixed-race children, who remain a tiny share of the overall population but grew 46%—or roughly 900,000—between 2000 and 2010.

The Census population counts don't specify how much change came from births compared with immigration.

Shifts in the youth population's racial makeup suggest the US could become a "majority-minority" nation—where non-Hispanic whites account for less than half of the population—before the 2042 date that the Census Bureau has estimated in the past, according to Mr. Frey. This has already spelled big changes in the nation's schools, where the black-white divide of the past has become a more complex mix of race, language and religion.

The changing makeup of the US could play a significant role in setting national priorities, especially as Washington grapples with debt obligations that are sparking fights over which entitlement programs to cut and by how much. "Politically, an age-race divide could create even sharper divisions between candidates and parties that espouse more or less government support for measures benefiting the young, like education or affordable housing, and those benefiting the old, like Social Security or Medicare," Mr. Frey wrote in the report.

http://online.wsj.com/article/SB10001424052748703806304576245030067903412.html

Chapter 3 Ethnic Groups in the United States

The United States is a diverse country racially and ethnically. White Americans are the racial majority and are spread throughout the country; racial and ethnic minorities, composing one fourth of the population, are concentrated in coastal and metropolitan areas. The Black American or African American population is concentrated in the South, and also spread throughout parts of the Northeast and Midwest. Black Americans make up the largest racial minority in the United States.

White Americans make up 74% of the total population per the 2006 American Community Survey (ACS). Black Americans compose 13.5% of the population. Asian Americans are concentrated in the Western states; 47% of them reside there, mostly in California and Hawaii. Half of the American Indian population resides in the West; there were 4.1 million in 2000, including those of partial ancestry. The Inuit population is mainly found in Alaska, and more than three quarters of the Native Hawaiian and Pacific Islander population is found in the West, mostly in Hawaii and California. The population of those described as "two or more races" resides mostly in the West and South, where a combined 69% of all multiracial Americans reside. Americans of "Some other race" — a catchall, non-standard category almost all of whose members are reclassified as white in official documents — are nearly all Hispanic or Latino in ancestral or national origin, and 44% lived in the West in 2006.

Hispanic and Latino Americans form 14.8% of the total population, they form a racially and ethnically diverse ancestral group, constituting the nation's largest collated ancestral minority. Hispanics and Latinos are most concentrated in the West, where they represent 27% of the population, corresponding to 43% of the group's population nationwide.

In the 2000 census, Americans self-described as belonging to these racial groups:

• White: those having origins in any of the original peoples of Europe, the Middle East, or North Africa.

• Black or African American: those having origins in any of the black racial groups of Sub-Saharan Africa.

• American Indian or Alaska Native, also called Native Americans: those having origins in any of the original peoples of North, Central and South America, and who maintain tribal affiliation or community attachment.

• Asian, also called Asian American: those having origins in any of the original peoples of the Far East, Southeast Asia, and the Indian subcontinent; frequently specified as Chinese American, Korean American, Indian American, Filipino American, Vietnamese American, Japanese American, etc.

• Native Hawaiian or Other Pacific Islander: those having origins in any of the original peoples of Hawaii, Guam, Samoa, or other Pacific Islands.

• Some other race: respondents write in the race they consider themselves to be, if different from the foregoing categories. This category captures responses such as Mestizo, Creole, and Mulatto, but among the write-in entries reported in the 2000 census were also South African, Moroccan, Belizean, Mexican, Puerto Rican, Cuban and Wesort, mixed, interracial, and others.

• Two or more races, also known as multiracial: those who check off and/or write in more than one race. There is no actual option labelled "Two or more races" on census and other forms; instead, people who report more than one race are categorized together in subsequent processing. Any number, up to all six, of the foregoing racial categories can be reported by any respondent.

3.1 White Americans

The majority of the 300 million people currently living in the United States consists of White Americans, who trace their ancestry to the original peoples of Europe. Fifty-three percent of white Americans are of colonial ancestry, and 47 percent are the descendants of ancestors who came to America after 1790. Approximately 63 percent of white Americans are of English, Irish, Scottish or Welsh descent. Eighty-six percent of US whites are of Northwestern European ancestry, and 14 percent are of Southern and Eastern European extraction.

White Americans are the majority in forty-nine of the fifty states, with Hawaii as the exception. The District of Columbia, which is not a state, also has a non-white majority. Non-Hispanic Whites, however, are the majority in forty-six states, with Hawaii, New Mexico, California, and Texas, as well as the District of Columbia, as the exceptions. The latter five have "minority majorities", i. e. minority groups are a majority of their populations.

The non-Hispanic White percentage (68 in 2006) tends to decrease every year, and this sub-group is expected to become a plurality of the overall US population after the year 2050. However, White Americans overall (non-Hispanic Whites together with White Hispanics) will remain the majority, at 73.1% (or 303 million out of 420 million) in 2050, from 80% in 2006 (per the Population Estimates Program, not the ACS; it is 76% in the ACS, as previously noted).

Even though a high proportion of the population has two or more ancestries, only slightly more than one ancestry was stated per person. This means that the percentages listed are significantly dependent on subjective perception of which of several ancestry lines is relevant.

A large number of individuals (7.2% of the US population) listed their ancestry as American on the 2000 census. According to the United States Census Bureau, the number of people in the US who reported American and no other ancestry increased from 12. 4 million in 1990 to 20. 2 million in 2000. This increase represents the largest numerical growth of any ethnic group in the United States during the 1990s.

The descendants of Dutch and Hanoverian settlers, whose countries were non-simultaneously in personal union with the British monarchy, often identify with the successor countries today, namely Netherlands and Germany. This helps colonial diasporas(离散)fit in more with current nations.

The largest Central European ancestry was Polish (both Catholic Poles and Ashkenazi Jews), and the largest Eastern European ancestry was Russian (includes a recent influx of Ashkenazi Jews). There were other significant ancestries from Central, Eastern and Southern Europe, as well as from French Canada. Most who registered as French American are descended from colonists of Catholic New France — exiled Huguenots quickly assimilated into the relevant British population of the Thirteen Colonies and were immediately seen and self-regarded as subjects of the Crown under the old Plantagenet claim.

Other ethnic European origins included are Dutch/Flemish, Lithuanian, Latvian, former Yugoslavs, Greek, Hungarian, Portuguese, Czech, Slovak, Australian, and New Zealander. A comparatively small fraction of recent immigrants are non-Hispanic whites, but the largest numbers come from Canada, Poland, Russia, Ukraine, and the United Kingdom. In addition to direct Spanish ancestry, including the Isleños of Louisiana and the Hispanos of the Southwest, most White Hispanics are of Mexican, Puerto Rican, and Cuban ancestry.

According to the 2006 ACS, there are 1.5 million Arab Americans, accounting for 0.5% of the American population. The largest subgroup was by far the Lebanese Americans, with 481,675, and 3 million descendants, nearly a third of the Arab American population. Most Lebanese descend from immigrants of the late 18th century through the early 19th century. Over 1/4 of all Arab Americans claimed two ancestries, having not only Arab ancestry but also non-Arab. Among them, 14.7% reported Irish, 13.6% reported Italian, and 13.5% reported German ancestry in the 2000 census. Assyrians(亚述人)were also listed in the US census under Assyrian/Chaldean/Syriac.

3.2 Black Americans

About 13.5% of the American people are Black or African American, most of whom are primarily descendants of Africans who lived through the Slavery era in the US between 1619 and the 1860s and were emancipated during the American Civil War. Black Americans are the largest racial minority as opposed to Hispanics and Latinos, who are the largest "ethnic" minority. The historical national origin of the majority of Black Americans is untraceable, as most African nations were named centuries after they arrived in the United States; the continent of Africa serves as an indicator of geographic origin and a descriptive term. Starting in the 1970s, the black population has been bolstered by immigration from the Caribbean, especially Jamaica, Haiti, Cuba, Trinidad and

Tobago, Belize, Barbados and the Dominican Republic, as well as from South America, primarily from Guyana, Brazil, Panama, Colombia, and Venezuela. More recently, starting in the 1990s, there has been an influx of African immigrants to the United States, due to the instability in political and economic opportunities in various nations in Africa.

Historically, most African Americans lived in the Southeast and South Central states of Alabama, Georgia, South Carolina, Louisiana, Mississippi and Texas. Since World War I there occurred the Great Migration of rural black Americans to the industrial Northeast, urban Midwest and, in a smaller wave, to the West Coast that lasted until 1960. Today, most African Americans (56%) live in the Southern US and in urban areas, but are increasingly moving to the suburbs. Historically, any person with any sub-Saharan African ancestry, even if they were mostly white, were designated and classified as "black", according to the "one drop theory," by which any Black African ancestry made the person "black" in legal sense. Today, the US census in law and practice does not declare any person to belong in any race or ethnicity without the prior consent of that person.

Out of Africa and Thrown into Slavery

Unlike other ethnic groups that came to the United States more or less voluntarily (with the exception of American Indian, who inhabited in North America before the first white settlers arrived), African Americans were brought to the "New World" in the early 1600s against their will. They were at first small in number and used as indentured servants. By the late 1600s, however, permanent enslavement had become the fate of these colored people from the Cribbean andAfrica, and their status was subsequently relegated to that of property. Due to the severe shortage of labor supply in the then vast land of wilderness and the huge profits that colonists gained from slave labor, white settlers from then onward were actively engaged in the notorious slave trade. In this way, the white slave traders managed to ship to the "New World" thousands of tons of "human cargo" in chains. By the time of the American Revolution, black slaves accounted for about 20 percent of the total population of the colonies.

Black slaves were brought to the United States primarily to be used as agricultural labor force in the South, growing tobacco, rice, and later on, cotton. In the North, as the climate is not suitable for plantation crops, relatively few slaves were used there. So, for a long time in American history, slavery had been a regional issue, confined mostly to the South.

As slavery became part and parcel of southern way of life and got embedded in its social structure, southern whites tightened their control over black slaves and exploited them to the maximum degree possible. Laws were made to regulate the conduct of slaves (the so-called black codes), and opposition to the institution, either in the form of abolitionist(废奴主义)literature or in the form of slaves' assembly, incurred zero tolerance from the ruling class in the South. Tension grew high between whites and blacks. In response to the iron-fisted approach of white Southerners, black slaves waged uprisings and rebellions across the South to demonstrate their unquenchable will for freedom and self-autonomy. Southern whites, in turn, increased their repression, leaving bloodshed sprinkling on the soil of southern plantations. It was not until the conclusion of the Civil War that the whole slave issue was finally brought to an end.

When World War I broke out and drew the United States into it, northern industries suddenly found their labor force drained out of the workshop and fighting in the war fronts. As the flow of immigrants from Europe stopped as a result of the war, the shortage of labor supply in most of northern industries had to be solved by attracting southern blacks to the North. With the outbreak of the Second World War, a much larger exodus of blacks occurred, and most of them settled in the industrial cities of the North and West. Once in the North and West, while blacks did obtain numerous benefits, these benefits of urban life came with a high price tag. Such familiar urban problems as poverty, unemployment, overcrowded housing, violence and crime became increasingly associated with black communities.

In the face of the indifference of the federal government toward the "black problems" and the pervasiveness of white racism in the North as well as in the South, black Americans in the 1950s started their legal struggle for desegregation. Led by the National Association for the Advancement of Colored People (NAACP), black Americans launched fierce attacks on the separate-but-equal doctrine. In 1954, the United States Supreme Court declared that racially segregated public schools were inherently unequal, because they did not provide equal educational opportunities for black Americans. Inspired by this decision, black Americans decided to try to end racial segregation and racial discrimination in all areas of American life, starting what later became known as the Civil Rights Movement.

Struggle for Civil Rights

Beginning with Montgomery bus boycott (抵制) in 1955, and March on Washington in 1963, black Americans engaged themselves in one battle after another across the country. Out of this Civil Rights Movement, there emerged such black leaders as Martin Luther King, Jr. and Malcolm X. In the view of the former, African Americans' civil rights should be achieved primarily through non-violent tactics and direct protest action. To the latter, however, equality and liberty should be in no way compromised and, therefore, all necessary means should be resorted to in order to attain the goals set by the Civil Rights Movement. In the first half of the 1960s, the Civil Rights Movement was largely dominated by Martin Luther King's ideology, and blacks were mainly using non-violent action to crash "the wall of segregation". To give him due credit, King-led movement achieved considerable success for the black people's civil rights, the most important of which included the passage of two acts: the Civil Rights Act of 1964 and the Voting Right Act of 1965. However, as the movement progressed, especially when blacks shifted their demands to social and economic equality, the US government first dragged its feet along, and then simply displayed its displeasure, blaming blacks for asking for too much. As black Americans would not settle for anything less than a full citizenship, tension between whites and blacks started to rise.

With the federal government retreating its ground on racial issue, and with the conservative political force gradually rearing its ugly head, non-violent action was now making little headway. Consequently, Malcolm X's advocacy of violence for violence gained ground in the Civil Rights Movement, particularly among urban black youth. The late 1960s witnessed dozens of race riots in American cities, when frustrated black youth fought street wars with white police, giving rise to growing militancy on the part of black radicals. On the surface, violent and non-violent action appears to be contradictory, but in reality, they act like yin-yang dualism, supplementing each other in their struggle for freedom and equality. The non-violent tactics for example, played along the line of American liberal tradition, helping to win sympathy and support from liberal whites. The violent action, on the other hand, more effectively drove home the seriousness of "black problems," compelling the dominant class to confront the race issues involving discrimination and segregation. In their own different ways, both efforts contributed to the black struggle for racial equality in the United States.

Such efforts have brought about sustained success for African Americans. In 1969, the Supreme Court ordered the desegregation(废除种族隔离)of all public schools, and later approved measures to force integration, such as racial quotas, the groupings of non-contiguous school districts and busing in order to achieve racial balance in the schools. More importantly, the civil rights laws of the 1960s eventually helped to reduce the amount of white prejudice toward black people in all parts of the country. The number of African Americans attending the nation's colleges and universities, holding elective public office, and earning higher incomes increased dramatically in the late 1960s and 1970s. Black political figures have now taken on national prominence and black voters have been courted by all serious politicians. In 1984 and 1988, for example, Jesse Jackson, a black leader who had worked with Martin Luther King in the 1960s, became the first African American to run for the presidency of the United States. Although he did not win, he received significant national attention and greatly influenced the policies of the Democratic party. Additionally, many African Americans are now mayors of major cities and member of Congress. They hold offices at all levels of government. In 1994, for instance, there were 7,000 black officials in the South, and about 40 black members of US Congress.

Equally important is the change of white people's perception of blacks. In 1983, for example, Congress overwhelmingly passed, and the president signed, a law, making the birthday of the late civil rights leader Martin Luther King, Jr. a national holiday. This was done, in part, to symbolize America's commitment to completing the promise of equality announced in the Declaration of Independence, and, in part, to give recognition to the great contributions made by black Americans to the United States. Also symbolically, perhaps, more than 80 percent of whites said in the late 1990s that they would vote a black for the president of the United States, someone like General Colin Powell, for example. Perhaps most impressive of all, Barack Obama, a black Senator, successfully secured the presidency of the United States in 2008. All this indicates that African Americans as a whole have made considerable progress over the past 40 years.

3.3 Asian Americans

A third significant minority is the Asian American population, comprising 13.1 million in 2006, or 4.4% of the US population. California is home to 4.5 million Asian Americans, whereas 512,000 live in Hawaii, where they compose the plurality at 40% of the islands' people. Asian Americans live across the country, and are also found in large numbers in New York City, Chicago, Boston, Houston, and other urban centers. It is by no means a monolithic(庞大的)group. The largest groups are immigrants or descendants of immigrants from the Philippines, China, India, Brunei, Malaysia, Vietnam, Cambodia, South Korea and Japan. While the Asian American population is generally a fairly recent addition to the nation's ethnic mix, relatively large waves of Chinese, Filipino and Japanese immigration happened in the mid to late 1800s.

Chinese

Many of the Chinese went to the United States as contract laborers or on money borrowed from Chiesese-American organizations that assumed a supervisory role toward them in the United States. Like other immigrants totally unfamiliar with the lauguage and culture of the United States, Chinese laborers often worked in gangs under the supervision of a fellow countryman. They were hard workers in agriculture, railroad building, and other taxing physical labor. They also worked cheaply and lived frugally, saving what they could to start their own business, or take money home when they returned to China.

By 1851, there were 25,000 Chinese in Cialifornia. By 1870, the number rose to 63,000 in the United States, almost all on the West Coast. In 1880, about 63,000 Chinese entered the United States, and in the middle of the 1880s, as a result of an exclusionary law directed against the Chinese (The Chinese Exclusion Act of 1882), the inflow of Chinese immigrants was drastically curtailed, down to less than 1,000 a year.

The reception of the Chinese immigrants was both harsh and violent. As Chinese immigrants were non-white and non-Christian, they were viewed as "strangers from a different shore," incapable of being assimilated into the mainstream culture. Additionally, they were feared as competitors, whose hard work and longer hours for low pay were said to drive down the standard of living of American labor. So labor unions in California were in the forefront of decades-long efforts to exclude Chinese and expel Chinese residents from the United States. With such an uproar against Chinese immigrants, Chinese residents in the West were either forced to leave or took the hardest, dirtiest and most menial jobs.

The Chinese reaction to the pervasive discrimination was withdrawal and inconspicuousness, much like the European Jews in the ghetto. Harassed by both violent mobs and legal impositions, Chinese immigrants usually tried to live in places where they were tolerated and got jobs urgently needed and few whites were interested in. That, in part, explained why most Chinese in the late 19th and early 20th centuries found themselves working as laundrymen or domestic servants. In addition to these two principal occupations, Chinese restaurants were another major source of jobs, located mostly in Chinese communities known as "Chinatown". Indeed, as late as 1920, more than half of all employed Chinese in the United States worked either in Laundries or restaurants. As a result, the Chinese hand laundry became an American institution, and so did the food made in Chinese restaurants for Americans.

With the passage of time, many Chinese managed to improve their lives in an impressive way. Some thrived in business in Chinatowns, while others made headway in the larger society outside Chinatowns. With this strengthened economic position, they sent their American-born Children to college and university, paving the way for Chinese Americans to enter professional occupations. As of 1940, only 3 percent of Chinese Americans in California were in the professions, while 8 percent of whites were. By 1950, the Chinese percentage had doubled to 6 percent, and the white percentage had risen to 10 percent. In the next decade, however, the proportion of Chinese who were professionals tripled to 18, passing the whites at 15.

During the Second World War, China and the United States became allies in their fight against the fascists. Under the pressure from the Chinese government, the US government repealed(废除)The Chinese Exclusion Act of 1882 in 1943, and passed new legislation, permitting limited immigration from China. Within a few years, more than 8,000 Chinese brought their wives to the United States, some of them after dsecades of separation. In the 1960s, many Chinese people left Hong Kong for the United States, settling mostly in the Chinatowns in San Francisco, New York, and later on, Chicago. These hordes of immigrants from Hong Kong doubled the Chinese population in the United States from 237,000 to 435,000. From then onwards, with the passage of the new immigration law of 1965, about 20,000 Chinese from Hong Kong and Taiwan legally entered the United States every year, and probably an equal number also entered illegally. After the normalization of relations between between China and the United States, the People's Republic of China was given its own annual quota for immigrants to the United States. Between 1965 and 1984, Chinese immigrants from Hong Kong, Taiwan, and Chinese mainland numbered 419,373, radically transforming the Chinese community from 61 percent American-born to 63 percent foreign-born.

Unlike the old immigration, which was composed mostly of men, the new immigration has included more women than men. Also, while the earlier immigrants had been peasants, the recent immigrants have originated not only from the working class, but also from the professional class. For instance, the number of scientists and engineers immigrating from Hong Kong and Taiwan skyrocketed from 36 in 1964 to 1,164 in 1970. Beginning in the 1980s, large numbers of students and scholars from the mainland went to study in the US, and upon the completion of their study, many of them decided to stay there, adding additional number of Chinese immigrants in the United States. The different class background of the new immigrants has led to the formation of a bipolar Chinese-American community—one divided between a colónized working class and an entrepreneurial professional middle class. In the mid-1980s, for example, about 51 percent of Chinese immigrants were employed in menial service and low-skilled, blue-collar work, while 42 percent were engaged in managerial and technical occupations. As a result, in New York City, there are now the "Downtown Chinese" of waiters and seamstresses as well as the affluent and professional "Uptown Chinese". Likewise, in southern California, there are Chinatowns in central Los Angeles as well as in Monterey Park—America's first suburban Chinatown.

On the whole, Chinese Americans today have higher income as well as higher occupational status than the average American. It is estimated that one-fourth of all employed Chinese Americans are working in scientific and professional fields. In politics, however, Chinese Americans have not been a high-profile ethnic groups. It is only in the recent ten to fifteen years that Chinese Americans have shown active participation in American politics, campaigning for local and state government positions. While there are still some pockets of poverty in Chinatown, many Chinese Americans are well-educated and quite prosperous.

Two or More Races

Multiracial Americans numbered 6. 1 million in 2006, or 2. 0% of the population. They can be any combination of races (White, Black or African American, Asian, American Indian or Alaska Native, Native Hawaiian or other Pacific Islander, "Some other race") and ethnicities. The US has a growing multiracial identity movement. Miscegenation or interracial marriage, most notably between whites and blacks, was deemed immoral and illegal in most states in early centuries. Demographers state that the American people are mostly multi-ethnic descendants of various immigrant nationalities culturally distinct until assimilation and integration took place in the mid 20th century.

3.4 Native Americans and Alaska Natives

Indigenous peoples of the Americas, such as American Indians and Inuit, made up 0.8% of the population in 2006, numbering 2.4 million. An additional 1.9 million declared part-Native American or American Indian ancestry. The legal and official designation of who is Native American by descent aroused controversy by demographers, tribal nations and government officials for many decades. The blood quantum laws are complex and contradictory in admittance of new tribal members, or for census takers to accept any respondent's claims without official documents from the US Bureau of Indian Affairs. Genetic scientists estimated that over 15 million other Americans may be one quarter or less of American Indian descent. Once thought to face extinction in race or culture, there has been a remarkable revival of Native American identity and tribal sovereignty in the 20th century. The Cherokee are at 800,000 full or part-blood degrees. 70,000 Cherokee live in Oklahoma in the Cherokee Nation, and 15,000 in North Carolina on remnants of their ancestral homelands. The second largest tribal group is the Navajo, who call themselves "Diné" and live on a 16-million acre (65,000 km^2) Indian reservation covering northeast Arizona, northwest New Mexico and southeast Utah. It is home to half of the 450,000 Navajo Nation members. The third largest group are the Lakota (a.k.a. Sioux) Nation located in the states of Minnesota, Montana, Nebraska, Wyoming; and North and South Dakota.

Of all the minority groups in the United States, American Indians, or Native Americans were the first to have settled down there. About 75,000 years before the birth of Christ, the ancestors of the Native Americans migrated from Eastern Asia across a land bridge to Alaska. 60,000 years later, the rising waters of the Pacific Ocean submerged this route under the Bering Strait. For 15,000 years, the new inhabitants of the Western Hemisphere had no contact with the rest of the world. These tribes of hunters slowly moved to warmer regions and adapted their economic and cultural lives to many climates.

With this transition, Native American history changed dramatically from a hunting to an agricultural economy. Beginning about 2000 BC, Native Americans in Mexico and Peru domesticated maize, or Indian corn. Through the centuries, these tribal peoples bred corn into and extremely large and nutritious plant. By cultivating corn, Native Americans achieved an agricultural surplus. Over time, as they developed more settled way of life, they worked out rather complex irrigation systems. When nomadic and semi-nomadic tribes of hunters came to these areas, they, too, quickly adapted themselves to this kind of settlement.

Encouraging European Settlers

When Europeans arrived in the American continent after Columbus' voyage, Native Americans soon found themselves the victims of their greed for gold, silver and other treasures. Horses, steel swords, and primitive muskets gave Europeans a great advantage over Indian inhabitants. Overwhelmed both in manpower and weaponry, Native Americans started their losing war with European invaders from the very beginning of their encounter. They fought bravely against white invaders under adverse conditions, and made gradual retreats into forests in the face of advancing conquerors. While they were eventually defeated by European invaders, Native Americans, nevertheless, left a great record of bravery and courage in the defense of their home. Conversely, while European whites triumphed over the Indians, they also left an inglorious record of brutality and cruelty in the conquest of the "New World".

When British colonists followed at Spaniards' heels to come to North America, they had three goals in mind: (1) to plant the Christian religion; (2) to traffic in goods; and (3) to conquer. In varying degrees, English colonists tried whatever means available and effective to materialize their goals. Missionaries viewed the Indians as heathens and went to great lengths to convert them into Christianity. Merchants considered the Indians to be easy trading partners, from whom they could profit tremendously. And ambitious conquistadors regarded the Indians as "wild beasts, unreasonable creatures and brutish savages," who had to be ruled with an iron hand. While their goals seemingly differed from one to another, and their means showed a great many variations, the overall objectives for the three groups of English colonists remained very much the same: to take whatever they could from the Indians.

Guided by these principles, English colonists, from the first day they set foot on the North American soil, engaged themselves in the ambitious plan to change the political, economic and cultural landscape of the continent. In the process of continental settlement, the English purchased land from the Indians when possible, and took land away from them by force if necessary. Driven by their insatiable desires for gold, furs, and, above all, land, English colonists and later Americans pushed Native Americans first from the East Coast to the areas east of the Mississippi River, and then from that region to the areas west of the Mississippi, and finally all the way down to the West Coast. Uprooted and constantly chased about, Indians not only found their peaceful family and community life disrupted, but to their great dismay, they also found their traditional culture ruined as a result of white conquest. Eventually, the overpowered Indians were driven to some remote interior areas, known nowadays as "Indian Reservations."

Aliens(外国人)in the Native Land

Reservations usually consist of those areas least desirable to whites. As such, this arrangement was not and has not been beneficial to Native Americans. First, when reservation policy was first introduced, Indians had no say over their own affairs on reservations, because US Supreme Court decisions in 1884 and 1886 denied them the right to become citizens. It is not until 1924 that the US Congress passed a law, making all Indians citizens of the United States. Second, at the beginning of their settlement, reservations were constantly harassed and attacked by whites, because white farmers and herders continually sought even remote Indian lands for their own purpose. Third, in setting up reservations, the federal government often ignored tribal integrity, even combining on the same reservations tribes that had habitually waged war with one another. This way of arrangement was detrimental to Indian tribes, either for their survival or for their cultural preservation. Last but not least, the reservation policy has cut off the outside contact with the Indian community, leaving them in perpetual backwardness.

Of course, not all Indians live on reservations. According to US 2003

Census estimate, about 2.8 million people in the United States may have some Indian blood. Out of this number, probably only one out of every four nowadays is a "reservation Indian." Indeed, no Indians are forced to stay on reservations, and among the younger generation, there has been a strong tendency to leave reservations for modern cities. In 1940, for example, there were fewer than 30,000 Indian city residents; but by the mid-1980s, Indian urban dwellers reached over 700,000. At present, it is estimated that a little over one third of Native Americans in the US live in the following three states: California, Arizona and Oklahoma. However, while charmed by the glamour of metropolitan landscape, Indians have also found it hard to live in modern American cities. Oftentimes, due to a cluster of factors such as discrimination, poor skills, and lack of political power, Indians, for years, have been among the poorest groups in American urban society. At present, more than 20 percent live below the poverty line, and their unemployment is higher than that of African Americans. Those with jobs frequently earn low wages, and only a very small well-educated elite enjoys a high standard of living.

In a way, those Indians, who remain on reservations have managed to maintain their culture to a certain extent. They keep their religious rituals in their own way; they pass down their folklore to their children; they hold their traditional dance, fairs, and festivals on regular basis; and they organize their social and family life in as much the same way as their ancestors did. In short, appalling as their living conditions are, Indians on reservations have been doing all they can to preserve their cultural heritage so as to keep this stream of human civilization to flow continuously.

3.5 Hispanic and Latino(拉丁美洲人)Americans

Ethnicity(种族渊源): Hispanic and Latino Americans

The question on Hispanic or Latino origin is separate from the question on race. Hispanic Latino Americans have origins in the Hispanophone countries of Latin America. Many respondents with Spain as their ancestral land also select this category, although they are not overtly included in the Government's definition. Self-identifying as being Hispanic or Latino and not Hispanic or Latino was neither explicitly allowed nor explicitly prohibited. On the Race question, Hispanic and Latino Americans choose from among the same categories as all Americans: no separate racial category exists for Hispanic and Latino Americans, as they do not make up a separate race. Thus each racial category contains Non-Hispanic or Latino and Hispanic or Latino Americans. For example: the White race category contains Non-Hispanic Whites and Hispanic Whites (White Hispanics); the Black or African American category contains Non-Hispanic Blacks and Hispanic Blacks (Black Hispanics); and likewise for all the other categories.

Americans of Hispanic origin do not form a race but an ancestral group known as "Hispanic or Latino", the largest ancestral minority in the country, composing 14.8% of the population in 2006. Mexican Americans made up 64% of this number, or 28 million, followed next by Puerto Rican Americans with 4 million. The Hispanic or Latino category is based on ancestral or national origin, not race, and is defined by the government as people who classify themselves in one of the specific Hispanic or Latino categories listed on the Census 2000 or ACS questionnaire—"Mexican," "Puerto Rican," or "Cuban"—as well as those who indicate that they are "other Spanish, Hispanic, or Latino." (ACS refers to the American Community Survey.) The inclusion of Spain was explicit in the 1990 census, but not so in the 2000 census and the American Community Survey definitions, although the term "Spanish", formerly used for the Hispanic or Latino group ("Persons of Spanish Origin", "Persons of Spanish Surname", etc) was retained, in "Spanish/Hispanic/Latino".

Hispanic and Latino Americans may be of any race. Their racial breakdown in 2006 was as follows: 52.3% White; 41.2% "Some other race"; 3.9% Two or more races; 1.4% Black or African American; 0.75% American Indian or Alaska Native; 0.35% Asian; and 0.09% Native Hawaiian or Other Pacific Islander.

The "Some other race" respondents usually identify by their national origin only (e. g. "Mexican", "Salvadoran", "Colombian" and 20 other nationalities). In Census 2000 data, the "some other race" category overlaps by 97% with the Hispanic/Latino category, suggesting that this group is virtually the only one using the category.

The spectacular growth of the Hispanic population through immigration and higher birth rates are noted as a partial factor for the US' population gains in the last quarter-century. The Bureau of the Census projects that by 2050 one-quarter of the population will be Hispanic. Bureau figures show the US population grew by 2. 8 million between July 1, 2004, and July 1, 2005. Hispanics accounted for 1. 3 million of that increase.

Immigration to the United States is what has produced its diverse population of today, and will continue to change its ethnic and racial makeup. A 2008 report from the Census Bureau projects that by 2042, non-Hispanic whites will no longer make up the majority of the population. This is a revision of earlier projections which projected this demographic change to take place in 2050.

Today, non-Hispanic whites make up about 68% of the population. This is expected to fall to 42% in 2050. The report foresees the Hispanic population rising from 15% today to 30% by 2050. Today African Americans make up 12% of the population, in 2050 they are projected to comprise 19% of the population. Asian Americans make up 5% of the population today and they are expected to make up 9% in 2050. The US has nearly 305 million people today.

Questions

1. What changes did the Civil Rights Movement of the 1960s bring to the black people, what about their life now?

2. Who are the people called Hispanics or Latinos in the United States? What are the political, social and cultural implications of the fast-growing population of Latinos in the US ?

3. Explain the maltreatment to the Chinese immigrants. Explain how recent Chinese immigrants differ from old Chinese immigrants.

4. American Indians of Native Americans are now a maiginal group in the US, how do they maintain their tradition?

Supplementary Reading 1

For Many Latinos, Racial Identity Is More Culture Than Color

By Mireya Navarro

Every decade, the Census Bureau spends billions of dollars and deploys hundreds of thousands of workers to get an accurate portrait of the American population. Among the questions on the census form is one about race, with 15 choices, including "some other race".

More than 18 million Latinos checked this "other" box in the 2010 census, up from 14.9 million in 2000. It was an indicator of the sharp disconnect between how Latinos view themselves and how the government wants to count them. Many Latinos argue that the country's race categories — indeed, the government's very conception of identity — do not fit them.

The main reason for the split is that the census categorizes people by race, which typically refers to a set of common physical traits. But Latinos, as a group in this country, tend to identify themselves more by their ethnicity, meaning a shared set of cultural traits, like language or customs.

So when they encounter the census, they see one question that asks them whether they identify themselves as having Hispanic ethnic origins and many answer it as their main identifier. But then there is another question, asking them about their race, because, as the census guide notes, "people of Hispanic, Latino or Spanish origin may be of any race," and more than a third of Latinos check "other."

This argument over identity has gained momentum with the growth of the Latino population, which in 2010 stood at more than 50 million. Census Bureau officials have acknowledged that the questionnaire has a problem, and say they are wrestling with how to get more Latinos to pick a race. In 2010, they tested different wording in questions and last year they held focus groups, with a report on the research scheduled to be released by this summer.

Some experts say officials are right to go back to the drawing table. "Whenever you have people who can't find themselves in the question, it's a bad question," said Mary C. Waters, a sociology professor at Harvard who specializes in the challenges of measuring race and ethnicity.

The problem is more than academic — the census data on race serves many purposes, including determining the makeup of voting districts, and monitoring discriminatory practices in hiring and racial disparities in education and health. When respondents do not choose a race, the Census Bureau assigns them one, based on factors like the racial makeup of their neighborhood, inevitably leading to a less accurate count.

Latinos, who make up close to 20 percent of the American population, generally hold a fundamentally different view of race. Many Latinos say they are too racially mixed to settle on one of the government-sanctioned standard races — white, black, American Indian, Alaska native, native Hawaiian, and a collection of Asian and Pacific Island backgrounds.

Some regard white or black as separate demographic groups from Latino. Still others say Latinos are already the equivalent of another race in this country, defined by a shared set of challenges.

"The issues within the Latino community — language, immigration status — do not take into account race," said Peter L. Cedeño, 43, a lawyer and native New Yorker born to Dominican immigrants. "We share the same hurdles."

At a time when many multiracial Americans are proudly asserting their mixed-race identity, many Latinos, an overwhelmingly blended population with Indian, European, African and other roots, are sidestepping or ignoring questions of race.

Erica Lubliner, who has fair skin and green eyes — legacies of her Jewish father and her Mexican mother — said she was so "conflicted" about the race question on the census form that she left it blank.

Ms. Lubliner, a recent graduate of the medical school at the University of California, Los Angeles, in her mid-30s, was only 9 when her father died, and she grew up steeped in the language and culture of her mother. She said she has never identified with "the dominant culture of white." She believes her mother is a mix of white and Indian. "Believe me, I am not a confused person," she said.

"I know who I am, but I don't necessarily fit the categories well."

Alejandro Farias, 23, from Brownsville, Tex., a supervisor for a freight company, sees himself simply as Latino. His ancestors came from the United States, Mexico and Portugal. When pressed, he checked "some other race."

"Race to me gets very confusing because we have so many people from so many races that make up our genealogical tree," he said.

Yet race matters. How Latinos identify themselves — and how the census counts them — affects the political clout of Latinos and other minority groups. Some studies have found that African-Latinos tend to be significantly more supportive of government-sponsored health care and much less supportive of the death penalty than Latinos who identify as white, a rift that is also found in the broader white and black populations.

This racial effect "weakens the political effectiveness of Latinos as a group," said Gary M. Segura, a political science professor at Stanford who has conducted some of the research.

A majority of Latinos identify themselves as white. Among them is Fiordaliza A. Rodriguez, 40, a New York lawyer who says she considers herself white because "I am light-skinned" and that is how she is viewed in her native Dominican Republic.

But she says there is no question that she is seen as different from the white majority in this country. Ms. Rodriguez recalled an occasion in a courtroom when a white lawyer assumed she was the court interpreter. She surmised the confusion had to do with ethnic stereotyping, "no matter how well you're dressed."

Some of the latest research, however, shows that many Latinos — like Irish and Italian immigrants before them — drop the Latino label to call themselves simply "white." A study published last year in the Journal of Labor Economics found that the parents of more than a quarter of third-generation children with Mexican ancestry do not identify their children as Latino on census forms.

Most of this ethnic attrition occurs among the offspring of parents or grandparents married to non-Mexicans, usually non-Hispanic whites. These Latinos tend to have high education, high earnings and high levels of English fluency. That means that many successful Latinos are no longer present in statistics tracking Latino economic and social progress across generations, hence many studies showing little or no progress for third-generation Mexican immigrants, said Stephen J. Trejo, an economist at the University of Texas at Austin and co-author of the study.

And a more recent study by University of Southern California researchers found that more than two million people, or 6 percent of those who claimed any type of Latin American ancestry on census surveys, did not ultimately identify as Latino or Hispanic. The trend was more prevalent among those of mixed parentage, who spoke only English and who identified as white, black or Asian when asked their race.

James Paine, whose father is half Mexican-American, said it never occurred to him to claim a Latino identity. Mr. Paine, 25, the owner of a real estate investment management company in La Jolla, Calif., spent summers with his Mexican-American aunt and attends his father's big family reunions every year (his mother is white of Irish and French descent). But he says he does not speak Spanish or live in a Latino neighborhood.

"If the question is 'What's your heritage?' I'd say Irish-Mexican," he said. "But the question is 'What are you?' and the answer is I'm white."

On the other side of the spectrum are black Latinos, who say they feel the sting of racism much the same as other blacks. A sense of racial pride has been emerging among many black Latinos who are now coming together in conferences and organizations.

Miriam Jimenez Roman, 60, a scholar on race and ethnicity in New York, says that issues like racial profiling of indigenous-looking and dark-skinned Latinos led her to appear in a 30-second public service announcement before the 2010 census encouraging Latinos of African descent to "check both: Latino and black." "When you sit on the subway, you just see a black person, and that's really what determines the treatment," she said. The 2010 census showed 1.2 million Latinos who identified as black, or 2.5 percent of the Hispanic population.

Over the decades, the Census Bureau has repeatedly altered how it asks the race question, and on the 2010 form, it added a sentence spelling out that "Hispanic origins are not races." The change helped steer 5 percent more Latinos away from "some other race," with the vast majority of those choosing the white category. Still, critics of the census questionnaire say the government must move on from racial distinctions based on 18th-century binary thinking and adapt to Americans' sense of self.

But Latino political leaders say the risk in changing the questions could create confusion and lead some Latinos not to mark their ethnicity, shrinking the overall Hispanic numbers.

Ultimately, said Angelo Falcon, president of the National Institute for Latino Policy and chairman of the Census Advisory Committee on the Hispanic Population, this is not just a tussle over identity, it is a political battle, too.

"It comes down to what yields the largest numbers for which group," he said.

*http://www. nytimes. com/*2012/01/14/*us/for-many-latinos-race-is-more-culture-than-color. html*? *_r*=1&*hp*

Supplementary Reading 2

Minority Report

White America's collapsing birth rate is changing the face of the country.

AMONG America's three-year-olds, a revolution is a foot. Children of that age are turning the country's demographics on its head. According to a recent study from the Census Bureau, the majority of them are now from groups normally considered minorities, chiefly Hispanics and blacks. The latest release of data from last year's decennial census confirms that whites still constitute a slender majority, 54%, of those under 18, and a larger one, 64%, of the population as a whole. But America's transformation into a much browner, more suburban, more southern and western place is rapid and relentless.

Over the past decade America's population has grown by 9.7%, to 309 million. Minorities accounted for 92% of that growth. The ranks of Hispanics swelled by 43%, to 51 million. The Asian population grew at the same rate, to 15 million. Blacks increased in number by 11%, to 38 million. All minority groups put together jumped by 29%, to 112 million. Minorities now form the majority in America's two most-populous states, California and Texas, as well as in Hawaii, New Mexico and Washington, D. C. They account for the majority of children in six more: Arizona, Florida, Georgia, Maryland, Mississippi and Nevada. And their numbers are growing particularly fast in previously lily-white places such as Iowa and New Hampshire.

Meanwhile America's white, non-Hispanic population grew by only 1. 2% from 2000 to 2010. In 15 of the 50 states, it shrank. California lost 5% of its whites; New Jersey and Rhode Island both shed 6%. The number of white children fell in 46 states, for an overall decrease of 10%. Whites, explains Bill Frey of the Brookings Institution, a think-tank, are older, have fewer children anyway and make up a relatively small proportion of immigrants, so their share of the population is destined to go on falling.

The giant sucking sound emanating from the South and West, another leitmotif of American demographics, continues unmuffled. Both regions grew by 14%, while the north-east and the Midwest managed just 3% and 4% growth respectively. People are fleeing the cold: there is a strong correlation between the average temperature in January and population growth, notes Edward Glaeser, a professor of economics at Harvard University. He also attributes the rapid expansion of cities like Atlanta, Dallas, and Houston to their cheap, abundant housing.

Even in the sunbelt, however, many rural areas are losing population. The trend is particularly acute in the plains states, but also pertains in much of the Midwest and the South. The proportion of Americans living in urban areas rose from 93. 2% in 2000 to 93. 7% last year, with big cities growing faster than small ones. Most of this growth occurred in the suburbs rather than the inner cities, Mr. Glaeser adds, with the more prosperous metropolitan areas and those with better educated residents growing especially fast. Areas with lots of manufacturing grew more slowly.

Michigan, with its long-suffering car industry, was the only state to see its population shrink over the decade, albeit by less than 1%. (Puerto Rico, an

American territory with economic troubles of its own, lost 2% of its inhabitants.)

What all this means for politics is the subject of some dispute. Right-wing analysts herald the ballooning population of the Republican-leaning states in the South and West and the relative stagnation of the Democratic bastions in theMidwest and north-east as proof of the superiority of Republican policies. What is more, they crow, faster growth is bringing more seats in the House of Representatives to Republican states, which could help to cement their current majority. Conservative Texas, for example, is gaining four seats in the reapportionment set in train by last year's census; liberal New York is losing two.

But Democrats counter that the growth the Republicans are celebrating comes from natural Democratic constituencies. Minorities, they point out, tend to vote Democratic, whereas the dwindling white, rural population is largely Republican. By this logic, Democratic infiltrators are gradually undermining Republicans' control over their territory from within. Barack Obama, after all, carried previously Republican-leaning western and southern states such as Colorado, Nevada, North Carolina and Virginia on his way to the White House in 2008. If he can maintain his share of the vote among blacks and Latinos, he will be hard to beat in 2012.

*http://www.economist.com/node/*18488452

Chapter 4 History of the United States

The first known inhabitants of what is now the United States are believed to have arrived over a period of several thousand years beginning sometime prior to 15,000 to 50,000 years ago by crossing Beringia into Alaska. Solid evidence of these cultures settling in what would become United States territory is dated to around 14,000 years ago.

Research has revealed much about the early Native American in North America. Christopher Columbus' men were the first documented Old Worlders to land in the territory of what is now the United States when they arrived in Puerto Rico during their second voyage in the year 1493. Juan Ponce de León, who arrived in Florida in 1513, is credited as being the first European to land in what is now the continental United States, although some evidence suggests that John Cabot might have reached what is presently New England in 1498.

The coming of Europeans began the colonial history of the United States. The Thirteen Colonies, British colonies that would become the original US states, were founded along what is now the country's east coast beginning in 1607, but various other European powers also founded settlements in what would become US territory, both before and later. Due to growing dissatisfaction with British rule, the thirteen British colonies fought the British army in the American Revolutionary War of the 1770s and issued a Declaration of Independence in 1776. In early 1781, the Articles of Confederation and Perpetual Union of the States were established, six months before the end of hostilities in the Revolutionary War. Two years later, Britain officially recognized the sovereignty and independence of the United States in the Treaty of Paris. After the nation split along state lines in 1861, the Civil War(内战)—the deadliest war in US history—reunified the country. In the nineteenth century, westward expansion of United States territory began, encouraged by the belief in Manifest Destiny, in which the United States would occupy all of North America east to west, from the Atlantic to the Pacific Oceans. By 1912, with the admission of Arizona to the Union, the US reached that goal. The outlying states of Alaska and Hawaii were both admitted in 1959.

Ratified in 1788, the Constitution serves as the supreme law in organizing the government; the Supreme Court is responsible for upholding Constitutional law. Many forms of social progress started in the nineteenth century; those advancements have been widely reflected in the Constitution. Slavery was abolished in 1865 by the Thirteenth Amendment to the United States Constitution; the following Fourteenth and Fifteenth Amendments respectively guaranteed citizenship for all persons naturalized within US territory and voting for people of all races. In later decades, civil rights were extended to women and African-Americans, following effective lobbying from social activists. The Nineteenth Amendment prohibited gender discrimination in voting rights; later, the Civil Rights Act of 1964 outlawed racial segregation in public places.

The Progressive Era marked a time of economic growth for the United States, advancing to the Roaring Twenties. However, the Wall Street Crash of 1929 led to the Great Depression, a time of economic downturn and mass unemployment. Consequently, the US government established the New Deal, a series of reform programs that intended to assist those affected by the Depression. The New Deal had varied success. However, once the US entered World War Ⅱ in December 1941, the economy quickly recovered, so much that the US became a world superpower by the dawn of the Cold War. During the Cold War, the US and the Soviet Union were the world's two superpowers, but with the end of the Cold War and the collapse of the Soviet Union, the United States became the world's only superpower.

Pre-Columbian Period

The earliest known inhabitants of what is now the United States are thought to have arrived in Alaska by crossing the Bering land bridge, at least 14,000 to 30,000 years ago. Some of these groups migrated south and east, and over time spread throughout the Americas. These were the ancestors to modern Native

Americans in the United States and Alaskan Native peoples, as well as all indigenous peoples of the Americas.

4.1 Colonial Period

After a period of exploration by people from various European countries, Spanish, Dutch, English, French, Swedish, and Portuguese settlements were established.

Columbus was the first European to set foot on what would one day become US territory when he came to Puerto Rico on November 19, 1493, during his second voyage.

In the 16th century, Europeans brought horses, cattle, and hogs to the Americas and, in turn, took back to Europe maize, potatoes, tobacco, beans, squash, and slave natives, many of whom died enroute.

Spanish Colonization

Spanish explorers came to what is now the United States beginning with Christopher Columbus' second expedition, which reached Puerto Rico on November 19, 1493. The first confirmed landing in the continental US was by a Spaniard, Juan Ponce de León, who landed in 1513 on a lush shore he christened La Florida.

Dutch Colonization

Nieuw-Nederland, or New Netherland, was the seventeenth century Dutch colonial province on the eastern coast of North America. Its capital, New Amsterdam, was located at the southern tip of the island of Manhattan on the Upper New York Bay and was renamed New York.

British Colonization

In 1607, the Virginia Company of London established the Jamestown

Settlement on the James River, named after King James I.

The strip of land along the eastern seacoast was settled primarily by English colonists in the 17th century, along with much smaller numbers of Dutch and Swedes. Colonial America was defined by a severe labor shortage that gave birth to forms of unfree labor such as slavery and indentured servitude, and by a British policy of benign(温和的)neglect (salutary neglect) that permitted the development of an American spirit distinct from that of its European founders. Over half of all European migrants to Colonial America arrived as indentured servants.

The first successful English colony was established in 1607, on the James River at Jamestown. The Plymouth Colony was established in 1620. The area of New England was initially settled primarily by Puritans who established the Massachusetts Bay Colony in 1630. The Middle Colonies, consisting of the present-day states of New York, New Jersey, Pennsylvania, and Delaware, were characterized by a large degree of diversity. The first attempted English settlement south of Virginia was the Province of Carolina, with Georgia Colony the last of the Thirteen Colonies established in 1733.

Political Integration and Autonomy

The French and Indian War (1754 - 1763) was a watershed event in the political development of the colonies. The influence of the main rivals of the British Crown in the colonies and Canada, the French and North American Indians, was significantly reduced. Moreover, the war effort resulted in greater political integration of the colonies, as symbolized by Benjamin Franklin's call for the colonies to "Join or Die". Following Britain's acquisition of French territory in North America, King George Ⅲ issued the Royal Proclamation of 1763 with the goal of organizing the new North American empire and stabilizing relations with the native Indians. In ensuing years, strains developed in the relations between the colonists and the Crown. The British Parliament passed the Stamp Act of 1765, imposing a tax on the colonies to help pay for troops stationed in North America following the British victory in the Seven Years' War. The British government felt that the colonies were the primary beneficiaries of this military presence, and should pay at least a portion of the expense. The colonists did not share this view. Rather, with the French and Indian threat diminished, the primary outside influence remained that of Britain. A conflict of economic interests increased with the right of the British Parliament to govern the colonies without representation being called into question.

The Boston Tea Party in 1773 was a direct action by colonists in the town of Boston to protest against the taxes levied by the British government. Parliament responded the next year with the Coercive Acts, which sparked outrage and resistance in the Thirteen Colonies. Colonists convened the First Continental Congress to coordinate their resistance to the Coercive Acts. The Congress called for a boycott of British trade, published a list of rights and grievances, and petitioned the king for redress of those grievances.

The Congress also called for another meeting in the event that their petition was unsuccessful in halting enforcement of the Coercive(强制的)Acts. Their appeal to the Crown had no effect, and so the Second Continental Congress was convened in 1775 to organize the defense of the colonies at the onset of the American Revolutionary War.

4.2 Formation of the United States of America

American Revolutionary War(1776 – 1789)

The Thirteen Colonies began a rebellion against British rule in 1775 and proclaimed their independence in 1776. They subsequently constituted the first thirteen states of the United States of America, which became a nation state in 1781 with the ratification of the Articles of Confederation and Perpetual Union. The 1783 Treaty of Paris represented the Kingdom of Great Britain's formal acknowledgement of the United States as an independent nation.

The United States defeated Britain with help from France, the United Provinces and Spain in the American Revolutionary War. The colonists' victory at Saratoga in 1777 led the French into an open alliance with the United States. It is a matter of debate which state was the first to recognize the United States, but the claim extends to the Republic of Ragusa (now the city of Dubrovnik), the Netherlands and Morocco.

In 1781, a combined American and French Army, acting with the support of a French fleet, captured a large British army led by General Charles Cornwallis at Yorktown, Virginia. The surrender of General Cornwallis ended serious British efforts to find a military solution to their American problem. In effect, "the United States was the first major colony successfully to revolt against colonial rule. In this sense, it was the first 'new nation'."

Declaration of Independence, but it actually shows the drafting committee presenting its work to the Congress

Side by side with the states' efforts to gain independence through armed resistance, a political union was being developed and agreed upon by them. The first step was to formally declare independence from Great Britain. On July 4, 1776, the Second Continental Congress, still meeting in Philadelphia, declared the independence of "the United States of America" in the Declaration of Independence. Although the states were still independent entities and not yet formally bound in a legal union, July 4 is celebrated as the nation's birthday. The new nation was dedicated to principles of republicanism, which emphasized civic duty and a fear of corruption and hereditary aristocracy.

A series of attempts to organize a movement to outline and press reforms culminated in the Congress calling the Philadelphia Convention in 1787. The structure of the national government was profoundly changed on March 4, 1789, when the American people replaced the confederation type government of the Articles with a federation type government of the Constitution. The new government reflected a radical break from the normative governmental structures of the time, favoring representative, elective government with a weak executive, rather than the existing monarchical structures common within the western traditions of the time. The system of republicanism borrowed heavily from the Enlightenment ideas and classical western philosophy: a primacy was placed upon individual liberty and upon constraining the power of government through a system of separation of powers. Additionally, the United States Bill of Rights was ratified on December 15, 1791 to guarantee individual liberties such as freedom of speech and religious practice and consisted of the first ten amendments of the Constitution.

Westward Expansion (1789 – 1849)

The Louisiana Purchase, in 1803, removed the French presence from the western border of the United States and provided US settlers with vast potential for expansion west of the Mississippi River. Slave importation from Africa became illegal in 1808, despite a growing plantation system in many southern states such as North Carolina and Georgia.

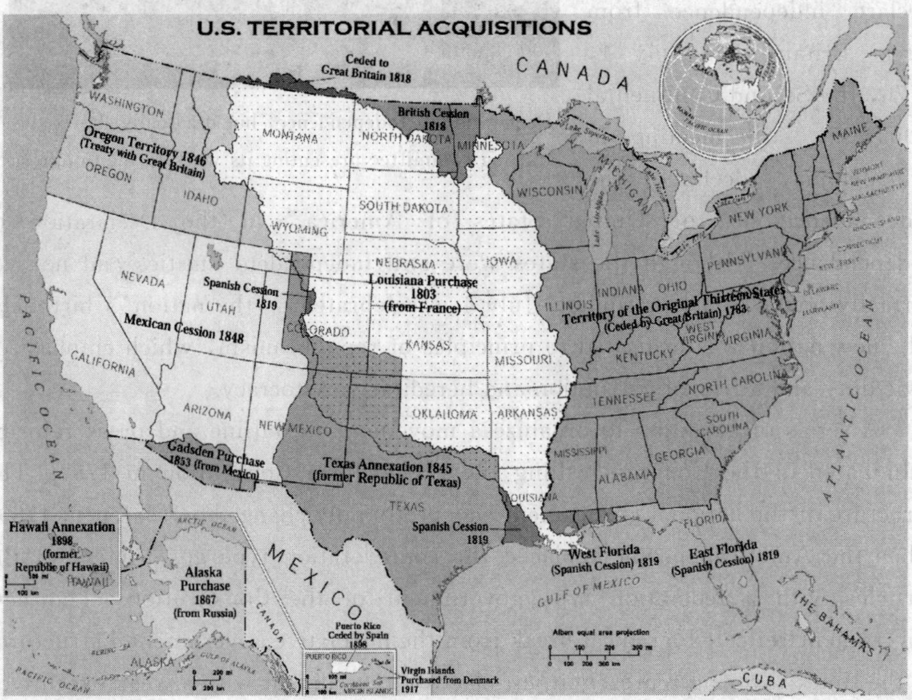

US Territorial Acquisitions

In 1830, Congress passed the Indian Removal Act, which authorized the president to negotiate treaties that exchanged Native American tribal lands in the eastern states for lands west of the Mississippi River. The act resulted most notably in the forced migration of several native tribes to the West, with several thousand people dying en route.

The Republic of Texas was annexed by president John Tyler in 1845. The US army, using regulars and large numbers of volunteers, defeated Mexico in 1848 during the Mexican-American War. Public sentiment in the US was divided as Whigs(辉格党)and anti-slavery forces opposed the war. The 1848 Treaty of Guadalupe Hidalgo ceded California, New Mexico, and adjacent areas to the United States, about thirty percent of Mexico. Westward expansion was enhanced further by the California Gold Rush, the discovery of gold in that state in 1848. Numerous "forty-niners" trekked to California in pursuit of gold; land-hungry European immigrants also contributed to the rising white population in the west. In 1849 cholera spread along the California and Oregon Trails. It is believed that over 150,000 Americans died during the two cholera pandemics between 1832 and 1849.

Settlers Crossing the Plains of Nebraska

4.3 Civil War Era

Civil War 1849 - 1865

In the middle of the 19th century, white Americans of the North and South were to reconcile fundamental differences in their approach to government, economics, society and African American slavery. The issue of slavery in the new territories was settled by the Compromise of 1850 brokered by Whig Henry Clay and Democrat Stephen Douglas; the Compromise included admission of California as a free state and the passage of the Fugitive Slave Act to make it easier for masters to reclaim runaway slaves. In 1854, the proposed Kansas-Nebraska Act abrogated the Missouri Compromise by providing that each new state of the Union would decide its stance on slavery. After Abraham Lincoln won the 1860 Election, eleven Southern states seceded from the union between late 1860 and 1861, establishing a rebel government, the Confederate States of America, on February 8, 1861.

By 1860, there were nearly four million slaves residing in the United States, nearly eight times as many from 1790; within the same time period, cotton production in the US boomed from less than a thousand tons to nearly one million tons per year. There were some slave rebellions, but they all failed and led to tighter slave oversight in the south. Harriet Beecher Stowe, daughter of minister Lyman Beecher, published her novel Uncle Tom's Cabin in 1852 in response to the passage of the Fugitive(逃跑的)Slave Act. The novel intended to express her views of the cruelty of slavery and sold nearly 300,000 copies during its first year of publication and was regarded by many, including President Lincoln, to be the book that started the Civil War. Numerous slaves also escaped their masters through the Underground Railroad, a term defining secret routes where abolitionists confidentially transported runaway slaves to "free state" territory; its most famous leader was Harriet Tubman.

The Civil War began on April 12, 1861, when Confederate forces attacked a US military installation at Fort Sumter in South Carolina. Along with the

Battle of Gettysburg

northwestern portion of Virginia, four of the five northernmost "slave states" did not secede and became known as the Border States. Emboldened by Second Bull Run, the Confederacy made its first invasion of the North when General Robert E. Lee led the Army of Northern Virginia across the Potomac River into Maryland. The Battle of Antietam near Sharpsburg, Maryland, on September 17, 1862, was the bloodiest single day in American history. Following the highly successful battles at Fredericksburg and Chancellorsville, Lee attempted to invade the North again, but during the invasion encountered once again the Army of the Potomac. In the devastating 3-day, Battle of Gettysburg, Lee suffered his greatest loss in what would turn out to be the bloodiest battle in the war. On the following day in the west, Union forces under the command of General Ulysses S. Grant gained control of the Mississippi River at the Battle of Vicksburg, thereby splitting the Confederacy. At the beginning of 1864, Lincoln made General Grant commander of all Union armies. Union General William Tecumseh Sherman captured Atlanta, Georgia, and from there started his "March to the Sea" that laid waste to about 20% of the farms in Georgia, until reaching the Atlantic Ocean at Savannah in December 1864. Lee surrendered his Army of Northern Virginia on April 9, 1865, at Appomattox Court House. Based on 1860 census figures, 8% of all white males aged 13 to 43 died in the war, including 6% in the North and an extraordinary 18% in the South.

Reconstruction and the Rise of Industrialization (1865–1890)

Reconstruction took place for most of the decade following the Civil War. During this era, the "Reconstruction Amendments" were passed to expand civil rights for black Americans. Those amendments included the Thirteenth Amendment, which outlawed slavery, the Fourteenth Amendment that guaranteed citizenship for all people born or naturalized within US territory, and the Fifteenth Amendment that granted the vote for all men regardless of race. While the Civil Rights Act of 1875 forbade discrimination in the service of public facilities, the Black Codes denied blacks certain privileges readily available to whites.

Following was the Gilded Age, a term that author Mark Twain used to describe the period of the late nineteenth century when there had been a dramatic expansion of American industry. Twain believed that this age was corrupted by such elements as land speculators, scandalous politics, and unethical business practices. By century's end, American industrial production and per capita income exceeded those of all other world nations and ranked only behind Great Britain. Later, an unprecedented wave of immigration served both to provide the labor for American industry and create diverse communities in previously undeveloped areas. From 1880 to 1914, peak years of immigration, more than 22 million people migrated to the United States. Abusive industrial practices led to the often violent rise of the labor movement in the United States. Influential figures of the period included John D. Rockefeller and Andrew Carnegie.

4.4 Two World Wars

Progressivism(进步主义), Imperialism, and World War Ⅰ(1890 - 1918)

After the Gilded(镀金的) Age came the Progressive Era, whose followers called for reform over perceived industrial corruption. Viewpoints taken by progressives included greater federal regulation of anti-trust laws and the industries of meat-packing, drugs, and railroads. Four new constitutional amendments—the Sixteenth through Nineteenth—resulted from progressive activism. The era lasted from 1900 to 1918, the year marking the end of World War Ⅰ.

US Federal government policy, since the James Monroe Administration, had been to move the indigenous population beyond the reach of the federal frontier into a series of Indian reservations. Tribes were generally forced onto small reservations as farmers and ranchers took over their lands.

The United States began its rise to international power in this period with substantial population and industrial growth domestically and numerous military ventures abroad, including the Spanish-American War. Also at stake were US interests in acquiring Cuba, an island nation fighting for independence from Spanish occupation; Puerto Rico and the Philippines were also two former Spanish colonies seeking liberation. In December 1898, representatives of Spain and the US signed the Treaty of Paris to end the war, with Cuba becoming an independent nation and Puerto Rico, Guam, and the Philippines becoming US territories. President Woodrow Wilson declared US entry into World War I in April 1917 following a yearlong neutrality policy; the US had previously shown interest in world peace by participating in the Hague Conferences. American participation in the war proved essential to the Allied victory.

Women's Suffrage(选举权)

These years of the early 20th century also saw the strengthening of the Women's Suffrage Movement. The movement had begun with the 1848 Seneca Falls Convention, organized by Elizabeth Cady Stanton and Lucretia Mott, and the Declaration of Sentiments demanding equal rights for women. The women's rights campaign during "first-wave feminism" was led by Mott, Stanton, Susan B. Anthony, and Sojourner Truth, Lucy Stone, and Julia Ward Howe, among others. By the end of the 19th century only several states had granted women full voting rights. In the early 20th century, protests became increasingly common as suffragette Alice Paul led parades through major cities and picketing of the White House. Finally, Wilson addressed the Congress

Alice Paul led parades in Women's Suffrage movement

on woman suffrage, urging them to pass a Constitutional amendment enfranchising women, which they did in 1919. It became law on August 26, 1920, after ratification by the 36th required state.

Post-World War I and the Great Depression(1918 - 1940)

Following World War I, the US grew steadily in stature as an economic and military world power. The United States Senate did not ratify the Treaty of Versailles imposed by its Allies on the defeated Central Powers; instead, the United States chose to pursue unilateralism, if not isolationism. The aftershock of Russia's October Revolution resulted in real fears of communism in the United States, leading to a three-year Red Scare and the US lost 675,000 people to the Spanish flu pandemic in 1918.

In 1920, the manufacture, sale, import and export of alcohol was prohibited by the Eighteenth Amendment to the United States Constitution. Prohibition encouraged illegal breweries and dealers to make substantial amounts of money selling alcohol illegally. The Prohibition ended in 1933, a failure. The 1920s were also known as the Roaring Twenties(兴旺的 20 年代), due to the great economic prosperity during this period. Jazz became popular among the younger generation, and thus was also called the Jazz Age.

An abandoned farm in South Dakota during the Dust Bowl, 1936

During most of the 1920s, the United States enjoyed a period of unbalanced prosperity: farm prices and wages fell, while new industries, and industrial profits grew. The boom was fueled by an inflated stock market, which later led to the a crash on October 29, 1929. The Hawley-Smoot Tariff, the Dust Bowl(干旱尘暴区), and the ensuing Great Depression led to government efforts to restart the economy and help its victims with Franklin D. Roosevelt's New Deal(新政).

The recovery was rapid in all areas except unemployment, which remained fairly high until 1940.

World War Ⅱ (1941 - 1945)

On December 7, 1941 Japan launched a surprise attack on the American naval base in Pearl Harbor, citing America's recent trade embargo(禁运) as justification. The following day, Franklin D. Roosevelt successfully urged a joint session of Congress to declare war on Japan, calling December 7, 1941 "a date which will live in infamy". Four days after the attack on Pearl Harbor, on December 11, Nazi Germany declared war on the United States, drawing the country into a two-theater war.

Battle against Germany

Upon entering the war, the United States and its allies decided to concentrate the bulk of their efforts on fighting Hitler in Europe, while maintaining a defensive position in the Pacific until Hitler was defeated. The United States's first step was to set up a large airforce in Britain to concentrate on bombing raids into Germany itself.

The American army's first ground action was fighting alongside the British, Australian and New Zealand armies in North Africa. By May 1943, the British 8th Army had expelled the Germans from North Africa and the Allies controlled this vital link until the end of the war. The American navy also played an active role in the Atlantic protecting the convoys bringing vital American war material to Britain. By midway through 1943, the Allies were fighting the war from Britain with unbroken supply lines, while at the same time Hitler's armies were very much on the back foot, with heavy bombing taking its toll on production.

By early 1944, a planned invasion of Western Europe was underway. What followed on June 6, 1944, was Operation Overlord, or D-Day. The largest war armada(舰队)ever assembled landed on the beaches of Normandy and began the penetration of Western Europe that eventually overthrew Hitler and Nazi Germany. Following the landing at Normandy, the Americans contributed greatly to the outcome of the war, with dogged fighting in the Battle of the

Ardennes and the Battle of the Bulge resulting in Allied victories against the Germans. The battles took a heavy toll on the Americans, who lost 19,000 men during the Battle of the Bulge alone. The allied bombing raids on Germany increased to unprecedented levels after the D-Day invasion, with over 70% of all bombs dropped on Germany occurring after this date. On April 30, 1945, with Berlin completely overrun with Russian forces and his country in tatters, Adolf Hitler committed suicide. On May 8, 1945, the war with Germany was over, following its unconditional surrender to the Allied forces.

Soldiers of the US Army 1st Infantry Division Landing
in Normandy on D-Day, June 6, 1944

Battle against Japan

Due to the United States commitment to defeating Hitler in Europe, the first years of the war against Japan was largely a defensive battle with the United States Navy attempting to prevent the Japanese Navy from asserting dominance of the Pacific region. Initially, Japan won the majority of its battles in a short period of time. Japan quickly defeated and created military bases in Guam, Thailand, Malaya, Hong Kong, Papua New Guinea, Indonesia and Burma. This was done virtually unopposed and with quicker speed than that of the German Blitzkrieg during the early stages of the war. This was important for Japan, as it had only 10% of the homeland industrial production capacity of the United States.

The turning point of the war was the Battle of Midway in June 1942. Following this, the Americans began fighting towards China where they could build an airbase suitable to commence bombing of mainland Japan with its B-29 Superfortress fleet. The Americans began by selecting smaller, lesser defended islands as targets as opposed to attacking the major Japanese strongholds. During this period, they inadvertently(无意地)triggered what would become their most comprehensive victory in the entire war.

The Pacific war became the largest naval conflict in history. The American Navy emerged victorious, after at one point being stretched near to the breaking point, with almost complete destruction of the Japanese Navy. The American forces were then poised for an invasion of the Japanese mainland, to force the Japanese into unconditional surrender. On April 12, 1945, President Franklin Delano Roosevelt died and Vice President Harry S. Truman was sworn in as the 33rd President of the United States. The use of atomic weapons against Japan was subsequently authorized. The decision to use nuclear weapons to end the conflict has been one of the most controversial decisions of the war. Supporters of the use of the bombs argue that an invasion would have cost an enormous numbers of lives, while opponents argue that the large number of civilian casualties resulting from the bombings was unjustified. The first bomb was dropped on Hiroshima(广岛)on August 6, 1945, and the second bomb was dropped on Nagasaki on August 9, 1945. On August 15, 1945, the Japanese surrendered unconditionally, ending World War Ⅱ.

4.5 The Cold War Era

Following World War Ⅱ, the United States emerged as one of the two dominant superpowers. The US Senate, on December 4, 1945, approved US participation in the United Nations (UN), which marked a turn away from the traditional isolationism of the US and toward more international involvement. The post-war era in the United States was defined internationally by the beginning of the Cold War, in which the United States and the Soviet Union attempted to expand their influence at the expense of the other, checked by each side's massive nuclear arsenal and the doctrine of mutual assured destruction. The result was a series of conflicts during this period including the Korean War and the tense nuclear showdown of the Cuban Missile Crisis. Within the United States, the Cold War prompted concerns about Communist influence, and also resulted in government efforts to focus mathematics and science toward efforts such as the space race.

In the decades after World War Ⅱ, the United States became a global influence in economic, political, military, cultural, and technological affairs. Beginning in the 1950s, middle-class culture had a growing obsession with consumer goods.

John F. Kennedy was elected President in 1960. Known for his charisma, he is so far the only Roman Catholic to be President. The Kennedys brought a new life and vigor to the atmosphere of the White House. During his time in office, the Cold War reached its height with the Cuban Missile Crisis in 1962. He was assassinated in Dallas, Texas, on November 22, 1963 by Lee Harvey Oswald.

The Civil Rights Movement (1955－1970)

Meanwhile, the American people completed a great migration from farms into the cities and experienced a period of sustained economic expansion. At the same time, institutionalized racism across the United States, but especially in the American South, was increasingly challenged by the growing Civil Rights movement. The activism of African American leaders Rosa Parks and Martin Luther King, Jr. led to the Montgomery Bus Boycott, which launched the movement. For years African Americans would struggle with violence against them,

Martin Luther King—March on Washington

but would achieve great steps towards equality with Supreme Court decisions, including Brown v. Board of Education and Loving v. Virginia, the Civil Rights Act of 1964, the Voting Rights Act of 1965, and the Fair Housing Act of 1968, which ended the Jim Crow laws that legalized racial segregation between Whites and Blacks. Martin Luther King, Jr., who had won the Nobel Peace Prize for his efforts to achieve equality of the races, was assassinated in 1968. Following his death other leaders led the movement, most notably King's widow, Coretta Scott King, who was also active, like her husband, in the Opposition to the Vietnam War, and in the Women's Liberation Movement. Over the first nine months of 1967, 128 American cities suffered 164 riots. The late 1960s and early 1970s saw the strengthening of Black Power, however the decade would ultimately bring about positive strides toward integration.

The Women's Movement (1963 – 1982)

A new consciousness of the inequality of American women began sweeping the nation, starting with the 1963 publication of Betty Friedan's best-seller, *The Feminine Mystique*, which explained how many housewives felt trapped and unfulfilled, assaulted American culture for its creation of the notion that women could only find fulfillment through their roles as wives, mothers, and keepers of the home, and argued that women were just as able as men to do every type of job. In 1966 Friedan and others established the National Organization for Women, or NOW, to act as an NAACP for women. Protests began, and the new "Women's Liberation Movement" grew in size and power, gained much media attention, and, by 1968, had replaced the Civil Rights Movement as the US's main social revolution. Marches, parades, rallies, boycotts, and pickets brought out thousands, sometimes millions; Friedan's Women's Strike for Equality (1970) was a nation-wide success. The Movement was factioned early on, however (NOW) on the left, the Women's Equity Action League (WEAL) on the right, the National Women's Political Caucus (NWPC) in the center, and more radical groups formed by younger women on the far left). Along with Friedan, Gloria Steinem was an important feminist leader, co-founding the NWPC, the Women's Action Alliance, and editing the Movement's magazine,

Ms. The proposed Equal Rights Amendment to the Constitution, passed by Congress in 1972 and favored by about seventy percent of the American public, failed to be ratified in 1982, with only three more states needed to make it law. However many federal laws, state laws (i. e. those ending spousal abuse and marital rape), Supreme Court rulings (i. e. ruling the equal protection clause of the Fourteenth Amendment applied to women), and state ERAs established women's equal status under the law, and social custom and consciousness began to change, accepting women's equality. The controversial issue of abortion, legalized in 1973 is still a point of feminist debate today.

The Counterculture Revolution and Cold War Détente (缓和)(1964－1980)

Amid the Cold War, the United States entered the Vietnam War, whose growing unpopularity fed already existing social movements, including those among women, minorities and young people. President Lyndon B. Johnson's Great Society social programs and the judicial activism of the Warren Court added to the wide range of social reform during the 1960s and 1970s. Feminism and the environmental movement became political forces, and progress continued toward civil rights for all Americans. The Counterculture Revolution swept through the nation and much of the western world in the late sixties and early seventies, dividing the already hostile environment but also bringing forth more liberated social views.

Johnson was succeeded by President Richard Nixon in 1969, who initially escalated the Vietnam War but soon was able to negotiate a peace treaty in 1973, effectively ending American involvement in the war. The war had cost the lives of 58,000 American troops and millions of Vietnamese. Nixon used a conflict in the Eastern Bloc between the Soviet Union and China to the advantage of the United States, bolstering relations with the People's Republic of China. A new era of Cold War relations known as détente (cooperation) was begun. The OPEC oil embargo led to a period of slow economic growth in 1973. Nixon's administration was brought to an ignominious close with the political scandal of Watergate in August 1974. During the years of his successor, Gerald Ford, the

American-backed South Vietnamese government collapsed.

The End of the Cold War (1980–1991)

Reagan took a hard line against the Soviet Union, proclaiming it to be the Evil Empire. Reagan ordered a massive buildup of the US military, incurring a costly budget deficit. Reagan introduced a complicated missile defense system known as the Strategic Defense Initiative (dubbed "Star Wars" by opponents) in which the US could, in theory, shoot down missiles by means of laser systems in space. Though it was never fully developed or deployed, the Soviets were genuinely concerned about the possible effects of the program and the research and technologies of SDI paved the way for the anti-ballistic missile systems of today. The Reagan administration also provided covert funding and assistance to anti-Communist resistance movements worldwide. Reagan's interventions against Grenada and Libya were popular in the US, though his backing of the Contra rebels was mired(深陷)in controversy. The arms-for-hostages scandal led to the convictions of such figures as Oliver North and John Poindexter. He shared many common views and goals with friend and ally Margaret Thatcher, the Prime Minister of the United Kingdom.

Reagan met with Soviet Leader Mikhail Gorbachev, who ascended to power in 1985, four times, and their summit conferences led to the signing of the INF Treaty. Gorbachev tried to save Communism in the Soviet Union first by ending the expensive arms race with America, then by shedding the East European empire in 1989. The Soviet Union collapsed in 1991, ending the US-Soviet Cold War.

4.6 The World Superpower

After the fall of the Soviet Union, the United States emerged as the world's sole remaining superpower and continued to involve itself in military action overseas, including the 1991 Gulf War. Following his election in 1992, President Bill Clinton oversaw unprecedented gains in securities values, a side effect of the digital revolution and new business opportunities created by the Internet. The

1990s saw one of the longest periods of economic expansion.

At the beginning of the new millennium, the United States found itself attacked by Islamic terrorism, with the September 11, 2001 attacks in which 19 extremists hijacked four transcontinental airliners and intentionally crashed two of them into the twin towers of the World Trade Center and one into the Pentagon. The passengers on the fourth plane, United Airlines Flight 93, revolted causing the plane to crash into a field in Somerset County, Pennsylvania. According to the 9/11 Commission Report, that plane was intended to hit the US Capitol Building in Washington. The twin towers of the World Trade Center collapsed, destroying the entire complex. The United States soon found large amounts of evidence that suggested that the terrorist group al-Qaeda, spearheaded by Osama bin Laden, was responsible for the attacks.

9/11 Attack by Terrorists in 2001

In response to the attacks, under the administration of President George W. Bush, the United States (with the military support of NATO and the political support of some of the international community) launched Operation Enduring Freedom which overthrew the Taliban regime in Afghanistan which had protected and harbored bin Laden and al-Qaeda. With the support of large bipartisan majorities, the US Congress passed the Authorization for Use of Military Force Against Iraq Resolution of 2002. With a coalition of other countries including Britain, Spain, Australia, Japan and Poland, in March 2003 President Bush ordered an invasion of Iraq dubbed Operation Iraqi Freedom which led to the overthrow and capture of Saddam Hussein. Using the language of 1998 Iraq Liberation Act and the Clinton Administration, the reasons cited by the Bush administration for the invasion included the spreading of democracy, the elimination of weapons of mass destruction (a key demand of the UN as well, though later investigations found parts of the intelligence reports to be inaccurate) and the liberation of the Iraqi people. This second invasion fueled protest marches in many parts of the world.

As of 2009, debates continue over abortion, gun control, same-sex marriage, immigration reform, and the ongoing war in Iraq. Although the new Democratic Congressional majority promised to withdraw US forces from Iraq, Congress continues to fund efforts in both Iraq and Afghanistan (however a withdrawal agreement has been agreed upon between the US and Iraqi governments). In the area of foreign policy, the US maintains ongoing talks, led by United States Secretary of State Hillary Rodham Clinton, with North Korea over its nuclear weapons program, as well as with Israel and the Palestinian Authority over a two-state solution to the Israeli-Palestinian conflict; the Palestinian-Israeli talks began in 2007, an effort spearheaded by United States Secretary of State Condoleezza Rice. The George W. Bush administration also increased allegations implicating Iran, and more recently Syria, in the development of weapons of mass destruction.

In December 2007, the United States entered the longest post-World War Ⅱ recession, which included a housing market correction, a subprime mortgage crisis(次贷危机), soaring oil prices, and a declining dollar value. In February 2008, 63,000 jobs were lost, a 5-year record for a single month. In September 2008, the crisis became much worse beginning with the government takeover of Fannie Mae and Freddie Mac followed by the collapse of Lehman Brothers. This economic crisis was considered the worst financial crisis since the Great Depression. By the end of 2008, the US had lost a total of 2.6 million jobs.

In the presidential election of 2008, Senator Barack Obama, having narrowly defeated Senator Hillary Rodham Clinton for the Democratic nomination, ran on a platform of "Hope and Change". This, coupled with the economic crisis, helped aid his and running-mate Joe Biden's victory against the Republican ticket of Senator John McCain and Governor Sarah Palin. On November 4, Obama became the first African American to be elected President of the United States; he was sworn into office as the 44th President on January 20, 2009.

Questions

1. Explain the"westward expansion" in detail.
2. What is the importance of the Philadelphia Convention?
3. Describe the rise of US industrialization.
4. How do you understand the progressivism in the US history?
5. How did the Great Depression influence America?
6. How did the 2008 Economic Recession happen?

Supplementary Reading 1

Roosevelt Aims for Economic Security with "Second New Deal"

Franklin Roosevelt's first three months as president was one of the most exciting periods in American politics. Roosevelt entered the White House in March nineteen thirty-three. The nation was in crisis. Banks across the country had closed their doors. The Great Economic Depression was at its lowest point.

Roosevelt and the Congress moved quickly to help people with little food or money. They launched a series of major economic programs.

This week in our series, we talk about the laws and policies of President Franklin Roosevelt including those known as the "Second New Deal".

Conditions improved within a year after Roosevelt took office. There was no question about that. Banks were open. More people had jobs. Farmers were doing better. And poor people were not so close to disaster as before. However, conditions were far from perfect. Ten million workers still did not have jobs. Young people leaving school were lucky to find any job at all. And most business owners were only earning small profits, if any at all.

After the worst crisis was past, some groups of Americans began to attack

Roosevelt and his programs. Conservatives were the first to break with the president. They accused Roosevelt of socialist economic policies.

Much more serious to Roosevelt was criticism from reformers within his own party. A number of popular leaders with strong ideas began to attract support from large numbers of Americans. Roosevelt saw his national unity falling apart. Conservatives were accusing him of socialism. Leftist opponents said he was doing too little to end the depression. He saw that he had to change his path.

Roosevelt knew he had little chance to re-gain the support of conservative Americans. His policies were too progressive. So, halfway through his first term as president, he began to support new reforms in an effort to win more support from the left.

The Supreme Court made the president's effort easier. Early in nineteen thirty-five, the court ruled that several of Roosevelt's earlier programs violated the constitution and ordered an end to them. Among them were major programs for farmers and industrial planning.

The court's decisions forced Roosevelt to create new programs and try new ideas. One of his first new actions was to support a plan for government controls on companies that supplied water and produced electricity.

Another was a measure to give jobs to workers. A third new law forced companies doing business with the federal government to pay workers a minimum wage. And the government also began enforcing a new law to control the actions of stock market traders and investment companies.

At the same time, Roosevelt began to attack large companies. He spoke about the importance of small businesses in a democracy. He warned the nation that large companies had too much power. And he called for new actions to increase business competition and control large companies.

Roosevelt supported, and Congress passed, two laws during this period that would change the lives of working Americans for years to come. The first law gave more power to labor unions. The second created a federal system to provide money for workers after they retired.

Roosevelt's administration had already supported labor unions in an earlier law. But that law was over-ruled by the Supreme Court. So in nineteen thirty-five, the Congress passed a new law called the National Labor Relations Act.

The act created a national labor relations group to help negotiate agreements between workers and business owners. It gave all workers the right to join or form a labor union. And it ordered business owners to negotiate with a union if it represented most of the workers.

The new law, for the first time, gave unions real power and negotiating rights.

The other very important law passed during this period created the national social security system. The law forced every worker and business owner to pay a small amount of money each month to the federal government. In exchange, the government paid money to workers who had retired or lost their jobs.

The new law did not serve everyone. Farmers, government workers, and a number of other groups were not included in the system. The plan also did nothing to help people who were already unemployed. A person had to have a job after the new system began and then lose it to get money.

However, the national social security law established a system that would grow and become a central part of American life.

Roosevelt also supported other new laws during this period that changed the American economy. A banking act gave the nation's central bank—the Federal Reserve Board—new power to control the total amount of money in use.

Another law increased taxes for rich people. A third law limited the power of major companies to gain control of local electric utility companies.

The new laws openly challenged the power of big companies, big banks, and big money. Roosevelt rejected the idea that government should cooperate with major companies. Instead, he accused many of the companies of ruining the economy and hurting the working man. He called on Congress to help small companies and the average American.

Perhaps the most important change during this period was that Roosevelt became willing to accept a federal budget that was not balanced. He began to agree with the ideas of Marriner Eccles, the head of the Federal Reserve Bank.

Eccles believed that government had a duty to spend extra money during times of economic crisis. The extra money, he said, would create jobs for more people. They could buy more goods. And this would increase economic growth.

Eccles believed that it was good policy for a government to spend more money than it earned through taxes during such periods. He argued that a growing economy would increase wages and bring in more tax money.

Roosevelt's administration had spent more money than it earned ever since it took office. But the president and his advisers did so only to end the economic crisis. They believed that it was a necessary evil. But Eccles and others told Roosevelt that it was not bad for the nation if the government spent more than it earned.

The British economist John Maynard Keynes published an influential book that supported the same policy. And Roosevelt and his top advisers began to accept the new idea.

Roosevelt's economic policies were known as the "New Deal". But the many changes he made during this period became known as the "Second New Deal".

They included some of the most important pieces of legislation in the history of the country, such as the National Labor Relations Act and the Social Security law. And Roosevelt's willingness to accept an unbalanced budget would be the first step toward federal budget deficits that would grow steadily in the years to come.

Budget deficits would jump under President Lyndon Johnson during the war in Vietnam. They would be an important cause of economic inflation in the United States and the world in the nineteen-seventies. And Americans would elect Ronald Reagan president in nineteen-eighty partly to try to bring federal spending under control.

In nineteen-thirty-five, however, most Americans agreed with Franklin Roosevelt that budget deficits were necessary to fight the serious economic depression.

*http://www. 51voa. com/VOA _ Special _ English/American-History-President-Roosevelt-Aims-for-Economic-Security-With-Second-New-Deal-*41386. *html*

Supplementary Reading 2

Kennedy and the Cuban Missile Crisis

Kennedy, a Democrat, defeated Republican Vice President Richard Nixon in one of the closest elections in United States history. He took office in January nineteen sixty-one.

After three months, Kennedy faced a major foreign policy failure.

On April seventeenth, armed Cuban exiles tried to invade Cuba, less one hundred fifty kilometers from the American state of Florida. They had been trained by the Central Intelligence Agency. Their goal was to overthrow the island's communist leader, Fidel Castro. In nineteen fifty-nine he and his guerrilla forces had overthrown Fulgencio Batista, the president who was supported by the United States.

US President John F. Kennedy reports to the nation on the Cuban missile crisis from the White House in Washington

The exiles came ashore at Cuba's Bay of Pigs. Most were killed or captured.

The last administration, under President Dwight Eisenhower, had planned the invasion. But Kennedy had approved it. After the failure, some Americans again wondered if the forty-three-year-old president had enough experience to lead the nation.

In May nineteen sixty-one, Kennedy went to Paris and met with French President Charles de Gaulle. Kennedy visited France with his wife Jacqueline, who spoke French and had studied there.

In June, Kennedy met in Vienna, Austria, with Soviet Premier Nikita Khrushchev. Khrushchev did not want to compromise on any issue. He threatened to have the East Germans block all movement into and out of the

Allied-controlled western half of Berlin.

In November, the East Germans, with Soviet support, started building the Berlin Wall to separate east and west. President Kennedy quickly announced a large increase in American military forces in Germany.

Less than a year later came the Cuban missile crisis. On October twenty-second, nineteen sixty-two, President Kennedy made an announcement to the American people.

JOHN KENNEDY: "This government, as promised, has maintained the closest surveillance of the Soviet military buildup on the island of Cuba. Within the past week, unmistakable evidence has established the fact that a series of offensive missile sites is now in preparation on that imprisoned island. The purpose of these bases can be none other than to provide a nuclear strike capability against the Western Hemisphere."

Upon receiving the first preliminary hard information of this nature last Tuesday morning at nine a. m., I directed that our surveillance be stepped up. And having now confirmed and completed our evaluation of the evidence and our decision on a course of action, this government feels obliged to report this new crisis to you in fullest detail.

"The characteristics of these new missile sites indicate two distinct types of installations. Several of them include medium range ballistic missiles, capable of carrying a nuclear warhead for a distance of more than one thousand nautical miles. Each of these missiles, in short, is capable of striking Washington, DC, the Panama Canal, Cape Canaveral, Mexico City, or any other city in the southeastern part of the United States, in Central America, or in the Caribbean area."

Kennedy had a warning for the Soviets.

JOHN KENNEDY: "It shall be the policy of this nation to regard any nuclear missile launched from Cuba against any nation in the Western Hemisphere as an attack by the Soviet Union on the United States, requiring a full retaliatory response upon the Soviet Union."

Kennedy and his national security advisers debated what to do about the Soviet missiles in Cuba. Should the United States launch an air strike and try to destroy them? What if some of the nuclear missiles escaped the attack?

Kennedy decided to use a naval blockade—he called it a "quarantine"—to prevent any more Soviet ships from reaching Cuba.

There were tense negotiations with the Soviets. Khrushchev demanded a promise that the United States would not invade Cuba. Kennedy agreed, and did so publicly. Secretly he also agreed to another demand. He promised that the United States would remove its Jupiter missiles based in Turkey, after the crisis was over.

The Cuban missile crisis lasted thirteen days. It raised fears of a nuclear war. But it ended peacefully when the Soviets agreed to remove their missiles from Cuba, and turned their ships around.

But the Cold War continued.

In Asia, the Kennedy administration tried to fight communism in Vietnam by increasing the number of American military advisers there.

The United States and the Soviet Union did make some progress on arms control. In nineteen sixty-three, the two countries agreed to ban tests of nuclear weapons except underground.

Kennedy also had to deal with domestic issues, including discrimination against blacks. His brother Robert was attorney general, the nation's top law enforcement official. The Justice Department took legal action against states in the South that violated laws on voting rights.

The administration also supported a voter registration campaign to sign up more black voters.

Robert Kennedy repeatedly called on National Guard troops to protect blacks when they tried to register to vote or attend white schools.

President Kennedy said the situation was causing a moral crisis in America. He decided it was time to propose a new civil rights law that would guarantee equal treatment for blacks in public places and jobs.

Congress did not pass a wide-reaching civil rights bill until nineteen sixty-four. By then Kennedy was no longer president.

In November nineteen sixty-three, he traveled to Texas. He hoped to settle a dispute in the Democratic Party in that state. The dispute might have affected his chances for re-election in nineteen sixty-four.

Kennedy arrived in Dallas in the late morning of November twenty-second.

The president and his wife were seated in the back of an open-topped car as his motorcade drove through the city. Suddenly, there were gunshots.

WALTER CRONKITE: "Here is a bulletin from CBS news. In Dallas, Texas, three shots were fired at President Kennedy's motorcade in downtown Dallas. The first reports say that President Kennedy has been seriously wounded by this shooting."

The motorcade raced to Parkland Memorial Hospital. But doctors could do little to save his life. This was how television newsman Walter Cronkite reported the news:

WALTER CRONKITE: "From Dallas, Texas—the flash apparently official—President Kennedy died at one p. m., Central Standard Time."

Police quickly arrested a suspect. Lee Harvey Oswald worked in a building near where Kennedy had been shot. People had seen him leave the building with a gun.

Lee Harvey Oswald was a man with a strange past. He was a former United States Marine. He was also a communist. He had lived for a while in the Soviet Union and had tried to become a Soviet citizen. He worked for a committee that supported the communist government in Cuba.

Police questioned Oswald about the shooting of President Kennedy. He told them he did not do it. After two days, officials decided to move him to a different jail.

Oswald was being led by two police officers. Suddenly, a man stepped forward. There was a shot. Oswald fell to the ground. Television cameras broadcast the events live.

The man who killed Oswald was Jack Ruby. He was a nightclub owner in Dallas. He said he shot Oswald to prevent the Kennedy family from having to live through a trial.

A commission investigated the assassination of John F. Kennedy. The chief justice of the United States, Earl Warren, led the investigation. In its report, the Warren commission said that Lee Harvey Oswald had acted alone. It said there was no plot to kill the president.

Many Americans never accepted that finding. Some blamed Fidel Castro or the Central Intelligence Agency. Others blamed organized crime.

President Kennedy was buried in Arlington National Cemetery, across the Potomac River from Washington. An Eternal Flame burns night and day by his grave.

http://www.51voa.com/VOA_Special_English/American-History-Kennedy-and-the-Cuban-Missile-Crisis-43483.html

Chapter 5 Politics of the United States

Politics of the United States takes place in the framework of a presidential, federal republic where the President of the United States (the head of state and head of government), United States Congress, and judiciary share federal powers, and the federal government shares sovereignty with the state governments. Federal and state elections generally take place within the lines of a two-party system, although this is not enshrined in law.

The executive branch is headed by the President and is independent of the legislature. Legislative power is vested in the two chambers of Congress, the Senate and the House of Representatives. Judicial power is exercised by the judicial branch (or judiciary), composed of the Supreme Court and lower federal courts. The judiciary's function is to interpret the United States Constitution as well as federal laws and regulations. This includes resolving disputes between the executive and legislative branches. The federal government of the United States was established by the Constitution. American politics has been dominated by two parties, the Democratic Party and the Republican Party, since the American Civil War, although other parties have also existed.

Major differences between the political system of the United States and that of most other developed democracies are the power of the Senate as the upper house of the legislature, the wide scope of power of the Supreme Court, the separation of powers between the legislature and the executive government, and the dominance of the two main parties—the United States being one of the world's developed democracies in which third parties have the least political influence.

5.1 Federal, State and Local Governments

The federal entity created by the Constitution is the dominant feature of the American governmental system. However, most persons are also subject to a state government, and all are subject to various units of local government. The latter include counties, municipalities, and special districts.

This multiplicity of jurisdictions reflects the country's history. The federal government was created by the states, which as colonies were established separately and governed themselves independently of the others. Units of local government were created by the colonies to efficiently carry out various state functions. As the country expanded, it admitted new states modeled on the existing ones.

State Government

States governments have the power to make laws on all subjects that are not granted to the national government or denied to the states in the US Constitution. These include education, family law, contract law, and most crimes. Unlike the national government, which only has those powers granted to it in the Constitution, a state government has inherent powers allowing it to act unless limited by a provision of the state or national constitution.

Like the national government, state governments have three branches: executive, legislative, and judicial. The chief executive of a state is its popularly elected governor, who typically holds office for a four-year term (although in a some states the term is two years). Except for Nebraska, which has unicameral legislature, all states have a bicameral legislature, with the upper house usually called the Senate and the lower house called the House of Representatives, the House of Delegates, Assembly or something similar. In most states, senators serve four-year terms, and members of the lower house serve two-year terms.

The constitutions of the various states differ in some details but generally follow a pattern similar to that of the federal Constitution, including a statement of the rights of the people and a plan for organizing the government. State constitutions are generally more detailed, however.

Local Government

There are 87,000 local governments, including 3,034 counties, 19,498 municipalities, 16,500 townships, 13,500 school districts, and 35,000 other special districts which deal with issues like fire protection. To a greater extent than on the federal or state level, the local governments directly serve the needs of the people, providing everything from police and fire protection to sanitary codes, health regulations, education, public transportation, and housing.

About 28% of the people live in cities of 100,000 or more population. City governments are chartered by states, and their charters detail the objectives and powers of the municipal government. For most big cities, cooperation with both state and federal organizations is essential to meeting the needs of their residents.

Types of city governments vary widely across the nation. However, almost all have some kind of central council, elected by the voters, and an executive officer, assisted by various department heads, to manage the city's affairs.

There are three general types of city government: the mayor-council, the commission, and the council-manager. These are the pure forms; many cities have developed a combination of two or three of them.

Mayor-Council. This is the oldest form of city government in the United States and, until the beginning of the 20th century, was used by nearly all American cities. Its structure is similar to that of the state and national governments, with an elected mayor as chief of the executive branch and an elected council that represents the various neighborhoods forming the legislative branch. The mayor appoints heads of city departments and other officials, sometimes with the approval of the council. He or she has the power of veto over ordinances — the laws of the city — and frequently is responsible for preparing the city's budget. The council passes city ordinances, sets the tax rate on property, and apportions money among the various city departments. As cities have grown, council seats have usually come to represent more than a single neighborhood.

The Commission. This combines both the legislative and executive functions in one group of officials, usually three or more in number, elected city-wide. Each commissioner supervises the work of one or more city departments. One is named chairperson of the body and is often called the mayor, although his or her power is equivalent to that of the other commissioners.

Council-Manager. The city manager is a response to the increasing complexity of urban problems, which require management expertise not often possessed by elected public officials. The answer has been to entrust most of the executive powers, including law enforcement and provision of services, to a highly trained and experienced professional city manager.

The city manager plan has been adopted by a large number of cities. Under this plan, a small, elected council makes the city ordinances and sets policy, but hires a paid administrator, also called a city manager, to carry out its decisions. The manager draws up the city budget and supervises most of the departments. Usually, there is no set term; the manager serves as long as the council is satisfied with his or her work.

County Government

The county is a subdivision of the state, sometimes — but not always — containing two or more townships and several villages. New York City is so large that it is divided into five separate boroughs, each a county in its own right. On the other hand, Arlington County, Virginia, the United State's smallest county located just across the Potomac River from Washington, D. C., is both an urbanized and suburban area, governed by a unitary county administration. In other cities, both the city and county governments have merged, creating a consolidated city-county government.

In most US counties, one town or city is designated as the county seat, and this is where the government offices are located and where the board of commissioners or supervisors meets. In small counties, boards are chosen by the county as a whole; in the larger ones, supervisors represent separate districts or townships. The board collects taxes for state and local governments; borrows and appropriates money; fixes the salaries of county employees; supervises elections; builds and maintains highways and bridges; and administers national, state, and county welfare programs. In very small counties, the executive and legislative power may lie entirely with a sole commissioner, who is assisted by boards to supervise taxes and elections. In some New England states, counties do not have any governmental function and are simply a division of land.

Town and Village Government

Thousands of municipal jurisdictions are too small to qualify as city governments. These are chartered as towns and villages and deal with such strictly local needs as paving and lighting the streets, ensuring a water supply, providing police and fire protection and waste management. Note that in many states the term "town" does not have any specific meaning—it is simply an informal term applied to populated places (both incorporated and unincorporated municipalities). And in some states, the term town is equivalent to how civil townships are used in other states.

The government is usually entrusted to an elected board or council, which may be known by a variety of names: town or village council, board of selectmen, board of supervisors, board of commissioners. The board may have a chairperson or president who functions as chief executive officer, or there may be an elected mayor. Governmental employees may include a clerk, treasurer, police and fire officers, and health and welfare officers.

One unique aspect of local government, found mostly in the New England region of the United States, is the town meeting. Once a year — sometimes more often if needed — the registered voters of the town meet in open session to elect officers, debate local issues, and pass laws for operating the government. As a body, they decide on road construction and repair, construction of public buildings and facilities, tax rates, and the town budget. The town meeting, which has existed for more than three centuries in some places, is often cited as the purest form of direct democracy, in which the governmental power is not delegated, but is exercised directly and regularly by all the people.

5.2 Political Culture

Most schools in the United States teach the Declaration of Independence, Constitution, Bill of Rights, and the writings of the Founding Fathers as the definition of the country's governing ideology. Among the core tenets of this ideology(意识形态)are the following:

• Democracy: The government is answerable to citizens, who may change it through elections.

• Equality before the law: The laws should attach no special privilege to any citizen. Government officials are subject to the law just as others are

• Freedom of religion and separation of church and state: The government can neither support nor suppress religion.

• Freedom of speech: A marketplace of ideas.

At the time of the United States' founding, the economy was predominantly one of agriculture and small private businesses, and state governments left welfare issues to private or local initiative. As in the UK and other industrialized countries, laissez-faire ideology was largely discredited during the Great Depression. Between the 1930s and 1970s fiscal policy was characterized by the Keynesian consensus(共识), a time during which modern American liberalism dominated economic policy virtually unchallenged. Since the late 1970s and early 1980s, however, laissez-faire ideology has once more become a powerful force in American politics. While the American welfare state expanded more than threefold after WWⅡ, it has been at 20% of GDP since the late 1970s. Today, modern American liberalism, and modern American conservatism are engaged in a continuous political battle, characterized by what the Economist describes as "greater divisiveness close, but bitterly fought elections".

Prior to World War Ⅱ the United States pursued a policy of noninterventionism in foreign affairs by not taking sides in conflicts between foreign powers. The country abandoned this policy when it became a superpower, and the country mostly supports internationalism.

5.3 Political Parties and Elections

The United States Constitution is silent on the subject of political organizations, mainly because most of the founding fathers disliked them. Yet, major and minor political parties and groups soon arose.

In partisan elections, candidates are nominated by a political party or seek public office as an independent. Each state has significant discretion in deciding how candidates are nominated, and thus eligible to appear on the election ballot (投票). Typically, major party candidates are formally chosen in a party primary or convention, whereas minor party and Independents are required to complete a petitioning process. Registered Democrats, Republicans and independents in millions as of 2004.

Political Parties

The completelist of political parties in the United States is vast. However, there are two main parties in presidential contention:

- Democratic Party
- Republican Party

Each of these two parties shares a degree of national attention by attaining the mathematical possibility of its nominee becoming President of the United States—i. e. , having ballot access for its presidential candidate in states whose collective total is at least half of the Electoral College votes.

Organization of American Political Parties

American political parties are more loosely organized than those in other countries. The two major parties, in particular, have no formal organization at the national level that controls membership, activities, or policy positions, though some state affiliates do. Thus, for an American to say that he or she is a member of the Democratic or Republican party, is quite different from a Briton's stating that he or she is a member of the Labour party. In the United States, one can often become a "member" of a party, merely by stating that fact. In some US states, a voter can register as a member of one or another party and/or vote in the primary election for one or another party, but such participation does not restrict one's choices in any way; nor does it give a person any particular rights or obligations with respect to the party, other than possibly allowing that person to vote in that party's primary elections (elections that determine who the candidate of the party will be). A person may choose to attend meetings of one local party committee one day and another party committee the next day. The sole factor that brings one "closer to the action" is the quantity and quality of participation in party activities and the ability to persuade others in attendance to give one responsibility.

Party identification becomes somewhat formalized when a person runs for partisan office. In most states, this means declaring oneself a candidate for the nomination of a particular party and intent to enter that party's primary election for an office. A party committee may choose to endorse one or another of those who is seeking the nomination, but in the end the choice is up to those who choose to vote in the primary, and it is often difficult to tell who is going to do the voting.

The result is that American political parties have weak central organizations and little central ideology, except by consensus. A party really cannot prevent a person who disagrees with the majority of positions of the party or actively works against the party's aims from claiming party membership, so long as the voters who choose to vote in the primary elections elect that person. Once in office, an elected official may change parties simply by declaring such intent.

At the federal level, each of the two major parties has a national committee that acts as the hub for much fund-raising and campaign activities, particularly in presidential campaigns. The exact composition of these committees is different for each party, but they are made up primarily of representatives from state parties, affiliated organizations, and other individuals important to the party. However, the national committees do not have the power to direct the activities of individual members of the party.

When a party controls the White House, the President is party leader and controls the national committee. Otherwise the leadership is diffuse.

Both parties also have separate campaign committees which work to elect candidates at a specific level. The most significant of these are the Hill committees, which work to elect candidates to each house of Congress.

State parties exist in all fifty states, though their structures differ according to state law, as well as party rules at both the national and the state level.

Political Pressure Groups

Special interest groups advocate the cause of their specific constituency. Business organizations will favor low corporate taxes and restrictions of the right to strike, whereas labor unions will support minimum wage legislation and protection for collective bargaining. Other private interest groups — such as churches and ethnic groups — are more concerned about broader issues of policy that can affect their organizations or their beliefs.

One type of private interest group that has grown in number and influence in recent years is the political action committee or PAC. These are independent groups, organized around a single issue or set of issues, that contribute money to political campaigns for US Congress or the presidency. PACs are limited in the amounts they can contribute directly to candidates in federal elections. There are no restrictions, however, on the amounts PACs can spend independently to advocate a point of view or to urge the election of candidates to office. PACs today number in the thousands.

"The number of interest groups has mushroomed, with more and more of them operating offices in Washington, D. C., and representing themselves directly to Congress and federal agencies," says Michael Schudson in his 1998 book The Good Citizen: A History of American Civic Life. "Many organizations that keep an eye on Washington seek financial and moral support from ordinary citizens. Since many of them focus on a narrow set of concerns or even on a single issue, and often a single issue of enormous emotional weight, they compete with the parties for citizens' dollars, time, and passion."

The amount of money spent by these special interests continues to grow, as campaigns become more and more expensive. Many Americans have the feeling that these wealthy interests — whether corporations or unions or PACs organized to promote a particular point of view — are so powerful that ordinary citizens can do little to counteract their influences.

General Developments

Many of America's Founding Fathers hated the thought of political parties. They were sure quarreling factions would be more interested in contending with each other than in working for the common good. They wanted individual citizens to vote for individual candidates, without the interference of organized groups — but this was not to be.

By the 1790s, different views of the new country's proper course had already developed, and those who held these opposing views tried to win support for their cause by banding together. The followers of Alexander Hamilton, the Hamiltonian faction, took up the name "Federalist"; they favored a strong central government that would support the interests of commerce and industry. The followers of Thomas Jefferson, the Jeffersonians and then the "Anti-Federalists," took up the name "Democratic-Republicans"; they preferred a decentralized agrarian republic in which the federal government had limited power. By 1828, the Federalists had disappeared as an organization, replaced by the Whigs, brought to life in opposition to the election that year of President Andrew Jackson. Jackson's presidency split the Democratic-Republican party: Jacksonians became the Democratic Party and those following the leadership of John Quincy Adams became the "National Republicans." The two-party system, still in existence today, was born. (Note: The National Republicans of John Quincy Adams is not the same party as today's Republican Party.)

In the 1850s, the issue of slavery took center stage, with disagreement in particular over the question of whether or not slavery should be permitted in the country's new territories in the West. The Whig Party straddled the issue and sank to its death after the overwhelming electoral defeat by Franklin Pierce in 1852 presidential election. Ex-Whigs joined the Know Nothings or the newly-formed Republican Party. While the Know Nothing party was short lived, it was the Republicans that would survive the intense politics leading up to the Civil War. The primary Republican policy was that slavery be excluded from all the territories. Just six years later, this new party captured the presidency when Abraham Lincoln won the election of 1860. By then, parties were well established as the country's dominant political organizations, and party allegiance had become an important part of most people's consciousness. Party loyalty was passed from fathers to sons, and party activities — including spectacular campaign events, complete with uniformed marching groups and torchlight parades — were a part of the social life of many communities.

By the 1920s, however, this boisterous folksiness had diminished. Municipal reforms, civil service reform, corrupt practices acts, and presidential primaries to replace the power of politicians at national conventions had all helped to clean up politics.

Development of the Two-party System in the United States

Since the 1790s the country has been run by two major parties. The United States does not have a parliamentary system, in which governing coalitions are formed after elections, so coalitions are formed before elections under the umbrella of the party organizations. In the absence of a parliamentary system, third parties cannot thrive. Since the Civil War, the two major parties have been called the Republican and Democratic parties. Many minor or third political parties appear from time to time. They tend to serve a means to advocate policies that eventually are adopted by the two major political parties. At various times the Socialist Party, the Farmer-Labor Party and the Populist Party for a few years had considerable local strength, then faded away. At present the Libertarian Party is the most successful third party.

Most officials in America are elected from single-member districts and win office by beating out their opponents in a system for determining winners called first-past-the-post—the one who gets the plurality wins, (which is not the same thing as actually getting a majority of votes). This encourages the two-party system.

Another critical factor has been ballot access law. Originally voters went to the polls and publicly stated which candidate they supported. Later on, this developed into a process whereby each political party would create its own ballot and thus the voter would put the party's ballot into the voting box. In the late nineteenth century, states began to adopt the Australian Secret Ballot Method, and it eventually became the national standard. The secret ballot method ensured that the privacy of voters would be protected (hence government jobs could no longer be awarded to loyal voters) and each state would be responsible for creating one official ballot. The fact that state legislatures were dominated by Democrats and Republicans provided these parties an opportunity to pass discriminatory laws against minor political parties, yet such laws did not start to arise until the first Red Scare that hit America after World War I. State legislatures began to enact tough laws that made it harder for minor political parties to run candidates for office by requiring a high number of petition signatures from citizens and decreasing the length of time that such a petition could legally be circulated.

It should also be noted that while the overwhelming majority of elected officials do identify with a political party, the political parties of the United States are much more individualistic than in other political systems (i. e. in a parliamentary system). More often than not, party members will "toe the line" and support their party's policies, but it is important to note that they are free to vote against their own party and vote with the opposition ("cross the aisle") whenever they please.

"In America the same political labels—Democratic and Republican—cover virtually all public officeholders, and therefore most voters are everywhere mobilized in the name of these two parties," says Nelson W. Polsby, professor of political science, in the book *New Federalist Papers: Essays in Defense of the Constitution*. "Yet Democrats and Republicans are not everywhere the same. Variations—sometimes subtle, sometimes blatant—in the 50 political cultures of the states yield considerable differences overall in what it means to be, or to vote, Democratic or Republican. These differences suggest that one may be justified in referring to the American two-party system as masking something more like a hundred-party system."

Political Spectrum of the Two Major Parties

During the 20th century the overall political philosophy of both the Republican Party and the Democratic Party underwent a dramatic shift from their earlier philosophies. From the 1860s to the 1950s the Republican Party was considered to be the more classically liberal of the two major parties and the Democratic Party the more classically conservative/populist of the two.

This changed a great deal with the presidency of Democrat Franklin D. Roosevelt, whose New Deal included the founding of Social Security as well as a variety of other federal services and public works projects. Roosevelt's success in the twin crises of the Depression and World War Ⅱ led to a sort of polarization in national politics, centered around him; this combined with his increasingly liberal policies to turn FDR's Democrats to the left and the Republican Party further rightward.

During the 1950s and the early 1960s both parties essentially expressed a more centrist approach to politics on the national level and had their liberal, moderate, and conservative wings influential within both parties.

From the early 1960s, the conservative wing became more dominant in the Republican Party, and the liberal wing became more dominant in the Democratic Party. The 1964 presidential election heralded the rise of the conservative wing among Republicans. The liberal and conservative wings within the Democratic Party were competitive until 1972, when George McGovern's candidacy marked the triumph of the liberal wing. This similarly happened in the Republican Party with the candidacy and later landslide election of Ronald Reagan in 1980, which marked the triumph of the conservative wing.

By the 1980 election, each major party had largely become identified by its dominant political orientation. Although strong showings in the 1990s by reformist independent Ross Perot pushed the major parties to put forth more centrist presidential candidates like Bill Clinton and Bob Dole, polarization in the congress was said by some to have been cemented by the Republican takeover of 1994, though others say that this polarization had existed since the late 1980's when the Democrats were in control of both houses of Congress.

Liberals within the Republican Party and conservatives within the Democratic Party and the Democratic Leadership Councilneoliberals(新自由主义者) have typically fulfilled the roles of so-called political mavericks(不合常规的人), radical centrists, or brokers of compromise between the two major parties. They have also helped their respective parties gain in certain regions that might not ordinarily elect a member of that party; the Republican Party has used this approach with centrist Republicans such as Rudy Giuliani, George Pataki, Richard Riordan and Arnold Schwarzenegger. The 2006 elections sent many centrist or conservative Democrats to state and federal legislatures including several, notably in Kansas and Montana, who switched parties.

Elections in the United States

The United States has a federal government, with elected officials at the federal (national), state and local levels. On a national level, the head of state, the President, is elected indirectly by the people, through an Electoral College. In modern times, the electors virtually always vote with the popular vote of their state. All members of the federal legislature, the Congress, are directly elected. There are many elected offices at the state level, each state having at least an elective governor and legislature. There are also elected offices at the local level, in counties and cities. It is estimated that across the whole country, over one million offices are filled in every electoral cycle.

Both federal and state laws regulate elections. The United States Constitution defines (to a basic extent) how federal elections are held, in Article One and Article Two and various amendments. State law regulates most aspects of electoral law, including primaries, the eligibility of voters (beyond the basic constitutional definition), the running of each state's electoral college, and the running of state and local elections. The financing of elections has always been controversial, because private sources of finance make up substantial amounts of campaign contributions, especially in federal elections. Voluntary public funding for candidates willing to accept spending limits was introduced in 1974 for presidential primaries and elections. The Federal Elections Commission, created in 1975 by an amendment to the Federal Election Campaign Act has the responsibility to disclose campaign finance information, to enforce the provisions of the law such as the limits and prohibitions on contributions, and to oversee the public funding of US presidential elections. The federal government has also been involved in attempts to increase voter turnout, by measures such as the National Voter Registration Act of 1993.

Suffrage

Suffrage is nearly universal for citizens 18 years of age and older. All 50 states, as well as the District of Columbia, contribute to the electoral vote for President. However, the District, and other US holdings like Puerto Rico and Guam, lack the states' representation in Congress. These constituencies do not have the right to choose any political figure outside their respective areas. Each commonwealth, territory, or district can only elect a non-voting delegate to serve in the House of Representatives.

Voting rights are sometimes restricted as a result of felony conviction, but such laws vary widely by state. Election of the president is an indirect suffrage: Voters vote for electors, who in turn vote for President. In theory, these electors vote as they please, but in modern practice they do not vote against the wishes of their constituencies (though they have abstained from voting in protest).

Campaign Finance

Successful participation, especially in federal elections, requires large amounts of money, especially for television advertising. This money is very difficult to raise by appeals to a mass base, although in the 2008 election, candidates from both parties had success with raising money from citizens over the Internet, as had Howard Dean with his Internet appeals. Both parties generally depend on wealthy donors and organizations—traditionally the Democrats depended on donations from organized labor while the Republicans relied on business donations. Since 1984, however, the Democrats' business donations have surpassed those from labor organizations. This dependency on donors is controversial, and has led to laws limiting spending on political campaigns being enacted. Opponents of campaign finance laws cite the First Amendment's guarantee of free speech, and challenge campaign finance laws on the grounds that they attempt to circumvent (回避) the people's constitutionally-guaranteed rights. Even when laws are upheld, the complication of compliance with the First Amendment requires careful and cautious drafting of legislation, leading to laws that are still fairly limited in scope, especially in comparison to those of other countries such as the United Kingdom, France or Canada.

Presidential Elections

The President and the Vice President are elected together in a Presidential election. The election is indirect, the winner being determined by votes cast by electors of the Electoral College. In modern times, voters in each state select a slate of electors from a list of several slates designated by different parties or candidates, and the electors typically promise in advance to vote for the candidates of their party (whose names usually appear on the ballot rather than those of the individual electors). The winner of the election is the candidate with at least 270 Electoral College votes. It is possible for a candidate to win the electoral vote, and lose the (nationwide) popular vote (receive fewer votes nationwide than the second ranked candidate). Until the Twelfth Amendment to the United States Constitution of 1804, the runner-up in a Presidential election became the Vice President.

Electoral College (选举团) votes are cast by individual states by a group of electors, each elector casts one electoral college vote. In modern times, with electors usually committed to vote for a party candidate in advance, electors that vote against the popular vote in their state are called faithless electors, and occurrences are rare. State law regulates how states cast their electoral college votes. In all states except Maine and Nebraska, the candidate that wins the most votes in the state receives all its electoral college votes (a "winner takes all" system). From 1969 in Maine, and from 1991 in Nebraska, two electoral votes are awarded based on the winner of the statewide election, and the rest (two in Maine, three in Nebraska) go to the highest vote-winner in each of the state's congressional districts. Incumbent Presidents and challengers usually seek to have a "balanced ticket", so that the Presidential candidate and the Vice Presidential candidates have complementary political support and political roles, allowing them to do well among different constituencies. Usually, there is some kind of balance, for example geographical, ideological, or in terms of (especially federal) government experience. The nominated Vice Presidential candidate is called the "running mate". Although incumbent Presidents can be challenged in the primaries, none have lost their party's nomination in recent times (although Gerald Ford in 1976 came close). The last incumbent President to not seek a second term was Lyndon B. Johnson, who stepped down after serving the remainder of John F. Kennedy's term and another full term (he was eligible for another term).

Democrat Barack Obama, the 44th US President and the first African American to hold the office.

The electoral college has long been criticized, for several reasons. It has been criticized for being undemocratic by definition, since through it the President is elected indirectly rather than a direct system of election. Another criticism is that it creates inequality between voters in different states during the Presidential election. Usually, only voters in swing states determine the outcome of the election and as a result, it is claimed that the vast majority of Americans, who live in non-competitive states, are largely ignored by political campaigns. If the electoral college were abolished and if the whole country were treated as one district for Presidential elections, then the result would not depend on crucial swing states. It also creates inequality in that the populations of very small states, which have a minimum of 3 Electoral College votes, are overrepresented compared with voters from larger states. For example, Wyoming has a population of 493,782 and 3 EC votes, 164,594 people per EC vote. California has a population of 33,871,648 and 55 EC votes, 615,848 people per EC vote.

Abolishing the college and replacing it with a national direct system would also prevent a candidate from receiving fewer votes nationwide than their opponent, but still winning more electoral votes, which last occurred in the 2000 Presidential election. Also, the electoral college discriminates against candidates who do not have support concentrated in several states. In 1992, Ross Perot won 18.9% of the national vote, but received no electoral college votes. The electoral college would require a constitutional amendment to be abolished, and since three-quarters of state legislatures would be required to ratify an amendment that would effectively redistribute voting power from many small states to numerically fewer large states, it is thought that an amendment would fail.

5.4 Law of the United States

The law of the United States consists of many levels of codified and uncodified forms of law, of which the most important is the United States Constitution, the foundation of the federal government of the United States. The Constitution sets out the boundaries of federal law, which consists of constitutional acts of Congress, constitutional treaties ratified by Congress, constitutional regulations promulgated by the executive branch, and case law originating from the federal judiciary.

The Constitution and federal law are the supreme law of the land, thus circumscribing state and territorial laws in the fifty US states and in the territories. In the unique dual-sovereign system of American federalism (actually tripartite when one includes Indian reservations), states are the plenary sovereigns, while the federal sovereign possesses only the limited supreme authority enumerated in the Constitution. Indeed, states may grant their citizens broader rights than the federal Constitution as long as they do not infringe on any federal constitutional rights. Thus, most US law (especially the actual "living law" of contract, tort (侵权), criminal, and family law experienced by the majority of citizens on a day-to-day basis) consists primarily of state law, which can and does vary greatly from one state to the next.

At both the federal and state levels, the law of the United States was originally largely derived from the common law system of English law, which was in force at the time of the Revolutionary War. However, US law has diverged greatly from its English ancestor both in terms of substance and procedure, and has incorporated a number of civil law innovations.

General Overview

Sources of Law

In the United States, the law is derived from four sources. These four sources are constitutional law, statutory law, administrative regulations, and the common law (which includes case law). The most important source of law is the United States Constitution. All other law falls under and is subordinate to that document. No law may contradict the Constitution.

Constitutionality

Where Congress enacts a statute that conflicts with the Constitution, the Supreme Court may find that law unconstitutional and declare it invalid.

Notably, a statute does not disappear automatically merely because it has been found unconstitutional; it must be deleted by a subsequent statute. Many federal and state statutes have remained on the books for decades after they were ruled to be unconstitutional. However, under the principle of stare decisis(照章办事), no sensible lower court will enforce an unconstitutional statute, and any court that does so will be reversed by the Supreme Court. Conversely, any court that refuses to enforce a constitutional statute (where such constitutionality has been expressly established in prior cases) will risk reversal by the Supreme Court.

American Common Law

The United States and most Commonwealth countries are heirs to the common law legal tradition of English law. Certain practices traditionally allowed under English common law were expressly outlawed by the Constitution, such as bills of attainder and general search warrants.

As common law courts, US courts have inherited the principle of stare decisis. American judges, like common law judges elsewhere, not only apply the law, they also make the law, to the extent that their decisions in the cases before them become precedent for decisions in future cases.

The actual substance of English law was formally "received" into the United States in several ways. First, all US states except Louisiana have enacted "reception statutes" which generally state that the common law of England (particularly judge-made law) is the law of the state to the extent that it is not repugnant to domestic law or indigenous conditions. Some reception statutes impose a specific cutoff date for reception, such as the date of a colony's founding, while others are deliberately vague. Thus, contemporary US courts often cite pre-Revolution cases when discussing the evolution of an ancient judge-made common law principle into its modern form, such as the heightened duty of care traditionally imposed upon common carriers.

Second, a small number of important British statutes in effect at the time of the Revolution have been independently reenacted by US states. Two examples that many lawyers will recognize are the Statute of Frauds (still widely known in the US by that name) and the Statute of 13 Elizabeth (the ancestor of the Uniform Fraudulent Transfers Act). Such English statutes are still regularly cited in contemporary American cases interpreting their modern American descendants.

However, it is important to understand that despite the presence of reception statutes, much of contemporary American common law has diverged significantly from English common law. The reason is that although the courts of the various Commonwealth nations are often influenced by each other's rulings, American courts rarely follow post-Revolution Commonwealth rulings unless there is no American ruling on point, the facts and law at issue are nearly identical, and the reasoning is strongly persuasive.

Early on, American courts, even after the Revolution, often did cite contemporary English cases. This was because appellate(上诉的)decisions from many American courts were not regularly reported until the mid-19th century; lawyers and judges, as creatures of habit, used English legal materials to fill the gap. But citations to English decisions gradually disappeared during the 19th century as American courts developed their own principles to resolve the legal problems of the American people. The number of published volumes of American reports soared from eighteen in 1810 to over 8,000 by 1910. Today, in the words of Stanford law professor Lawrence Friedman: "American cases rarely cite foreign materials. Courts occasionally cite a British classic or two, a famous old case, or a nod to Blackstone; but current British law almost never gets any mention." Foreign law has never been cited as binding precedent, but merely as a reflection of the shared values of Anglo-American civilization or even Western civilization in general.

Questions

1. Introduce the core tenets of the ideology of the United States.
2. Analyze the political spectrum of the two major parties in the US.
3. Analyze the process of Presidential election. What is the role of Electoral College?

Supplementary Reading 1

The Right Republican

Although the Presidency is theirs for the taking, America's Republicans are in danger of throwing it away.

IN JANUARY the battle to become the world's most powerful person begins—with small groups of Iowans "caucusing" to choose a Republican nominee for the White House. It is a great opportunity for them. Barack Obama is clearly beatable. No President since Franklin Roosevelt has been re-elected with unemployment as high as it is now; Mr. Obama's approval rating, which tends to translate accurately into vote-share, is down in the mid-40s. Swing states like Florida, Ohio and even Pennsylvania look well within the Republicans' grasp.

Yet recent polls show the president leading all his rivals: an average of two points ahead of Mitt Romney, eight points over Ron Paul and nine points over Newt Gingrich, according to *RealClearPolitics. com.* No doubt some rather flawed personalities play a part in that; but so does the notion that something has gone badly wrong with the party of Abraham Lincoln, Theodore Roosevelt and Ronald Reagan. Rather than answering the call for a credible right-of-centre, pro-business party to provide independents, including this newspaper, with a choice in November, it is saddling its candidate with a set of ideas that are cranky, extreme and backward-looking.

That matters far beyond this election—and indeed America's shores. Across the West nations are struggling to reform government. At their best the Republicans have combined a muscular foreign policy with sound economics, individualism and entrepreneurial pragmatism. It is in everybody's interests that they become champions of such policies again. That is not impossible, but there is a lot of catching up to do.

Please sign on the dotted line.

Optimists will point out that the Republicans, no less than the Democrats, tend to flirt with extremes in the primaries, then select an electable moderate (with Mr Romney being the likely winner this time). America is a conservative place; every Republican nominee, including those The Economist has backed in the past, has signed up to pretty uncompromising views on God, gays and guns. But even allowing for that, the party has been dragged further and further to the right. Gone are the days when a smiling Reagan could be forgiven for raising taxes and ignoring abortion once in office. As the Republican base has become ever more detached from the mainstream, its list of unconditional demands has become ever more stringent.

Nowadays, a candidate must believe not just some but all of the following things: that abortion should be illegal in all cases; that gay marriage must be banned even in states that want it; that the 12m illegal immigrants, even those who have lived in America for decades, must all be sent home; that the 46m people who lack health insurance have only themselves to blame; that global warming is a conspiracy; that any form of gun control is unconstitutional; that any form of tax increase must be vetoed, even if the increase is only the cancelling of an expensive and market-distorting perk; that Israel can do no wrong and the "so-called Palestinians", to use Mr. Gingrich's term, can do no right; that the Environmental Protection Agency, the Department of Education and others whose names you do not have to remember should be abolished.

These fatwas explain the rum list of candidates: you either have to be an unelectable extremist who genuinely believes all this, or a dissembler prepared to tie yourself in ever more elaborate knots (the flexible Mr. Romney). Several promisingly pragmatic governors, including Mitch Daniels, Chris Christie and Jeb Bush, never even sought the nomination. Jon Huntsman, the closest thing to a moderate in the race (who supports gay marriage and action to combat climate change), is polling in low single figures.

More depressingly, the fatwas have stifled ideas, making the Republican Party the enemy of creative positions it once pioneered. The idea of requiring every American to carry health insurance (thus broadening the insurance pool and reducing costs) originated in the conservative Heritage Foundation as a response to Clinton-care, and was put into practice by then-Governor Romney in Massachusetts. All this Mr. Romney has had to disavow, just as Mr. Gingrich has had to recant his ideas on climate change, while Rick Perry is still explaining his appalling laxity as governor of Texas in allowing the children of illegal immigrants to receive subsidised college education.

On the economy, where this newspaper has often found the most common ground with the Republicans, the impact has been especially unfortunate. America's commercial classes are fed up with a president they associate with big government, red tape and class warfare. A Republican could stake out a way to cut the deficit, reform taxes and refashion government. But instead of businesslike pragmatism, there is zealotry. The candidates have made a fetish out of never raising taxes (even when it involves getting rid of loopholes), while mostly ignoring tough decisions about cutting spending on defence or pensions. Such compassionless conservatism (slashing taxes for the rich and expenditure on the poor) comes with little thought as to which bits of government spending are useful. Investing in infrastructure, redesigning public education and maintaining unemployment benefits in the worst downturn since the Depression are hardly acts of communism.

We didn't leave you; you left us.

Elections are decided in the middle. If the Republicans choose an extreme candidate, they can hardly be surprised if independents plump for Mr. Obama, or look to a third-party candidate. But there could be two better outcomes for them.

The first would be if Mr. Romney secures a quick victory, defies his base and moves firmly to the centre. In theory, there is enough in his record to suggest that he may yet be the chief executive America needs, though such boldness is asking a lot of a man who still seems several vertebrae short of a backbone (John McCain, a generally braver man, flunked it in 2008). The alternative is that the primary race grinds to a stalemate, with neither Mr. Romney nor one of his rivals able to secure victory. Then a Bush, Daniels or Christie just might be tempted into the contest. It is a sad commentary that this late in the day "the right Republican" does not even seem to be running yet.

*http://www.economist.com/node/*21542180

Supplementary Reading 2

Political Struggle in Congress Delayed, Not Resolved

By Robert Pear

WASHINGTON — When Congress handily passed a bill to set payroll, tax rates, jobless benefits and medicare doctors' fees for the next two months, it seemed to end an epic political struggle between President Obama and Republicans on Capitol Hill. In fact, that was just the beginning.

Every issue in dispute remains unresolved, waiting to be addressed when Congress returns next month for an election-year session in which agreements could be even more elusive.

Basically, the new law, signed on Friday by Mr. Obama, preserves the status quo through February, so House and Senate negotiators can try to reach longer-term agreements on the Social Security payroll tax, unemployment insurance, Medicare and a few other issues, like the shape of the welfare program that provides cash assistance to more than 4.6 million poor people.

The law says that Mr. Obama shall grant a permit within 60 days for construction of the Keystone XL oil pipeline, from Canada to the Gulf Coast, unless he finds that the project "would not serve the national interest." Republicans in Congress are already looking for additional ways to put pressure on Mr. Obama if he blocks the pipeline or delays a decision.

Under growing political pressure, House Republican leaders accepted the two-month extension of payroll tax relief. But many rank-and-file members of the House Republican caucus said they doubted that the tax break would do much to stimulate the economy and saw no urgent need to continue it for 10 more months. By contrast, Mr. Obama and Congressional Democrats say the payroll tax cut is needed to bolster the economy.

An extension of the tax cut and jobless benefits "should be a formality," Mr. Obama said. But he added, "We have a lot more work to do," and said he expected "some tough fights."

Even if Democrats and Republicans could agree on extending the payroll tax cut, they fundamentally disagree about how to offset the additional cost, $100 billion for the last 10 months of 2012.

The Senate majority leader, Harry Reid of Nevada, made clear on Friday that Democrats would keep pressing for a tax surcharge on individual income over $1 million — a demand dropped by Democrats in talks that led to the two-month compromise.

"There should be a fair tax on rich people," Mr. Reid said.

With a few exceptions, Republicans in Congress have opposed a "millionaires' tax," saying it would hurt the economy and people who create jobs.

House Republicans would pay for the legislation, in part, by freezing the pay of federal employees through September 2013.

Democrats generally oppose that idea.

A 20-member conference committee will try to work out differences between the House and the Senate on a yearlong bill. Mr. Reid said he had appointed Senator Benjamin L. Cardin of Maryland to the panel because he knew that Mr.

Cardin would guard the interests of federal employees. More than 275,000 federal workers live in Maryland.

The fate of the main federal-state welfare program, Temporary Assistance for Needy Families, was largely overlooked in the fight over payroll taxes. Money and the legal authority for the welfare program were due to run out on Dec. 31.

Jennifer Hrycyna Wagner, the welfare director in Illinois, said state officials around the country feared a possible interruption in benefits and services for "our most vulnerable residents."

Congress extended the program for two months, but its future beyond that is up in the air. If Congress provides additional welfare money, it is likely to come with new conditions.

Many states deliver cash assistance using electronic benefit transfer cards. The House has voted twice this month to forbid use of the cards at any liquor store, casino or strip club — any "retail establishment which provides adult-oriented entertainment in which performers disrobe or perform in an unclothed state for entertainment."

Several states have been embarrassed by the disclosure that welfare recipients were claiming benefits at such places.

Representative Gwen Moore, Democrat of Wisconsin, opposed the restriction, saying it would "humiliate and marginalize" poor people.

"In many neighborhoods," she said, "the closest A. T. M. is located in a nearby liquor store."

Some state officials also question the provision. Miki Allard, a spokeswoman for the Nevada Department of Health and Human Services, said: "It may be very appropriate for our public assistance recipients to access benefits from casino machines. A large proportion of our clients work in casinos. They are not there to gamble. They are there to work."

A bigger fight looms over unemployment insurance. House Republicans want to reduce the maximum duration of benefits to 59 weeks, from 99. They would allow states to require drug testing. And they would require most recipients of jobless benefits to search for work and to enroll in G. E. D. programs if they had not completed high school. Republicans also want to allow waivers of federal law so some states could divert money from the payment of benefits to the retraining of workers. Democrats oppose most of those ideas, saying they would cut a lifeline for millions of people who have been out of work for a year or more.

Senator Jack Reed, Democrat of Rhode Island, will be a member of the House-Senate conference committee. In picking him, Mr. Reid noted that Rhode Island had high unemployment and said "no one in the Senate has been more protective of the unemployed."

The negotiators will also try to find a new way to pay doctors treating Medicare patients, to avoid the continual threat of deep cuts in fees.

Unless Congress steps in, doctors will see a 27 percent reduction in Medicare reimbursements in March. As a result of such cuts, lawmakers say, many older Americans could lose access to their doctors, because doctors would be less willing to take Medicare patients.

One of the five House Democrats named to the conference committee, Representative Allyson Y. Schwartz of Pennsylvania, is drafting legislation to scrap the current payment formula, which penalizes doctors if Medicare spending on physician services exceeds annual goals linked to growth of the nation's economy.

http://www.nytimes.com/2011/12/27/us/politics/congress-delays-political-struggle.html?_r=1&scp=1&sq=December+26+2011&st=nyt

Chapter 6 Religion in the United States

Religion in the United States is remarkable both in its high adherence level as well as its diversity. The First Amendment to the country's Constitution prevents the government from having any authority in religion, and guarantees the free exercise of religion. A majority of Americans report that religion plays a "very important" role in their lives, a proportion unusual among developed nations, though similar to other nations in the Americas. Many faiths have flourished in the United States, including imports spanning the country's multicultural heritage as well as those founded within the country, and have led the United States to become the most religiously diverse country in the world.

The majority of Americans identify themselves as Christians (76%) while non-Christian religions (including Buddhism, Hinduism, Islam, Judaism, and others) collectively make up about 4% of the adult population. Another 15% of the adult population identified as having no religious affiliation. According to the American Religious Identification Survey, religious belief varies considerably across the country: 59% of Americans living in Western states report a belief in God, yet in the South (the "Bible Belt") the figure is as high as 86%.

Several of the original Thirteen Colonies were established by English settlers who wished to practice their own religion without discrimination: the Massachusetts Bay Colony was established by Puritans, Pennsylvania by Quakers, and Maryland by Roman Catholics. Although some individual states retained established churches well into the nineteenth century, the United States was the first nation to have no official religion. Modeling the provisions concerning religion within the Virginia Statute for Religious Freedom, the framers of the Constitution rejected any religious test for office, and the First Amendment specifically denied the federal government any power to enact any law respecting either an establishment of religion or prohibiting its free exercise. The decision was mainly influenced by Reformation ideals, but was also a consequence of the pragmatic concerns of minority religious groups and small states that did not want to be under the power or influence of a national religion that did not represent them.

Main Religious Preferences of Americans

According to a 2007 survey, the following is the order of religious preferences in the United States:

- Christianity: (78.4%)
    - Protestantism(新教)(51.3%)
    - Roman Catholicism (23.9%)
    - Mormon (1.7%)
    - Jehovah's Witness (0.7%)
    - Orthodox Church (0.6%)
    - other Christian (0.3%)
- Unaffiliated, including atheist(无神论者)or agnostic(不可知论者)(16.1%)
- Judaism (1.7%)
- Buddhist (0.7%)
- Islam (0.6%)
- Hinduism (0.4%)
- other (1.2%)

More recent studies show that the overall percentage of Americans identifying themselves as Christians is sliding. Christianity in the United States has become more polarized with the numbers of evangelical Christians increased which, according to the studies, also contributed to the increasing numbers of Americans who are rejecting religion completely. Around half of American adults leave the faith tradition of their upbringing to either switch allegiances(忠诚)or abandon religious affiliation altogether.

Monument honoring the right to worship, Washington, D. C.

Washington National Cathedral in Washington, D. C.

Crystal Cathedral, a Protestant megachurch in California

A Presbyterian(长老派)church; most Americans identify as Christian

6.1 Christianity

The largest religion in the US is Christianity, practiced by the majority of the population (76% in 2008). Roughly 51.3% of Americans are Protestants, 23.9% are Catholics, and 1.7% are Mormons (the name commonly used to refer to members of The Church of Jesus Christ of Latter-day Saints), and 1.6% to various other Christian denominations. Christianity was introduced during the period of European colonization.

By the 2009 Yearbook of American and Canadian Churches of the National Council of Churches, the Roman Catholic Church is the largest single denomination with a membership of 67,117,016, and Southern Baptist Convention ranks second at 16,266,920.

The Hispanics/Latinos, Irish, Italians, Polish, French, Spanish, Hungarians, German, and Lebanese brought Catholicism, while Northern European peoples introduced Protestantism. Among Protestants, adherents to Anglicanism, Baptism, Calvinism, Puritanism, Presbyterianism, Lutheranism, Quakerism, Amish, Methodism and Moravian Church were the first to settle to the US, spreading their faith in the new country. Greek, Russian, Central and Eastern European, Middle Eastern, Ethiopian, and South Indian immigrants brought Eastern Orthodoxy and Oriental Orthodoxy to the United States. These branches of Christianity have since spread beyond the boundaries of ethnic immigrant communities and now include multi-ethnic membership and parishes.

Since then, American Christians developed in their own path. During the Great Awakenings interdenominational evangelicalism(派系间的福音派), Pentecostalism(五旬节教派)and Christian fundamentalism emerged, along with new Protestant denominations such as Adventism, and new branches of Restorationism, particularly Jehovah's Witnesses and The Church of Jesus Christ of Latter-day Saints, also commonly referred to as Mormonism. Today, with 16.6 million adherents (5.3% of the total population), Southern Baptist is the largest of more than 200 distinctly named Protestant denominations. Of the total population, Evangelicals comprise 26.3%, and Mainline Protestants 16%. The strength of various sects varies greatly in different regions of the country, with rural parts of the South (except Louisiana and the Hispanic community, which both consist mainly of Catholics), having many evangelicals but very few Catholics, while urbanized areas of the north Atlantic states and Great Lakes, as well as many industrial and mining towns, are heavily Catholic, though still quite mixed. As of 1990, nearly 72% of the population of Utah was Mormon, as well as 26% of neighboring Idaho. Lutheranism is most prominent in the Upper Midwest, with North Dakota having the highest percentage, 35% according to a 2001 survey.

Despite its status as the most widespread and influential religion in the US, Christianity is undergoing a continuous relative decline in demographics. While the absolute number of Christians rose from 1990 to 2008 as the overall population increased, the actual percentage of Christians dropped from 86.2% to 76.0%. A nationwide telephone interview of 1,002 adults conducted by The

Barna Group found that 70% of American adults believe that God is "the all-powerful, all-knowing creator of the universe who still rules it today," and that 9% of all American adults and 0.5% young adults hold to what the survey defined as a "biblical worldview".

6.2 Other Religions

No Religion

A 2001 survey directed by Dr. Ariela Keysar for the City University of New York indicated that, amongst the more than 100 categories of response, "no religious identification" had the greatest increase in population in both absolute and percentage terms. This category included atheists, agnostics, humanists, deists(自然神论), and others with no theistic(有神论的) religious beliefs or practices. Figures are up from 14.3 million in 1990 to 34.2 million in 2008, representing a proportionate increase from 8% of the total in 1990 to 15% in 2008. Another nation-wide study puts the figure of unaffiliated persons at 16.1%.

In a 2006 nationwide poll, University of Minnesota researchers found that despite an increasing acceptance of religious diversity, atheists were generally distrusted by other Americans, who rated them below Muslims, recent immigrants and other minority groups in "sharing their vision of American society". They also associated atheists with undesirable attributes such as criminal behavior, rampant materialism, and cultural elitism.

Judaism

After Christianity and no-religion, Judaism is the third-largest religious affiliation in the US, though this identification is not necessarily indicative of religious beliefs or practices. Jews have been present in what is now the US since the 17th century, though large scale immigration did not take place until the 19th century, largely as a result of persecutions in parts of Eastern Europe. The CIA

Fact Book estimates 1% of Americans belong to this group. Approximately 25% of this population lives in New York City.

A significant number of people identify themselves as American Jews on ethnic and cultural grounds, rather than religious ones. For example, 19% of self-identified American Jews believe God does not exist, notwithstanding God's existence to be integral to Jewish religious beliefs. The 2001 ARIS study projected from its sample that there are about 5.3 million adults in the American Jewish population: 2.83 million adults (1.4% of the US adult population) are estimated to be adherents of Judaism; 1.08 million are estimated to be adherents of no religion; and 1.36 million are estimated to be adherents of a religion other than Judaism.

According to the 2001 National Jewish Population Survey, 4.3 million American Jews have some sort of strong connection to the Jewish community, whether religious or cultural. Jewishness is generally considered an ethnic identity as well as a religious one. Among the 4.3 million American Jews described as "strongly connected" to Judaism, over 80% have some sort of active engagement with Judaism, ranging from attendance at daily prayer services on one end of the spectrum to as little as attending Passover Seders or lighting Hanukkah candles on the other. Of these 4.3 million strongly connected Jews, 46% belong to a synagogue. Among those who belong to a synagogue, 38% are members of Reform synagogues, 33% Conservative, 22% Orthodox, 2% Reconstructionist, and 5% other types. The survey also discovered that Jews in the Northeast and Midwest are generally more observant than Jews in the South or West. Reflecting a trend also observed among other religious groups, Jews in the Northwestern United States are typically the least observant.

In recent years, there has been a noticeable trend of secular American Jews, called baalei teshuva, returning to a more religious, in most cases, Orthodox, style of observance. It is uncertain how widespread or demographically important this movement is at present.

The Jewish community in the United States is composed predominantly of Ashkenazi Jews who emigrated from Central and Eastern Europe, and their US-born descendants. There are, however, small numbers of older (and some recently arrived) communities of Sephardi Jews with roots tracing back to 15th century Iberia (Spain, Portugal, and North Africa).

There are Mizrahi Jews (from the Middle East, Caucasia and Central Asia), as well as much smaller numbers of Ethiopian Jews, Indian Jews, Kaifeng Jews and others from various smaller Jewish ethnic divisions.

Buddhism

Buddhism entered the US during the 19th century with the arrival of the first immigrants from Eastern Asia. The first Buddhist temple was established in San Francisco in 1853 by Chinese Americans.

During the late 19th century Buddhist missionaries from Japan came to the US. Simultaneously to these processes, US intellectuals started to take interest in Buddhism.

Estimates of the number of Buddhists in the United States vary between 0.5% and 0.9%.

Unitarian Universalism

Unitarian Universalism (UUism)(唯一神教派) came into existence as a unique religion when the Unitarian Universalist Association (UUA) was founded in 1961 as a consolidation of the American Unitarian Association and the Universalist Church in America. Unitarian Universalism is a theologically liberal religious movement characterized by its support of a "free and responsible search for truth and meaning". Unitarian Universalism is a covenantal religion. Members do not share a creed; rather they are unified by their shared search for spiritual growth. Unitarian Universalists draw on many different sources and have a wide range of beliefs and practices.

Being historically derived from Unitarianism and Universalism, Unitarian Universalism traces its roots to Christian Protestantism, however, the theological significance of both Unitarianism and Universalism had significantly expanded beyond the traditional understanding prior to their decision to combine their efforts at the continental level as Unitarian Universalists. Many UUs appreciate and value aspects of Islamic, Christian and Jewish spirituality, but the extent to which the elements of any particular faith tradition are incorporated into one's personal spiritual practices is a matter of personal choice in keeping with Unitarian Universalism's creedless, non-dogmatic approach to spirituality and faith development.

As a result of these historical roots, Unitarian Universalist congregations and fellowships tend to retain some Christian traditions such as Sunday worship that includes a sermon and singing of hymns, despite the fact that they do not necessarily identify themselves as Christians.

According to the 2007 survey published by the Pew Forum on Religion & Public Life, 3% of US adults or approximately 340,000 individuals identified themselves as Unitarian Universalist.

Belief in God

The phrase "In God We Trust" first appeared on a US coin on the 2-cent piece of 1864, and has been on all coins and paper bills since 1957. It was declared the national motto by Congress in 1956. The one dollar Federal Reserve Note of October 1957 was the first US paper money with the motto. The US Pledge of Allegiance was modified in 1954 to add the phrase "under God". Various polls have been conducted to determine Americans' actual beliefs regarding God:

- A 2006 online Harris Poll of 2010 US adults (18 and older) found that 73% of those surveyed said that they believed in a God, 11% said they believed there was no God, and 16% said that they were not sure whether or not there was a God. The believers in God included 58% of respondents who said they were "absolutely certain", and 15% who said they were "somewhat certain" that there is a God. The believers in no God included 6% who were "absolutely certain", and 6% who were "somewhat certain" that there is no God. About 29% believed that God "controls what happens on Earth", while a plurality (44%) believed that God "observes but does not control what happens on Earth". The poll also showed that an "absolute certain" belief in God is correlated to age: only 43%-45% of those aged 18 - 29 were "absolutely certain" that God exists, while 54%

of those aged 30 – 39 were "absolutely certain" that God exists, and 63%–65% of those aged 40 and older were "absolutely certain" that God exists.

Church Attendance

Gallup International indicates that 41% of American citizens report they regularly attend religious services, compared to 15% of French citizens, 10% of UK citizens, and 7.5% of Australian citizens.

6.3 Religion and Politics

The US guarantees freedom of religion and some churches in the US take strong stances on political subjects.

Politicians frequently discuss their religion when campaigning, and many churches and religious figures are highly politically active. However, to keep their status as tax-exempt organizations they must not officially endorse a candidate. There are Christians in both the Democratic Party and the Republican Party, but evangelical Christians tend to support the Republican Party whereas more liberal Christians and secular voters tend to support the Democratic Party.

Every President and Vice President, with the exception of the present President, Barack Obama, was raised in a family with affiliations with Christian religions. Only former President John F. Kennedy, and current Vice President Joe Biden were raised in Roman Catholic families. Two former Presidents, Richard Nixon and Herbert Hoover, were raised as Quakers. All the rest were raised in families affiliated with Protestant Christianity. However, many Presidents have themselves had only a nominal affiliation with churches, and some never joined any church. Jefferson and Monroe were Deists (with Jefferson later expressing agreement with much of Unitarianism).

Questions

1. What is the religious life like in American people's life?

2. Christianity is a major religion in the US, What is the role Christianity plays in Americans' livese?

Supplementary Reading 1

The Faith (and Doubts) of Our Fathers

What did the makers of America believe about God and religion? The subject is stirring the very rancour they wanted to avoid.

IN THE year of our Lord 1816 two grand old men of the American Revolution corresponded eagerly about the work they had recently done, in their rural retirement, on the Bible. Ex-President Thomas Jefferson thanked his old friend Charles Thomson, a co-sponsor of the Declaration of Independence, for sending a copy of his newly completed synopsis of the Gospels.

At a time when many modern Americans are arguing feverishly over the real significance of the nation's religious and political beginnings, such letters can be dynamite. So let the contents of this exchange be noted carefully. Thomson, like most members of the first American Congress, which he had served as secretary, was a committed member of a church—in his case Presbyterian—but he still felt that there might be things in the Bible that organised Christianity hadn't grasped. So he spent years re-translating the scriptures; the ex-president approved.

But Jefferson, like most of the top figures in the American Revolution, was far more of a sceptic in religious matters. He was fascinated by metaphysics but he had no time for the mystical. In contrast with today's vituperative exchanges, these differences did not stop the two gentlemen maintaining a warm correspondence. But Jefferson's approach to redacting the Bible involved something more radical than translation. He literally snipped out everything supernatural: miracles, the Virgin birth, the resurrection. The result was his own, non-mystical account of the life of Jesus. He told his old comrade: "I too have made a wee little book from the same materials which I call the 'Philosophy of Jesus.' It is a paradigma of his doctrines, made by cutting the pages out of the book and arranging them on the pages of a blank book ... A more beautiful or precious morsel ... I have never seen. It is a document in proof that I am a real Christian, that is to say, a disciple of the doctrines of Jesus, very different from the Platonists who call me infidel and themselves Christians."

If Jefferson was a Christian of any kind, he was an idiosyncratic one. He admired Jesus as a moral teacher but like many of America's revolutionaries, he had a visceral loathing for priestcraft. Jefferson blamed Saint Paul, the early Church, and even the Gospel writers for distorting the mission of Jesus, which, as he saw it, had been to reverse the decadence of the Jewish religion. Starting from the (correct) proposition that mystical ideas originating from Plato were influential when Christian theology was being developed, he castigated followers of the Greek philosopher for corrupting what he saw as the original Christian message.

Did Jefferson believe in God? Certainly not the Christian idea of a God in three Persons; he saw that notion as incomprehensible and therefore impossible for a rational person to accept. One view is that like many of America's founders, he was a Deist, believing in a Creator who set the universe and its laws in motion but did not intervene thereafter. (The Deist God has been described as rather like a rich aunt in Australia—benevolent, a long way off, and mostly leaving the world to its own devices.)

The shape of the Earth, for example, he ascribed to a Creator's genius. "Had He created the Earth perfectly spherical, its axis might have been perpetually shifting by the influence of the other bodies of the system," Jefferson once told Thomson. Others think Jefferson's views were somewhere between Deism and traditional Theism. In language that some modern American conservatives can pounce on, he once asked whether the young republic's liberties could be secure without "a conviction in the minds of the people that these liberties are a gift from God". But that does not imply he held such convictions. Although we know what Jefferson did not believe, it is harder to say what he did believe.

Between now and the 2012 presidential election, many pronouncements by the founding fathers—especially but not only on the subject of Christianity—will be parsed and dissected with passion by both sides. Liberals, keen to protect the American variety of secularism from what they see as a resurgence of zealotry, will stress the rationalist leanings of most of the revolution's protagonists; religious conservatives will point out that the revolution's foot-soldiers were generally people of faith who would be shocked, for example, by the idea of banning prayer in schools.

Believers in the idea that America was established as a Christian state scored a hit last year when the Texas school board, a politicised body in which evangelicals control crucial votes, ordered up textbooks laying out this view. Given the size of the Texan market, school-book publishers across the country often follow its lead. The best-known advocate of the "Christian nation" theory is a Texan, an author and evangelist called David Barton, who has been writing on the subject since the 1980s.

Among his recent claims are that the founding fathers rejected Darwinism (although they pre-dated Charles Darwin), and that they broke away from Britain in order to abolish slavery. In fact the southern states only joined the Revolution on the understanding that slavery would not be questioned. Strange as his views may sound to most scholars, Mr. Barton's philosophy is taken seriously in Republican circles. When Rick Perry, the Texas governor and presidential candidate, held a day of prayer for the nation in August, Mr. Barton was an acknowledged endorser. One of Mr. Barton's admirers is Newt Gingrich, the former House speaker who argues that American history has been distorted by secular historians to play down the role of faith. "I never listen to David Barton without learning a whole lot of new things," Mr. Gingrich has said.

It is easy to see why politicians are attracted by the assertion that America was founded as a Christian land, and is hence called to be a place of exceptional virtue. It elegantly fuses two beliefs: Christianity itself, and belief in American history as another sacred narrative, one that sees the founders as people of near-infallible wisdom and virtue waging a noble war against the forces of darkness.

If Mitt Romney, a Mormon, and Mr. Gingrich confirm their place as front-runners for the Republican nomination, debates over sacred texts and stories—from the Book of Mormon to the days of prayer and fasting decreed by the first Congress—could take some unpredictable turns, even if Mr. Romney tries to avoid them. As a political slogan, citing the founders (to condemn welfare, as Mr. Perry does) is a formidable weapon; invoking Jesus Christ (to make the case against the minimum wage, as Mr. Barton does) is even stronger medicine. Arguments that use both sources at once can seem almost irresistible.

Academic historians are bemused at times by the inquiries they get from people with no previous interest in the nation's beginnings: what did America's creators really believe? Jill Lepore, a Harvard professor who deconstructs the uses and abuses of the past, is wary of would-be historians with an agenda. For her, the founders' genius lay in their willingness to cast doubt on fixed ways of thinking inherited from the past. So to make them final arbiters is to traduce their spirit.

Nor, indeed, were the fathers of one mind. They did not spend their time producing pearls of unanimously agreed wisdom. They quarrelled bitterly. Indeed, if something about this period still resonates in modern politics, it may be the fathers' disputes, and the subtle points each side brought to bear. The tug-of-war between Alexander Hamilton, who successfully campaigned for an American central bank and other federal authorities, and Jefferson, who favoured states' rights, is in many ways still going on.

Linda Bilmes, a public policy professor at Harvard, sees in Hamilton's argument a practical application of the metaphysical belief that man is neither utterly wicked nor naturally virtuous; it followed, Hamilton thought, that honest, competent administration was needed to maximise the chances of virtue prevailing.

Above all, the fathers were pragmatists. The exigencies of war with Britain, and survival in an unconquered frontier, gave them little choice. Take George Washington. Unlike Jefferson, Washington does not seem to have had much personal interest in matters philosophical. He was a general and politician, not a theologian. Still, when exhorting troops before battle, or addressing fellow citizens of the republic, he could use religious rhetoric. "No people can be bound to acknowledge the invisible hand, which conducts the affairs of men, more than the people of the United States," he declared in his inaugural address. But these circumlocutions were typical of his references to God.

As his biographer Ron Chernow observes, Washington spoke of "Destiny" or the "author of our being" or simply "Heaven". Another favourite term was "Providence"—a word often used by Freemasons, a movement of which

Washington was an active member. For those who know where to look, the Washington home at Mount Vernon is full of Masonic symbols, one Masonic researcher has written. But on this matter, Ms. Lepore cautions against over-interpretation: the Masons were just one of the gentlemen's clubs where squires liked to gather.

Virtually absent from Washington's pronouncements was any reference to Jesus. He did not take communion—for most Christians, the most important rite of their faith—and he did not summon a Christian minister to his death bed. Was Jefferson right, then, to claim that "[Washington] thinks it right to keep up appearances but is an unbeliever"? Washington was certainly a diplomat. Although he remained formally Anglican, as president he wrote friendly letters to many Christian and Jewish communities and attended their services. And when he needed a job done on the estate, he was firm, for his time, about the irrelevance of religion: "If they are good workmen," he said, "they may be Mahometans, Jews or Christian of any sect, or they may be atheists."

As every American youngster has been taught, one thing that Washington, Jefferson and all the founders did believe in was religious freedom. They were appalled by the fusion of religious and political power, epitomised by the divine right of kings.

The emphasis on freedom seems clearer than anything else about the founding texts. People may still argue over whether those texts have any religious inspiration at all. The constitution contains little reference to any deity, while the Declaration of Independence appeals to "Nature's God"—a formula that sounds more Deistic than Christian. But the constitution's first amendment seems crystal-clear on the subject of freedom: it bars Congress from establishing any religion, or from erecting any barrier to the free exercise of religion.

Yet for all the sonorous beauty of much early American writing on the subject, religious liberty too should be seen as something pragmatic—a hard-nosed solution to the problem of stitching together a country out of 13 colonies with diverse populations and different religious arrangements. Nine colonies had established churches at the time of the Revolution; most of these regimes sputtered on for several decades afterwards. The religious scene in the colonies ranged from the strict Puritan communities of New England to the suffocating

Anglican regime of Virginia. In New England, Anglican clergy acted as fifth columnists for the crown; Virginia had an Anglican American culture of its own. Maryland had always been a comfortable place for Catholics.

It was all a big, volatile mess, to which a regime of religious liberty was the best solution. Among the many impulses behind the Revolution was a network of Presbyterians and other non-conformists who loathed Anglicans' entitlements. The advocates of "Christian history" rightly point out that conventional scholars sometimes underestimate the role of low-church Protestant zeal as a source of revolutionary fervour. Non-conformists resented the fact that, as Holly Brewer of the University of Maryland has noted, the monarch in some ways had more sway over American Anglicans than he did over the Church of England. This Anglican (and crown) privilege so infuriated dissenting Christians that it spurred them to form countervailing networks across state boundaries. But neither Presbyterian nativism, or any other sectarian impulse, would have sufficed to underpin a revolution.

As things turned out, the founding fathers—and above all Jefferson—had a much broader vision of the danger that religious intolerance of all kinds posed to the new republic. To see how sectarianism was trumped, it is worth looking at the state where freedom of conscience was first established, after a fight—Virginia.

That battle's heroes, including four of the first five presidents of the United States, were Virginian gentlemen. Jefferson saw the establishment of religious freedom in his native Virginia—overthrowing an Anglican establishment in which he, as a vestryman, had played a part—as one of his greatest feats. On his instructions, his tombstone records three things: his authorship of the Declaration of Independence, his creation of the University of Virginia (pointedly built around a library, not a church), and religious liberty in his home state.

The dismantling of Virginia's Anglican regime began in 1776, with a sonorous declaration that "the duty which we owe to our Creator, and the manner of discharging it, can be directed only by reason and conviction, not by force or violence". This ensured there would be no repeat of the incident two years earlier when a Baptist minister was whipped and jailed for preaching without a licence. The state church was finally dislodged in 1786, when a Bill for

Establishing Religious Freedom, penned by Jefferson, was passed after a lively debate in which Madison, who had been appalled by the jailing of Baptist ministers in his neighbourhood, prevailed. Madison went on to frame the Bill of Rights for the republic, including its vital provisions on liberty of conscience.

Virginia's church establishment was ended by a coalition of free-thinking gentlemen like Jefferson and Madison, and non-conformists who resented the curbs on their ability to worship and preach. One of the few conventionally devout figures in the revolution's front ranks was also one of the few opponents of full religious freedom: John Jay, the second secretary of state. A staunch New York Anglican, he could not stomach the idea of freedom for Catholics. But he was defeated by fellow founders who thought the cohesion of the state should trump any sectarian concern.

On the face of things, the victory for religious liberty, first in Virginia and then in the American republic, was so decisive that no venerator of the founders could plausibly challenge it. Yet Mr. Barton, the advocate-in-chief of Christian history, has raised his standard over that very issue. The argument centres on a famous phrase of Jefferson's, cherished by secularists, which calls for a "wall of separation" between church and state. Jefferson used that formula in a letter to some Baptists who asked him what exactly the constitution's framers had meant when outlawing the establishment of a state religion. Mr. Barton's line is that the "wall" works only one way, as does the constitution's ban on a state religion. This principle does not, he says, exclude governance by Christian principles; all it bars is state interference in church life or theology. This argument has been adopted by many other Christian conservatives since he first made it 20 years ago. (A minority of evangelicals take a different view; they think the founding fathers were indeed hopeless freethinkers, and conclude that good Christians should avoid politics. But that is a hard corner to argue.)

There is a great irony about all these disputes over America's creators, whether they pit Christian against Christian, or religious types against secularists. Regardless of their own views on the spiritual, people like Madison, Washington and Jefferson were intensely concerned for the welfare and cohesion of the new republic. They worried not only about religious wars as such but about political disputes which were "religious" in their intensity. They wanted to create a state and political system to which people with utterly different ideas about metaphysics, and many other things, could offer unconditional loyalty. People who disagree over legal or economic matters ought to be able to respect one another and compromise; people who disagree over things they regard as ultimate—and therefore see one another as heretics—usually can't.

The religious or non-religious character of the constitution (and what children should learn about it) is only one of many issues on which it is hardly possible, these days, to have a calm debate. Perhaps all sides should ponder the words of Jefferson in his first inaugural address: "Let us reflect that, having banished from our land that religious intolerance under which mankind so long bled and suffered, we have yet gained little if we countenance a political intolerance as despotic, as wicked, and capable of as bitter and bloody persecutions."

*http://www.economist.com/node/*21541718

Supplementary Reading 2

America Becoming Less Christian, Survey Finds

America is a less Christian nation than it was 20 years ago, and Christianity is not losing out to other religions, but primarily to a rejection of religion altogether, a survey published Monday found.

Seventy-five percent of Americans call themselves Christian, according to the American Religious Identification Survey from Trinity College in Hartford, Connecticut. In 1990, the figure was 86 percent.

William Donohue, president of the Catholic League said he thinks a radical shift towards individualism over the last quarter-century has a lot to do it.

"The three most dreaded words are thou shalt not," he told Lou Dobbs. "Notice they are not atheists—they are saying I don't want to be told what to do with my life."

At the same time there has been an increase in the number of people expressing no religious affiliation.

The survey also found that "born-again" or "evangelical" Christianity is on the rise, while the percentage who belong to "mainline" congregations such as the Episcopal or Lutheran churches has fallen.

One in three Americans consider themselves evangelical, and the number of people associated with mega-churches has skyrocketed from less than 200,000 in 1990 to more than 8 million in the latest survey.

The rise in evangelical Christianity is contributing to the rejection of religion altogether by some Americans, said Mark Silk of Trinity College.

"In the 1990s, it really sunk in on the American public generally that there was a long-lasting 'religious right' connected to a political party, and that turned a lot of people the other way," he said of the link between the Republican Party and groups such as the Moral Majority and Focus on the Family.

"In an earlier time, people who would have been content to say, 'Well, I'm some kind of a Protestant,' now say 'Hell no, I won't go,'" he told CNN.

Silk also said the revelation that some Catholic priests had sexually abused children—and senior figures in the church hierarchy had helped to hide it—drove some Catholics away from religion.

And, he said, it is now more socially acceptable than it once was to admit having no religion.

"You're not declaring yourself a total pariah. The culture has changed in a way that makes it easier to say, 'No, I don't have a religion. Even in the past year, Mitt Romney and Barack Obama feel obliged to talk about 'those of no faith,'" he pointed out. Obama mentioned people without faith in his inaugural address in January, making him the first president to do so.

http://articles.cnn.com/2009-03-09/living/us.religion.less.christian_1_american-religious-identification-survey-christian-nation-evangelical?_s=PM:LIVING

Chapter 7 Education in the United States

Education in the United States is mainly provided by the public sector, with control and funding coming from three levels: federal, state, and local. Child education is compulsory. A sub-type of compulsory education is public education. Public education is universal at the primary and secondary levels (known inside the United States as the elementary and high school levels). At these levels, school curricula, funding, teaching, and other policies are set through locally elected school boards with jurisdiction over school districts. School districts are usually separate from other local jurisdictions, with independent officials and budgets. Educational standards and standardized testing decisions are usually made by state governments. The ages for compulsory education vary by state, beginning at ages five to eight and ending at the ages of fourteen to eighteen. A growing number of states are now requiring compulsory education until the age of 18.

Compulsory education requirements can generally be satisfied by educating children in public schools, state-certified private schools, an approved home school program or in an orphanage. In most public and private schools, education is divided into three levels: elementary school, middle school (sometimes called junior high school), and high school (sometimes referred to as secondary education). In almost all schools at these levels, children are divided by age groups into grades, ranging from kindergarten (followed by first grade) for the youngest children in elementary school, up to twelfth grade, the final year of high school. The exact age range of students in these grade levels varies slightly from area to area.

Post-secondary education, better known as "college" in the United States, is generally governed separately from the elementary and high school system, and is described in a separate section below.

In the year 2000, there were 76.6 million students enrolled in schools from kindergarten through graduate schools. Of these, 72 percent aged 12 to 17 were judged academically "on track" for their age (enrolled in school at or above grade level). Of those enrolled in compulsory education, 5.2 million (10.4 percent) were attending private schools. Among the country's adult population, over 85 percent have completed high school and 27 percent have received a bachelor's degree or higher. The average salary for college or university graduates is greater than $51,000, exceeding the national average of those without a high school diploma by more than $23,000, according to a 2005 study by the US Census Bureau. The United States school system includes over 5,000 Montessori(蒙台梭利)schools.

The country has a reading literacy rate at 98% of the population over age 15, while ranking below average in science and mathematics understanding compared to other developed countries. In 2008, there was a 77% graduation rate from high school, below that of most developed countries.

The poor performance has pushed public and private efforts such as the No Child Left Behind Act. In addition, the ratio of college-educated adults entering the workforce to general population (33%) is slightly below the mean of other developed countries (35%) and rate of participation of the labor force in continuing education is high. A 2000s study by Jon Miller of Michigan State University concluded that "A slightly higher proportion of American adults qualify as scientifically literate than European or Japanese adults."

School Grades

In the US public education begins with early childhood programs at the age of three or four. Children are then placed in year groups known as grades, beginning with kindergarten and culminating in twelfth grade. The US uses ordinal numbers for naming grades, unlike Canada and Australia where cardinal numbers are preferred. Thus, Americans are more likely to say "First Grade" rather than "Grade One". Typical ages and grade groupings in public and private schools may be found through the US Department of Education. Many different variations exist across the country.

Education in the United States

Level/Grade	Typical age (at end of the school year)
Preschool	
Various optional programs, such as Head Start	Under 6
Pre-Kindergarten	3,4
Kindergarten	4,5
Elementary School	
1st Grade	6 – 7
2nd Grade	7 – 8
3rd Grade	8 – 9
4th Grade	9 – 10
5th Grade	10 – 11
Middle School	
6th Grade	11 – 12
7th Grade	12 – 13
8th Grade	13 – 14
High school	
9th Grade (Freshman)	14 – 15
10th Grade (Sophomore)	15 – 16
11th Grade (Junior)	16 – 17
12th Grade (Senior)	17 – 18
Post-secondary education	
Tertiary education (College or University)	Ages vary (usually four years, referred to as Freshman, Sophomore, Junior and Senior years)

Continued

Level/Grade	Typical age (at end of the school year)
Vocational education	Ages vary
Graduate education	
Adult education	

Preschool

There are no mandatory public prekindergarten or crèche(托儿所)programs in the United States. The federal government funds the Head Start preschool program for children of low-income families, but most families are on their own with regard to finding a preschool or childcare.

In the large cities, there are sometimes upper-class preschools catering to the children of the wealthy. Because some upper-class families see these schools as the first step toward the Ivy League, there are even counselors who specialize in assisting parents and their toddlers through the preschool admissions process.

7.1 Elementary and Secondary Education

Schooling is compulsory for all children in the United States, but the age range for which school attendance is required varies from state to state. Most children begin elementary education with kindergarten (usually five to six years old) and finish secondary education with twelfth grade (usually eighteen years old). In some cases, pupils may be promoted beyond the next regular grade. Some states allow students to leave school between 14 - 17 with parental permission, before finishing high school; other states require students to stay in school until age 18.

Most parents send their children to either a public or private institution. According to government data, one-tenth of students are enrolled in private schools. Approximately 85% of students enter the public schools, largely because they are "free" (tax burdens by school districts vary from area to area).

Most students attend school for around six hours per day, and usually anywhere from 175 to 185 days per year. Most schools have a summer break period for about two and half months from June through August. This break is much longer than in some other nations. The other option available and being taken up by some schools is Year-round school.

Parents may also choose to educate their own children at home; 1.7% of children are educated in this manner.

Elementary School

Elementary school is a school of kindergarten through fifth grade (sometimes, the first eight grades or up to fourth grade or sixth grade), where basic subjects are taught. Elementary school provides and often remain in one or two classrooms throughout the school day, with the exceptions of physical education ("P.E." or "gym"), library, music, and art classes. There are (as of 2001) about 3.6 million children in each grade in the United States.

Typically, the curriculum within public elementary education is determined by individual school districts. The school district selects curriculum guides and textbooks that are reflective of a state's learning standards and benchmarks for a given grade level. Learning Standards are the goals by which states and school districts must meet adequate yearly progress (AYP) as mandated by No Child Left Behind. This description of school governance is simplistic at best, however, and school systems vary widely not only in the way curricular decisions are made but also in how teaching and learning take place. Some states and/or school districts impose more top-down mandates than others. In many schools, teachers play a significant role in curriculum design and there are few top-down mandates. Curricular decisions within private schools are made differently than in public schools and in most cases without consideration for NCLB.

Public Elementary School teachers typically instruct between twenty and thirty students of diverse learning needs. A typical classroom will include children with identified special needs as listed in Individuals with Disabilities Act IDEA to those that are cognitively, athletically or artistically gifted. At times an individual school district identifies areas of need within the curriculum. Teachers and advisory administrators form committees to develop supplemental materials to support learning for diverse learners and identify enrichment for textbooks. Many school districts post information about the curriculum and supplemental materials on websites for public access. Teachers receive a book to give to the students for each subject and brief overviews of what they are expected to teach. In general, a student learns basic arithmetic and sometimes rudimentary algebra in mathematics, English proficiency (such as basic grammar, spelling, and vocabulary), and fundamentals of other subjects. Learning standards are identified for all areas of curriculum by individual States, including those for math, social studies, science, physical development, the fine arts as well as reading. While the concept of State Learning standards has been around for some time, No Child Left Behind has mandated standards exist at the State level.

Elementary School teachers are trained with emphases on human cognitive and psychological development and the principles of curriculum development and instruction earning either a Bachelors or Masters Degree in Early Childhood and Elementary Education. The teaching of social studies and science are often underdeveloped in some elementary school programs and some attribute this to the fact that elementary school teachers are trained as generalists. However, teachers attribute this to the priority placed on developing reading, writing and math proficiency in the elementary grades and the amount of time needed to do so. Reading, writing and math proficiency greatly affect performance in social studies, science and other content areas. Certification standards for teachers are determined by individual States, with individual colleges and universities determining the rigor of the college education provided for future teachers. Some states require content area tests, as well as instructional skills tests for teacher certification in that state. Social studies may include key events, documents, understandings, and concepts in American history and geography, and in some programs, state or local history and geography; science varies widely. Most States have predetermined the number of minutes that will be taught within a given content area. As No Child Left Behind focuses on reading and math as primary targets for improvement, other instructional areas have received less attention. There is much discussion within educational circles about the justification and impact of singularly focusing on reading and math as tested areas for improvement.

Secondary Education

As part of education in the United States, secondary education usually covers grades 6, 7, 8, 9, or 10 through 12.

Junior and Senior High School

Middle school and Junior high school are any school intermediate between elementary school and senior high school. It usually includes sixth, seventh and eighth grade; for "Junior high", ninth grade. Middle school is often used instead of junior high school when demographic factors increase the number of younger students. At this time, students are given more independence as choosing their own classes. Usually, starting in ninth grade, grades become part of a student's official transcript. Future employers or colleges may want to see steady improvement in grades and a good attendance record on the official transcript. Therefore, students are encouraged to take much more responsibility for their education.

Senior high school is a school attended after junior high school. High school is often used instead of senior high school and distinguished from junior high school.

Basic Curricular Structure

Generally, at the high school level, students take a broad variety of classes without special emphasis in any particular subject. Curricula vary widely in quality and rigidity; for example, some states consider 65 (on a 100-point scale) a passing grade, while others consider it to be as low as 60 or as high as 75.

The following subjects are fairly universally required in the United States:

• Science (usually two years minimum, normally biology, chemistry and physics)

• Mathematics (usually two years minimum, normally including algebra(代数), geometry(几何), algebra Ⅱ, and/or precalculus/trigonometry 三角学)

• English (usually four years minimum, including literature, humanities, etc)

• Social Science (usually three years minimum, including various history, government/economics courses)

• Physical education (at least one year)

Many states require a "health" course in which students learn about anatomy (解剖), nutrition, first aid, sexuality, and birth control. Anti-drug use programs are also usually part of health courses. In many cases, however, options are provided for students to "test out" or complete independent study to meet this requirement. Foreign language and some form of art education are also a mandatory part of the curriculum in some schools.

Electives

Many high schools offer a wide variety of Elective courses, although the availability of such courses depends upon each particular school's financial resources and desired curriculum emphases.

Common types of electives include:

• Visual arts (drawing, sculpture, painting, photography, film)

• Performing arts (drama, band, chorus, orchestra, dance)

• Technology education ("Shop"; woodworking, metalworking, automobile repair, robotics)

• Computers (word processing, programming, graphic design)

• Athletics (cross country, football, baseball, basketball, track and field, swimming, tennis, gymnastics, water polo, soccer, wrestling, cheerleading, Volleyball, lacrosse, ice hockey, field hockey, boxing, skiing/snowboarding)

• Publishing (journalism/student newspaper, yearbook/annual, literary magazine)

• Foreign languages (Spanish, French are common; Chinese, Latin, Greek, German, Italian, Arabic, and Japanese are less common)

• Junior Reserve Officers' Training Corps

Advanced Courses

Many high schools provide Advanced Placement (AP) or International Baccalaureate (IB) courses. These are special forms of honors classes where the curriculum is more challenging and lessons more aggressively paced than standard courses. AP or IB courses are usually taken during the 11th or 12th grade of high school.

Most post-secondary institutions take AP or IB exam results into consideration in the admissions process. Because AP and IB courses are intended to be the equivalent of the first year of college courses, post-secondary institutions may grant unit credit, which enables students to graduate early. Other institutions use examinations for placement purposes only: students are exempted from introductory course work but may not receive credit towards a concentration, degree, or core requirement. Institutions vary in the selection of examinations they accept and the scores they require to grant credit or placement, with more elite institutions tending to accept fewer examinations and requiring higher scoring. The lack of AP, IB, and other advanced courses in impoverished inner-city high schools is often seen as a major cause of the greatly differing levels of post-secondary education these graduates go on to receive, compared with both public and private schools in wealthier neighborhoods.

Also, in states with well-developed community college systems, there are often mechanisms by which gifted students may seek permission from their school district to attend community college courses full-time during the summer, and part-time during the school year. The units earned this way can often be transferred to one's university, and can facilitate early graduation. Early college entrance programs are a step further, with students enrolling as freshmen at a younger-than-traditional age.

Home Schooling

There were 1.5 million children that were home schooled in 2007, up 74% from 1999 when the US Department of Education first started keeping statistics. This was 2.9% of all children.

Many select moral or religious reasons for home schooling their children. The second main category is "unschooling", those who prefer a non-standard approach to education.

Most homeschooling advocates are wary of the established educational institutions for various reasons. Some are religious conservatives who see nonreligious education as contrary to their moral or religious systems, or who wish to add religious instruction to the educational curriculum (and who may be unable to afford a church-operated private school, or where the only available school may teach views contrary to those of the parents). Others feel that they can more effectively tailor a curriculum to suit an individual student's academic strengths and weaknesses, especially those with singular needs or disabilities. Still others feel that the negative social pressures of schools (such as bullying, drugs, crime, sex, and other school-related problems) are detrimental to a child's proper development. Parents often form groups to help each other in the homeschooling process, and may even assign classes to different parents, similar to public and private schools.

Opposition to homeschooling comes from varied sources, including teachers' organizations and school districts. The National Education Association, the largest labor union in the United States, has been particularly vocal in the past. Opponents' stated concerns fall into several broad categories, including fears of poor academic quality, loss of income for the schools, and religious or social extremism, or lack of socialization with others. At this time, over half of states have oversight into monitoring or measuring the academic progress of home schooled students, with all but ten requiring some form of notification to the state.

Grading Scale

In schools in the United States children are continually assessed throughout the school year by their teachers, and report cards are issued to parents at varying intervals. Generally the scores for individual assignments and tests are recorded for each student in a grade book, along with the maximum number of points for each assignment. At any time, the total number of points for a student when divided by the total number of possible points produces a percent grade, which can be translated to a letter grade. Letter grades are often but not always used on report cards at the end of a marking period, although the current grade may be available at other times (particularly when an electronic grade book connected to an online service is in use). Although grading scales usually differ from school to school, the most common grade scale is letter grades—"A" through "F"—derived from a scale of 0 – 100 or a percentile. In some areas, Texas or Virginia for example, the "D" grade (or that below 70) is considered a failing grade. In other jurisdictions, such as Hawaii, a "D" grade is considered passing in certain classes, and failing in others.

Example Grading Scale

I,E,N,U or F	D			C			B			A		
	−		+	−		+	−		+	−		+
Below 60	60—	63—	67—	70—	73—	77—	80—	83—	87—	90—	93—	97—
Percent	62	66	69	72	76	79	82	86	89	92	96	100

Standardized Testing

Under the No Child Left Behind Act, all American states must test students in public schools statewide to ensure that they are achieving the desired level of minimum education, such as on the Regents Examinations in New York, or the Florida Comprehensive Assessment Test (FCAT), and the Massachusetts Comprehensive Assessment System (MCAS); students being educated at home or in private schools are not included. The act also requires that students and schools show "adequate yearly progress." This means they must show some improvement each year. When a student fails to make adequate yearly progress, No Child Left Behind mandates that remediation through summer school and/or tutoring be made available to a student in need of extra help.

During high school, students (usually in 11th grade) may take one or more standardized tests depending on their postsecondary education preferences and their local graduation requirements. In theory, these tests evaluate the overall level of knowledge and learning aptitude of the students. The SAT and ACT are the most common standardized tests that students take when applying to college. A student may take the SAT, ACT, or both depending upon the post-secondary institutions the student plans to apply to for admission. Most competitive schools also require two or three SAT Subject Tests, (formerly known as SAT Ⅱ s), which are shorter exams that focus strictly on a particular subject matter. However, all these tests serve little to no purpose for students who do not move on to post-secondary education, so they can usually be skipped without affecting one's ability to graduate.

Extracurricular Activities(课外活动)

A major characteristic of American schools is the high priority given to sports, clubs and activities by the community, the parents, the schools and the students themselves. Extracurricular activities are educational activities not falling within the scope of the regular curriculum but under the supervision of the school. These activities can extend to large amounts of time outside the normal school day; home-schooled students, however, are not normally allowed to participate. Student participation in sports programs, drill teams, bands, and spirit groups can amount to hours of practices and performances. Most states have organizations that develop rules for competition between groups. These organizations are usually forced to implement time limits on hours practiced as a prerequisite for participation. Many schools also have non-varsity sports teams, however these are usually afforded less resources and attention. The idea of having sports teams associated with high schools is relatively unique to the United States in comparison with other countries.

Sports programs and their related games, especially football and/or basketball, are major events for American students and for larger schools can be a major source of funds for school districts. Schools may sell "spirit" shirts to wear to games; school stadiums and gymnasiums are often filled to capacity, even for non-sporting competitions.

High school athletic competitions often generate intense interest in the community. Inner city schools serving poor students are heavily scouted by college and even professional coaches, with national attention given to which colleges outstanding high school students choose to attend. State high school championship tournaments football and basketball attract high levels of public interest.

In addition to sports, numerous non-athletic extracurricular activities are available in American schools, both public and private. Activities include Quizbowl, musical groups, marching bands, student government, school newspapers, science fairs, debate teams, and clubs focused on an academic area (such as the Spanish Club) or cultural interests (such as Key Club).

Education of Students with Special Needs

In the United States, education for students with special needs is structured to adhere as closely as possible to the same experience received by typically developing peers. This concept was developed with the passing of IDEA. This law directed states to develop opportunities for children with special needs to be educated within the public education system.

Students with special needs must have the opportunity to be with typically developing peers in the mainstream school. For example: recess, cafeteria, assemblies, hallways, regular classes, etc. This process is known as mainstreaming(回归主流). Special education (educational programs required to assist special needs students) must be provided for these students for mainstreaming to be possible. Students with special needs attend special schools only if their need for very specialized services makes mainstreaming impossible. The level of mainstreaming that is provided varies greatly within different school districts. For example, larger school districts are often able to provide more adequate and quality care for those with special needs rather than smaller school districts.

Students with special needs are required to attend the same amount of time as typically developing peers. Students receiving special education services are entitled by law to an annual review of yearly progress as well as an evaluation every three years to determine the needs for continued services. Parents who have specific desires for their child's education must act as advocates to assure their child's best interests are being met.

To more clearly identify special needs students, the federal government defined thirteen categories of special needs. These included autism, deaf-blindness, deafness, hearing impairment, mental retardation, multiple disabilities, orthopedic (整形) impairment, other health impairment (损害), serious emotional disturbance, specific learning disability, speech or language impairment, traumatic brain injury, and visual impairment. The key to overcoming special needs in the mainstream school for students is:

- Attending sessions (i. e. resource room) during the day to supplement regular or special classroom instruction. The goal of these programs is for students to learn compensatory strategies and study skills to enable them to succeed in mainstream classes. These sessions are generally for students who are fully included into the general educational environment.

- Students with similar needs are placed together in a self-contained classroom if their education cannot be satisfactorily achieved in the general educational environment. In other words, these classrooms are provided for students who do not benefit educationally, socially or emotionally from a standard classroom placement. These classrooms, commonly known as *special classes*, are taught by teachers with training in adapting curricula to meet the needs of students with special needs.

According to the National Association of School Nurses, 5% students in 2009 have a seizure disorder, another 5% have ADHD and 10% have mental or emotional problems. 17% of students are considered obese and 32% are overweight.

Educating Children with Disabilities

IDEA is a federal law that requires states to ensure that all school districts provide services to meet the individual needs of students with special needs. Students must be placed in the Least Restrictive Environment (LRE). This means that school districts must meet with the parents to develop an Individualized Education Program that determines best placement for their child. School districts that fail to provide an appropriate placement for students with special needs can be taken to due process wherein parents may legally and formally submit their grievances and demand appropriate services for their child. All special needs students are entitled to a free and appropriate public education (FAPE).

The federal government supports the standards developed in the Individuals with Disabilities Education Improvement Act of 2004. The law mandates that schools must accommodate students with special needs as defined by the act, and specifies methods for funding the (sometimes large) costs of providing them with the necessary facilities.

Criticism

At-risk students (those with educational needs that aren't associated with a disability) are often placed in classes with students with minor disabilities. Critics assert that placing at-risk students in the same classes as disabled students may impede the educational progress of both the at-risk and the disabled students.

Public and Private Schools

The United States has an education system decentralized by state. There are no national schools.

K–12 students in most areas have a choice between free tax-funded public schools, or privately-funded private schools.

Public school systems are supported by a combination of local, state, and federal government funding. Because a large portion of school revenues come from local property taxes, public schools vary widely in the resources they have available per student. Class size also varies significantly from one district to another. Curriculum decisions in public schools are made largely at the local and state levels; the federal government has limited influence. In most districts, a locally elected school board runs schools. The school board appoints an official called the superintendent of schools to manage the schools in the district. The largest public school system in the United States is in New York City, where more than one million students are taught in 1,200 separate public schools. Because of its immense size—there are more students in the system than residents in eight US states—the New York City public school system is nationally influential in determining standards and materials, such as textbooks.

Admission to individual public schools is usually based on residency. To compensate for differences in school quality based on geography, school systems serving large cities and portions of large cities often have "magnet schools" that provide enrollment to a specified number of non-resident students in addition to serving all resident students. This special enrollment is usually decided by lottery with equal numbers of males and females chosen. Some magnet schools cater to gifted students or to students with special interests, such as the sciences or performing arts. Admission to some of these schools is highly competitive and based on an application process.

Private schools in the United States include parochial (教区的) schools (affiliated with religious denominations), non-profit independent schools, and for-profit private schools. Private schools charge varying rates depending on geographic location, the school's expenses, and the availability of funding from sources, other than tuition. For example, some churches partially subsidize private schools for their members. Some people have argued that when their child attends a private school, they should be able to take the funds that the public school no longer needs and apply that money towards private school tuition in the form of vouchers; this is the basis of the school choice movement.

5,072,451 students attended 33,740 private elementary and secondary schools in 2007. 74.5% of these were white, non-Hispanic, 9.8% were black, 9.6% were Hispanic. 5.4% were Asian or Pacific Islander, and 0.6% were American Indian. Average school size was 150.3 students. There were 456,266 teachers. The number of teachers per student was about 11. 65% of seniors in private schools in 2006 - 7 went on to attend a 4-year college.

Private schools have various missions: most of them take sports very seriously and recruit athletes heavily, some cater to college-bound students seeking a competitive edge in the college admissions process; others are for gifted students, students with learning disabilities or other special needs, or students with specific religious affiliations. Some cater to families seeking a small school, with a nurturing, supportive environment. Unlike public school systems, private schools have no legal obligation to accept any interested student. Admission to some private schools is highly selective. Private schools also have the ability to permanently expel persistently unruly students, a disciplinary option not always legally available to public school systems. Private schools offer the advantages of smaller classes, under twenty students in a typical elementary classroom, for example; a higher teacher/student ratio across the school day, greater individualized attention and in the more competitive schools, expert college placement services. Unless specifically designed to do so, private schools usually cannot offer the services required by students with serious or multiple learning, emotional, or behavioral issues. Although reputed to pay lower salaries than public school systems, private schools often attract teachers by offering high-quality professional development opportunities, including tuition grants for advanced degrees. According to elite private schools themselves, this investment in faculty development helps maintain the high quality program that they offer.

An August 17, 2000 article by the Chicago Sun-Times refers to the Roman Catholic Archdiocese(大主教的管区)of Chicago Office of Catholic Schools as the largest private school system in the United States.

7.2 College and University

Post-secondary education in the United States is known as college or university and commonly consists of four years of study at an institution of higher learning. There are 4.352 colleges, universities, and junior colleges in the country. In 2008, 36% of enrolled students graduated from college in four years. 57% completed their undergraduate requirements in six years, at the same college they first enrolled in.

Like high school, the four undergraduate grades are commonly called freshman, sophomore, junior, and senior years (alternatively called first year, second year, etc.). Students traditionally apply to receive admission into college, with varying difficulties of entrance. Schools differ in their competitiveness and reputation; generally, the most prestigious schools are private, rather than public. Admissions criteria involve the rigor and grades earned in high school courses taken, the students' GPA, class ranking, and standardized test scores (Such as the SAT or the ACT tests). Most colleges also consider more subjective factors such as a commitment to extracurricular activities, a personal essay, and an interview. While numerical factors rarely ever are absolute required values, each college usually has a rough threshold, below which admission is unlikely.

Once admitted, students engage in undergraduate study, which consists of satisfying university and class requirements to achieve a bachelor's degree in a field of concentration known as a major. (Some students enroll in double majors or "minor" in another field of study.) The most common method consists of four years of study leading to a Bachelor of Arts (B. A.), a Bachelor of Science (B. S.), or sometimes another bachelor's degree such as Bachelor of Fine Arts (B. F. A.), Bachelor of Social Work (B. S. W.), Bachelor of Engineering (B.

Eng.) or Bachelor of Philosophy (B. Phil.) Five-Year Professional Architecture programs offer the Bachelor of Architecture Degree (B. Arch.)

Professional degrees such as law, medicine, pharmacy, and dentistry, are offered as graduate study after earning at least three years of undergraduate schooling or after earning a bachelor's degree depending on the program. These professional fields do not require a specific undergraduate major, though medicine, pharmacy, and dentistry have set prerequisite courses that must be taken before enrollment.

Some students choose to attend a community college for two years prior to further study at another college or university. In most states, community colleges are operated either by a division of the state university or by local special districts subject to guidance from a state agency. Community colleges may award Associate of Arts (AA) or Associate of Science (AS) degree after two years. Those seeking to continue their education may transfer to a four-year college or university (after applying through a similar admissions process as those applying directly to the four-year institution). Some community colleges have automatic enrollment agreements with a local four-year college, where the community college provides the first two years of study and the university provides the remaining years of study, sometimes all on one campus. The community college awards theassociate's degree, and the university awards the bachelor's and master's degrees.

Graduate study, conducted after obtaining an initial degree and sometimes after several years of professional work, leads to a more advanced degree such as a master's degree, which could be a Master of Arts (MA), Master of Science (MS), Master of Business Administration (MBA), or other less common master's degrees such as Master of Education (MEd), and Master of Fine Arts (MFA). After additional years of study and sometimes in conjunction with the completion of a master's degree, students may earn a Doctor of Philosophy (Ph. D.) or other doctoral degree, such as Doctor of Arts, Doctor of Education, Doctor of Theology, Doctor of Medicine, Doctor of Pharmacy, Doctor of Physical Therapy, or Juris Doctor. Some programs, such as medicine, have formal apprenticeship procedures post-graduation, such as residencies(实习期) and internships, which must be completed after graduation and before one is considered fully trained. Other professional programs like law and business have no formal apprenticeship requirements after graduation (although law school graduates must take the bar exam to legally practice law in nearly all states).

Entrance into graduate programs usually depends upon a student's undergraduate academic performance or professional experience as well as their score on a standardized entrance exam like the Graduate Record Examination (GRE-graduate schools in general), the Medical College Admission Test (MCAT), or the Law School Admission Test (LSAT). Many graduate and law schools do not require experience after earning a bachelor's degree to enter their programs; however, business school candidates are usually required to gain a few years of professional work experience before applying. Only 8.9 percent of students ever receive postgraduate degrees, and most, after obtaining their bachelor's degree, proceed directly into the workforce.

Cost

The vast majority of students (up to 70 percent) lack the financial resources to pay tuition up front and must rely on student loans and scholarships from their university, the federal government, or a private lender. All but a few charity institutions charge all students tuition, although scholarships (both merit-based and need-based) are widely available. Generally, private universities charge much higher tuition than their public counterparts, which rely on state funds to make up the difference. Because each state supports its own university system with state taxes, most public universities charge much higher rates for out-of-state students.

Annual undergraduate tuition varies widely from state to state, and many additional fees apply. In 2009, average annual tuition at a public university (for residents of the state) was $7,020. Tuition for public school students from outside the state is generally comparable to private school prices, although students can often qualify for state residency after their first year. Private schools are typically much higher, although prices vary widely from "no-frills" private schools to highly specialized technical institutes. Depending upon the type of school and program, annual graduate program tuition can vary from $15,000 to as high as $50,000. Note that these prices do not include living expenses (rent, room/board, etc.) or additional fees that schools add on such as "activities fees" or health insurance. These fees, especially room and board, can range from $6,000 to $12,000 per academic year (assuming a single student without children).

The mean annual Total Cost (including all costs associated with a full-time post-secondary schooling, such as tuition and fees, books and supplies, room and board), as reported by the Census Bureau for the school year 2001/2, according to the various college years was as follows:

- College years 1 to 2: $9,489 (per year)
- College years 3 to 4: $11,901 (per year)
- Total, four year schooling: $42,780
- College years 5 or plus: $13,669 (per year)
- Vocational, technical, business or other: $7,401 (per year)

College costs are rising at the same time that state appropriations for aid are shrinking. This has led to debate over funding at both the state and local levels. From 2002 to 2004 alone, tuition rates at public schools increased by just over 14 percent, largely due to dwindling state funding. A more moderate increase of 6 percent occurred over the same period for private schools. Between 1982 and 2007, college tuition and fees rose three times as fast as median family income, in constant dollars.

To combat costs colleges have hired adjunct professors to teach. In 2008 these teachers cost about $1,800 per 3-credit class as opposed to $8,000 per class for a tenured professor. Two-thirds of college instructors were adjuncts. There are differences of opinion whether these adjuncts teach better or worse than regular professors. There is a suspicion that student evaluation of adjuncts, along with their subsequent continued employment, can lead to grade inflation.

The Status Ladder

American college and university faculty, staff, alumni, students, and applicants monitor rankings produced by magazines such as US News and World Report, Academic Ranking of World Universities, test preparation services such as The Princeton Review or another university itself such as the Top American Research Universities by the University of Florida's The Center. These rankings are based on factors like brand recognition, selectivity in admissions, generosity of alumni donors, and volume of faculty research. Fifty-five US universities are listed in the top 200 in the world in the THES—QS World University Rankings. A small percentage of students who apply to these schools gain admission.

Many Americans would also recognize the "top tier" to include the so-called "Little Ivies"; a handful of liberal arts colleges known for their high-quality instruction and academic rigor.

Certain public universities (sometimes referred to as "Public Ivies") are also recognized for their outstanding record in scholarship. Some of these institutions currently place among the elite in certain measurements of graduate education and research, especially among engineering and medical schools.

Each state in the United States maintains its own public university system, which is always non-profit. The State University of New York and the California State University are the largest public higher education systems in the United States; SUNY is the largest system that includes community colleges, while CSU is the largest without. Most areas also have private institutions, which may be for-profit or non-profit. Unlike many other nations, there are no public universities at the national level outside of the military service academies.

Prospective students applying to attend one of the five military academies require, with limited exceptions, nomination by a member of Congress. Like acceptance to "top tier" universities, competition for these limited nominations is intense and must be accompanied by superior scholastic achievement and evidence of "leadership potential".

Aside from these aforementioned schools, academic reputations vary widely among the "middle-tier" of American schools, (and even among academic departments within each of these schools.) Most public and private institutions fall into this "middle" range. Some institutions feature honors colleges or other rigorous programs that challenge academically exceptional students, who might otherwise attend a "top-tier" college. Aware of the status attached to the perception of the college that they attend, students often apply to a range of schools. Some apply to a relatively prestigious school with a low acceptance rate, gambling on the chance of acceptance, and also apply to a "safety school", to which they will (almost) certainly gain admission.

Lower status institutions include community colleges. These are primarily two-year public institutions, which individual states usually require to accept all local residents who seek admission, and offer associate's degrees or vocational certificate programs. Many community colleges have relationships with four-year state universities and colleges or even private universities that enable their students to transfer to these universities for a four-year degree after completing a two-year program at the community college.

Regardless of perceived prestige, many institutions feature at least one distinguished academic department, and most post-secondary American students attend one of the 2,400 four-year colleges and universities or 1,700 two-year colleges not included among the twenty-five or so 'top-tier' institutions. For this reason (among others), America's higher education status ladder remains highly controversial, and certainly not beyond reproach. For example, Reed College refuses to participate in institutional rankings, insisting that one cannot quantify the qualitative. Similarly, Bard College president Leon Botstein said of US News' annual rankings; "it is the most successful journalistic scam I have seen in my entire adult lifetime—corrupt, intellectually bankrupt and revolting."

7.3 Contemporary Education Issues

Major educational issues in the United States center on curriculum, funding, and control. Of critical importance, because of its enormous implications on education and funding, is the No Child Left Behind Act.

Curriculum Issues

Curricula in the United States vary widely from district to district. Not only do schools offer a range of topics and quality, but private schools may include religious classes as mandatory for attendance (raising the question of government funding vouchers; see below). This has produced camps of argument over the standardization of curricula and to what degree. These same groups often are advocates of standardized testing, which is mandated by the No Child Left Behind Act.

There is debate over which subjects should receive the most focus, with astronomy and geography among those cited as not being taught enough in schools.

English in the Classroom

A large issue facing curricula today is the use of the English language in teaching. English is spoken by over 95% of the nation, and there is a strong national tradition of upholding English as the de facto(事实上) official language. Some 9.7 million children aged 5 to 17 primarily speak a language other than English at home. Of those, about 1.3 million children do not speak English well or at all. While a few, mostly Hispanic, groups want bilingual education, the majority of school districts are attempting to use English as a Second Language (ESL) course to teach Spanish-speaking students English. In addition, many feel there are threats to the "integrity" of the language itself.

Attainment

Forty-four percent of college faculty believe that incoming students aren't ready for writing at the college level. Ninety percent of high school teachers believe exiting students are well-prepared.

Intelligent Design or Creationism(创造宇宙说)

In 1999 the School Board of the state of Kansas caused controversy when it decided to eliminate teaching of evolution in its state assessment tests. This caused outrage among scientists and average citizens alike, and intense media coverage and the national spotlight persuaded the board to eventually overturn the decision. As of 2005, such controversies have not abated. Not surprisingly, scientists stress the importance of evolution in the curriculum and most do not support the teaching of intelligent design or creationism in public school biology courses. Many fundamentalist religious and "family values" groups, on the other hand, claim that evolution is simply a "theory" (thereby misunderstanding this scientific term), and as such creationist(创造论者) ideas should therefore be taught alongside it as an "alternative viewpoint". While a majority of United States citizens approve of teaching evolution, many also support teaching intelligent design and/or creationism in public schools. Support for evolution was found to be greater among the better educated. US courts have ruled it is a violation of the separation of church and state to present creationism and intelligent design (declared to be the same thing under different names) as science or fact in public schools.

Sex Education

Today, sex education ("sex ed") in the United States is highly controversial. Many schools attempt to avoid the study as much as possible, confining it to a unit in health classes. There are few specifically sex education classes in existence. Also, because former President George W. Bush called for abstinence-only sex education and had the power to withhold funding, many schools backed away from instructing students in the use of birth control or contraceptives.

However, according to a 2004 survey, a majority of the 1001 parent groups polled wants complete sex education in the schools. The American people are heavily divided over the issue. Over 80% of polled parents agreed with the statement "Sex education in school makes it easier for me to talk to my child about sexual issues," while under 17% agreed with the statement that their children were being exposed to "subjects I don't think my child should be discussing." 10 percent believed that their children's sexual education class forced them to discuss sexual issues "too early". On the other hand, 49 percent of the respondents (the largest group) were "somewhat confident" that the values taught in their children's sex ed classes were similar to those taught at home, and 23 percent were less confident still. (The margin of error was plus or minus 4.7 percent.)

Funding

Funding for K－12 schools

According to a 2005 report from the OECD, the United States is tied for first place with Switzerland when it comes to annual spending per student on its public schools, with each of those two countries spending more than $11,000 (in US currency). Despite this high level of funding, according to the OECD, US public schools lag behind the schools of other developed countries in the areas of reading, math, and science.

According to a 2007 article in The Washington Post, the Washington, D. C. public school district spends $12,979 per student per year. This is the third highest level of funding per student out of the 100 biggest school districts in the US Despite this high level of funding, the school district has produced outcomes that are lower than the national average. In reading and math, the district's students score the lowest among 11 major school districts—even when poor children are compared with other poor children. 33% of poor fourth graders in the US lack basic skills in math, but in Washington, D. C., it's 62%. In 2004, the US Congress set up a voucher program for low income minority students in Washington, D. C. to attend private schools. The vouchers were $7,500 per student per year. The parents said their children were receiving a much better education from the private schools. In 2007, Washington, D. C. non-voting delegate Eleanor Holmes Norton said she wanted the voucher program to be eliminated, and that the public schools needed more money. Secretary of Education Arne Duncan supports retaining vouchers for the district only, as do some DC parent groups.

According to a 2006 study by the Goldwater Institute, Arizona's public schools spend 50% more per student than Arizona's private schools. The study also says that while teachers constitute 72% of the employees at private schools, they make up less than half of the staff at public schools. According to the study, if Arizona's public schools wanted to be like private schools, they would have to hire approximately 25,000 more teachers, and eliminate 21,210 administration employees.

During the 2006 - 2007 school year, a private school in Chicago founded by Marva Collins to teach low income minority students charged $5,500 for tuition, and parents said that the school did a much better job than the Chicago public school system. Meanwhile, during the 2007 - 2008 year, Chicago public school officials claimed that their budget of $11,300 per student was not enough.

In 1985 in Kansas City, Missouri, a judge ordered the school district to raise taxes and spend more money on public education. Spending was increased so much, that the school district was spending more money per student than any of the country's other 280 largest school districts. Although this very high level of spending continued for more than a decade, there was no improvement in the school district's academic performance.

Public school defenders answer that both of these examples are misleading, as the task of educating students is easier in private schools, which can expel or refuse to accept students who lag behind their peers in academic achievement or behavior, while public schools have no such recourse and must continue to attempt to educate these students. For this reason, comparisons of the cost of education in public schools to that of private schools is misleading; private school education can be accomplished with less funding because in most cases they only educate those students who are easiest to teach.

But not in all cases. For example, Marva Collins created her low cost private school specifically for the purpose of teaching low income African American children whom the public school system had labeled as being "learning disabled". One article about Marva Collins' school stated, "Working with students having the worst of backgrounds, those who were working far below grade level, and even those who had been labeled as 'unteachable,' Marva was able to overcome the obstacles. News of third grade students reading at ninth grade level, four-year-olds learning to read in a few months, outstanding test scores, disappearance of behavioral problems, second-graders studying Shakespeare, and other incredible reports, astounded the public."

According to a 1999 article by William J. Bennett, former US Secretary of Education, increased levels of spending on public education have not made the schools better. Among many other things, the article cites the following statistics:

- Between 1960 and 1995, US public school spending per student, adjusted for inflation, increased by 212%.
- In 1994, less than half of all US public school employees were teachers.
- Out of 21 industrialized countries, US 12th graders ranked 19th in math, 16th in science, and last in advanced physics.

Other commentators have suggested that the public school system has exhibited signs of success. SAT scores have risen consistently over the past decades, despite the fact that the pool of students taking the test has increased from an academic elite to a much more representative sampling of the population. Commentators have suggested that this increase in scores, coming as it does at a time when more students have started to take the test and the public schooling system has faced ever-increasing challenge, suggests that the US educational system is much more effective than is commonly believed, and that the negative cast common in public perception is due to negative propaganda disseminated by elements with a personal interest in discrediting or weakening public education.

Funding for schools in the United States is complex. One current controversy stems much from the No Child Left Behind Act. The Act gives the Department of Education the right to withhold funding if it believes a school, district, or even a state is not complying and is making no effort to comply. However, federal funding accounts for little of the overall funding schools receive. The vast majority comes from the state government and in some cases from local property taxes. Various groups, many of whom are teachers, constantly push for more funding. They point to many different situations, such as the fact that in many schools funding for classroom supplies is so inadequate that teachers, especially those at the elementary level, must supplement their supplies with purchases of their own.

Property taxes as a primary source of funding for public education have become highly controversial, for a number of reasons. First, if a state's population and land values escalate rapidly, many longtime residents may find themselves paying property taxes much higher than anticipated. In response to this phenomenon, California's citizens passed Proposition 13 in 1978, which severely restricted the ability of the Legislature to expand the state's educational system to keep up with growth. Some states, such as Michigan, have investigated or implemented alternate schemes for funding education that may sidestep the problems of funding based mainly on property taxes by providing funding based on sales or income tax. These schemes also have failings, negatively impacting funding in a slow economy.

Another issue is that many parents of private school and homeschooled children have taken issue with the idea of paying for an education their children are not receiving. However, tax proponents point out that every person pays property taxes for public education, not just parents of school-age children. Indeed, without it schools would not have enough money to remain open. Still, parents of students who go to private schools want to use this money instead to fund their children's private education. This is the foundation of the school voucher(证书) movement. School voucher programs were proposed by free-market advocates seeking competition in education, led by economist Milton Friedman, but have been criticized for damaging public schools, both in funding and diversity.

One of the biggest debates in funding public schools is funding by local taxes or state taxes. The federal government supplies around 8.5% of the public school system funds, according to a 2005 report by the National Center for Education Statistics. The remaining split between state and local governments averages 48.7 percent from states and 42.8 percent from local sources. However, the division varies widely. In Hawaii local funds make up only 1.7 percent, while state sources account for nearly 90.1 percent.

Funding for College

At the college and university level student loan funding is split in half; half is managed by the Department of Education directly, called the Federal Direct Student Loan Program (FDSLP). The other half is managed by commercial entities such as banks, credit unions, and financial services firms such as Sallie Mae, under the Federal Family Education Loan Program (FFELP). Some schools accept only FFELP loans; others accept only FDSLP. Still others accept both, and a few schools will not accept either, in which case students must seek out private alternatives for student loans.

Charter(特许)Schools

The charter-school movement was born in 1990. Charter schools have spread rapidly in the United States, members, parents, teachers, and students "to allow for the expression of diverse teaching philosophies and cultural and social life styles." Some scholars say that there is no statistically significant improvement in charter schools over public schools. 24 of the 25 studies on charter schools or voucher programs that feed charter and private schools show that there is significant improvement and 14 out of 15 studies show that charter schools even improve public education outcomes because of competition.

Control

There is some debate about where control for education actually lies. Education is not mentioned in the constitution of the United States. In the current situation, the state and national governments have a power-sharing arrangement, with the states exercising most of the control. Like other arrangements between the two, the federal government uses the threat of decreased funding to enforce laws pertaining to education. Furthermore, within each state there are different types of control. Some states have a statewide school system, while others delegate power to county, city or township-level school boards. However, under the Bush administration, initiatives such as the No Child Left Behind Act have attempted to assert more central control in a heavily decentralized system.

The US federal government exercises its control through the US Department of Education. Educational accreditation (鉴定合格) decisions are made by voluntary regional associations. Schools in the 50 states, the District of Columbia, the US Virgin Islands, Guam, and the Northern Mariana Islands, teach in English, while schools in the commonwealth of Puerto Rico teach in Spanish. Nonprofit private schools are widespread, are largely independent of the government, and include secular as well as parochial schools.

Competitiveness

The national results in international comparisons have often been far below the average of developed countries. In OECD's Programme for International Student Assessment 2003, 15 year olds ranked 24th of 38 in mathematics, 19th of 38 in science, 12th of 38 in reading, and 26th of 38 in problem solving. In the 2006 assessment, the US ranked 35th out of 57 in mathematics and 29th out of 57 in science. Reading scores could not be reported due to printing errors in the instructions of the US test booklets. US scores were far behind those of most other developed nations. While US teens perform poorly on these Programme for International Student Assessment tests, which emphasizes problem solving, US fourth and eighth graders tested above average on the Trends in International

Mathematics and Science Study tests, which emphasizes traditional learning.

Educational Attainment

The rise of the high school movement in the beginning of the 20th century was unique in the United States, such that, high schools were implemented with virtues like: property-tax funded tuition, openness, non-exclusivity, and were decentralized(分散的). For the countries of Europe the educational system in the middle of the 20th century still lacked many of these virtues, and were more apprentice-type and very exclusive. The educational system was different in the United States. The academic curriculum was designed to provide the students with a terminal degree. The students obtained general knowledge (such as mathematics, chemistry, composition, etc.) best applicable to the high geographic and social mobility in the United States. The provision of the high schools accelerated with the rise of second industrial revolution industry. The increase in office white collar and skilled blue-collar work in manufacturing reflected in the high demand for high schools. It was not until after WWⅡ that European and other industrialized nations began to follow the United States' efforts. Now the educational attainment of the US population is similar to that of many other industrialized countries with the vast majority of the population having completed secondary education and a rising number of college graduates that outnumber high school dropouts. As a whole the population of the United States is becoming increasingly more educated. Post-secondary education is valued very highly by American society and is one of the main determinants of class and status. As with income, however, there are significant discrepancies in terms of race, age, household configuration and geography. Overall the households and demographics featuring the highest educational attainment in the United States are also among those with the highest household income and wealth. Thus, while the population of the US is becoming increasingly educated on all levels, a direct link between income and educational attainment remains.

In 2007, Americans stood second only to Canada in the percentage of 35 to 64 year olds holding at least two-year degrees. Among 25 to 34 year olds, the country stands tenth. The nation stands 15 out of 29 rated nations for college completion rates, slightly above Mexico and Turkey.

Questions

1. What are the differences between public and private schools in the US?

2. What is K－12? What are the characteristics of elementary and secondary education in the US?

3. What is IDEA?

4. What's your impression of American contemprary educaiton issues?

Supplementary Reading 1

American Education

Colonial America

> Education, in its broadest sense, is the means of this social continuity of life.
>
> —John Dewey

European immigrants to **Colonial America** brought with them their culture, traditions and philosophy about education. Much of the formal educational system in the United States is rooted in the European or Western belief system. Though an indigenous population of Native Americans lived on the North American continent, their influence on the development of formal educational practice in America was minimal. Many tribes had not yet developed writing or a system of formal educational practice. Additionally, there was a systematic effort to eradicate this population as opposed to assimilating them.

Among the tribes that had developed written languages, the Cherokee tribe who originally lived in the Southern portion of the United States had developed a system of formal education to pass knowledge from one generation to the next. They, however, were methodically pushed out of their native territory in the early 1800's and forced to move to the Oklahoma territory, which limited their

A Native American

ability to influence educational practice in early America.

The English were the predominant settlers in the New World and as a result education in colonial America, was patterned on the English model. It originally developed as a two-track system with people from the lower classes receiving minimal instruction and only learning to read and write, calculate and receive religious instruction. The upper classes were allowed to pursue an education beyond the basics and oftentimes attended Latin grammar or secondary schools where they learned Greek and Latin and studied the classics in preparation for a college education.

Religion played an important rule in developing an educational system in the United States. The Puritans, a strict fundamentalist Protestant sect who immigrated to the New World for religious freedom beginning in 1609, believed that education was necessary in order to read the Bible to receive salvation. This was in line with the beliefs of the Protestant Reformers. Their schools made no distinction between religious and secular life and were also used to inspire children to endure the hardships of a life in the New World through religious devotion.

Teachers had some status in the community because they, along with the clergy, had more education than most of the population. However, their position was secondary to that of the clergy. Additionally, teachers had to be of high moral character, which came under intense scrutiny by the rest of the community. They also had many other duties besides teaching, such as cleaning the school, substituting for the minister, and ring the church bell.

The settlers in a particular area heavily influenced the development of schools and formal education in the American colonies. For example in the New England Colonies, which was primarily Puritan, religious instruction was of paramount importance. Puritans believed that people (children in particular) were inherently bad (sinners) and had to learn to behave. Salvation lay in learning to check one's natural instincts and behave as an adult.

The **Mid-Atlantic colonies** had a more diverse population consisting of the

Dutch, English, Irish, Scottish, German, etc. They were also more varied in their religious beliefs and therefore did not develop a common school system such as the one that prevailed in the New England colonies. Instead each group often developed their own schools which promoted their culture, religion and traditions. The Quakers who settled in the Philadelphia area in the 1680's believed in educating the populace. They were also tolerant of others' beliefs and ways of life. They had a strong influence on the development of education and established the first public school.

In the Southern Colonies, where society was more structured and stratified according to socioeconomic classes, the wealthy plantation owners developed their own system to prepare their sons for further education. Children from poorer households received a minimal education and slaves from Africa only learned what was necessary to attend their masters.

Here, religious instruction had an important role, but so too did the more rigorous education of secondary schools, where the sons of the wealthy learned the necessary subject matter to prepare them for college on the European continent. In 1636 Harvard College, the first post-secondary school on the North American continent, was established in the Boston, Massachusetts area and in 1693 the College of William and Mary in Williamsburg, Virginia was founded.

Dame Schools were one of the more common types of schools found in the colonies. They were often established by women, and more often than not run from the home of the person in charge. Students were charged a modest fee to attend. Education was basic, concentrating on reading, writing, and calculation. Attendance was often erratic and dependent on the season and work at home that needed to be done. For most females the dame school provided their only education and homemaking skills such as sewing were also included in the instructional process.

Requiring School Attendance

> Education is the transmission of civilization.
>
> —Ariel and Will Durant

The first compulsory education laws were passed in Massachusetts from 1642-1648. They were specifically oriented towards a segment of the population (non-Puritan) who was not providing their children with a proper education. Religious leaders were concerned about the rapid growth of the non-Puritan population and took these steps to maintain Puritan religious beliefs. The first act, called the Massachusetts Act of 1642 made education a state responsibility. While schools were not yet funded or required, education was and all children were supposed to learn how to read and write or parents would risk loss of custody of their children. The law was amended and strengthened in 1648.

The law requiring the establishment of schools was passed in 1647. All towns of fifty or more households were required to form a school and pay a teacher either out of private or public monies. In addition towns of one hundred or more households had to establish a secondary or Latin grammar school to prepare students to enter Harvard College.

Education in the Revolutionary Era.

> I know no safe depositary of the ultimate powers of the society but the people themselves; and if we think them not enlightened enough to exercise their control with a wholesome discretion, the remedy is not to take it from them, but to inform their discretion by education. This is the true corrective of abuses of constitutional power.
>
> —Thomas Jefferson to William C. Jarvis, 1820.

As the American colonies continued to grow and prosper, the European traditions that had previously guided the development of schools and education began to lose some of their influence. Though religion was still an important part of the curriculum, the need to build and maintain commerce, agriculture and shipping interests required a different focus. As generations were born and grew up in the American colonies, people began to see themselves as apart from their European roots and started to develop their own identity. The American Revolution was the culmination of this movement away from the European traditions and resulted in independence for the thirteen colonies from Great Britain. As the United States of America, the former colonists wanted to establish their independence in both thought and deed and saw education as a means to this end. Education was also seen as the tool that would both establish and promote the growth of concepts such as freedom, liberty, and democracy to insure that citizens would learn how to be responsible citizens and secure the United States as a nation for generations to come.

Benjamin Franklin (1706 - 1790) was a Renaissance man who had a profound influence in many different areas. He was a journalist and writer, establishing one of the first newspapers in the American colonies, a statesman and an ambassador to France, as well as one of the leaders in the American Revolution, an inventor, and an educator who founded the Philadelphia Academy, a secondary school that opened in 1751. This school followed Franklin's instructional curriculum that emphasized the more practical subjects such as modern languages, agriculture, accounting, etc. rather than the more traditional classical education such as employed by the Latin grammar schools.

Benjamin Franklin
(1706 - 1790)

Females for the most part received little or no formal education during the 17th and 18th centuries. Most were educated at home, although occasionally they attended dame schools. Sometimes a governess would be provided if the family was wealthy enough and girls were taught sewing, drawing, music, and languages such as French. Sarah Pierce established the Litchfield Female Academy in 1792 beginning with just two students and which eventually grew to 140 students. Almost 3000 girls were educated in this school. However, most females were not educated outside the home and formal education in secondary schools and colleges was reserved for males.

Thomas Jefferson (1743 - 1826), the third president of the United States, believed in the education of the common man as the most effective means of preserving the democratic ideal. He consistently advocated for free public education, even as early as 1779 when he tried to persuade the Virginia legislature to fund elementary and secondary schools. Though he was not successful in this particular endeavor, Jefferson still was able to exert an influence on the development of formal education in the United States. He went on to establish the University of Virginia and oversaw the adoption and implementation of many of his ideas regarding education.

Thomas Jefferson
(1743 - 1826)

A standard curriculum was difficult to achieve in a country as large and sparsely populated as the new United States of America. One of the means of promoting a curriculum that advocated the ideals of democracy and independence from England was the development of textbooks. Noah Webster (1758 - 1853) introduced his first text in 1783, a speller with an emphasis on developing patriotic and moral values as well as teaching children correct grammar and spelling. Webster's "blue books" as they were commonly known eventually sold over twenty-four million copies, a staggering number given the population of the United States at this time.

http://oregonstate.edu/instruct/ed416/ae2.html

Supplementary Reading 2

Like Ivies, Berkeley Adds Aid to Draw Middle-Class Students

By Jennifer Medina

LOS ANGELES — The University of California, Berkeley, announced Wednesday that it would offer far more financial aid to middle-class students starting next fall, with families earning up to $140,000 a year expected to contribute no more than 15 percent of their annual income, in what experts described as the most significant such move by a public institution.

As state budget cuts have led to rising tuition and fees at the University of California and other prestigious campuses across the nation, the middle class has increasingly been squeezed out of what was long seen as higher education's best balance between quality and affordability.

At Berkeley, officials said, the number of low-income and wealthy students has grown over the last several years, while the number from middle-class families has remained flat. That has raised concerns that some of the state's best and brightest are choosing private schools whose generous financial aid can erase differentials in sticker price or not enrolling at all. The cost of a year at Berkeley has risen sharply to $32,000.

"We see early signs that middle-income families who cannot access existing assistance programs are straining to meet college costs," said the Berkeley chancellor, Robert J. Birgeneau. "As a public institution we feel strongly that we need to sustain and expand access across the socioeconomic spectrum."

While several elite private universities — including the Ivy League triumvirate of Harvard, Princeton and Yale — offer similar programs for families with incomes up to $200,000, experts said that Berkeley was the first public university to do so. For the most part, public colleges have focused on merit scholarships to lure top students and aid for the poorest families to ensure access, but many now worry that approach has left out a wide group of families.

"Berkeley has really just changed the game," said Terry W. Hartle, senior vice president of the American Council on Education, which represents the nation's large research universities. "Other schools will follow if they can, but the problem is that most universities don't have the resources to match it. On the other hand, given how competitive colleges are with each other, they are certainly going to try."

At the University of Washington, where tuition, room and board amount to about $24,000, officials said they were trying to be creative with aid because they know that earnings are not increasing as fast as tuition amid cuts in education financing by the state.

"We're looking at our families and seeing that there is more financial need, not as many options in terms of a family's ability to borrow, and trying to find a way to make it work," said Kay Lewis, assistant vice president for student life at the University of Washington. "It really is an issue of access and trying to ensure that access for middle- and low-income students is something we are constantly thinking about."

Berkeley's definition of middle-class in creating its new financial aid program is a family with income between $80,000 and $140,000 a year. On top of the parental contribution of 15 percent of income, students would also have to pay about \$8,000 per year — generally a combination of loans, work-study and private scholarships. At the bottom end of the spectrum, that would make for a total payment of \$20,000, a 37.5 percent discount off the \$32,000 total of tuition, room and board for California residents. On the upper end, it would be about \$29,000, or a 10 percent discount.

(Out-of-state students, who make up 30 percent of Berkeley's freshman class this year, will get comparable discounts on the first \$32,000 of tuition and fees, but still have to pay an additional \$23,000.)

The announcement came a day after Gov. Jerry Brown of California announced a \$2.2 billion budget shortfall, and another severe round of cuts to state colleges and universities. A report by the College Board published this year showed that California's public universities had the nation's largest jump for in-state tuition in 2011–2012.

Although there are only a few anecdotal reports of middle-class students actually dropping out because of rising college costs, the issue has become a rallying cry of Occupy protesters around the country. Berkeley officials, like their counterparts elsewhere, are increasingly worried that some of the state's brightest students, who in previous generations would have chosen their campus because it was a bargain, are now being lured by private universities with big endowments to underwrite aid.

Indeed, in New Jersey, Seton Hall University announced a new plan this fall to give early applicants with top academic credentials a discount of up to two-thirds — making the cost comparable to that of Rutgers University, the elite public institution a few highway exits away.

Mark Kantrowitz, who tracks school aid programs on his Web site, FinAid.org, said, "When tuition is going up, that can have a chilling effect, but something like this has an emotional effect that works as a recruiting tool." He added, "It sends the message that we know everybody struggles to pay for college."

Berkeley officials said the program was expected to cost \$12 million a year and would be paid for from out-of-state and international student tuition, as well as private donations. Officials said they had recently received an \$8 million donation for financial aid and expect to raise more.

Fewer than 2,000 students from families with incomes over $80,000 received financial aid this year, officials said. They estimated that under the new policy, an additional 4,000 middle-class students would receive grants ranging from $3,600 to $16,000 next year. Officials said that the program was devised so that they could increase aid — most likely reducing the 15 percent contribution — if they raised more money, but acknowledged that they could also end up changing in the other direction if money fell short.

http://www.nytimes.com/2011/12/15/education/berkeley-increasing-aid-to-middle-class-students.html? ref=education

Chapter 8 Society and Customs

The society or culture of the United States is a Western culture, and has been developing since long before the United States became a country with its own unique characteristics and developments such as dialect, music, arts, cuisine, etc. Today the United States of America is a diverse and multi-cultural country as result of mass scale immigration from very many countries throughout its history.

Its chief early influences came from English and Irish settlers. British culture, due to colonial ties with Britain that spread the English language, legal system and other cultural inheritances, had a formative influence. Other important influences came from other parts of western Europe.

The United States has traditionally been known as a melting pot, but recent developments tend towards cultural diversity, pluralism and the image of a salad bowl rather than a melting pot. Due to the extent of American culture there are many integrated but unique subcultures within the United States. The cultural affiliations an individual in the United States may have commonly depend on social class, political orientation and a multitude of demographic characteristics such as ancestral traditions. The strongest influences on American culture came from northern European cultures, most prominently from Germany, Ireland and Britain. There are great regional and subcultural(次文化的) differences, making American culture mostly heterogeneous(多种多样的).

8.1 Social Class and Race

Social Class and Work

Though most Americans today identify themselves as middle class, American society and its culture are considerably more fragmented. Social class, generally described as a combination of educational attainment, income and occupational prestige, is one of the greatest cultural influences in America. Nearly all cultural aspects of mundane interactions and consumer behavior in the US are guided by a person's location within the country's social structure.

Distinct lifestyles, consumption patterns and values are associated with different classes. Early sociologist-economist Thorstein Veblen, for example, noted that those at the very top of the social ladder engage in conspicuous leisure as well as conspicuous consumption. Upper middle class persons commonly identify education and being cultured as prime values. Persons in this particular social class tend to speak in a more direct manner that projects authority, knowledge and thus credibility. They often tend to engage in the consumption of so-called mass luxuries, such as designer label clothing. A strong preference for natural materials and organic foods as well as a strong health consciousness tend to be prominent features of the upper middle class. Middle class individuals in general value expanding one's horizon, partially because they are more educated and can afford greater leisure and travels. Working class individuals take great pride in doing what they consider to be "real work", and keep very close-knit kin networks that serve as a safeguard against frequent economic instability. Working class Americans as well as many of those in the middle class may also face occupation alienation(疏远). In contrast to upper middle class professionals who are mostly hired to conceptualize, supervise and share their thoughts, many Americans enjoy only little autonomy or creative latitude in the workplace. As a result white collar professionals tend to be significantly more satisfied with their work. More recently those in the center of the income strata, who may still identify as middle class, have faced increasing economic insecurity, supporting the idea of a working class majority.

Political behavior is affected by class; more affluent individuals are more likely to vote, and education and income affect whether individuals tend to vote for the Democratic or Republican party. Income also had a significant impact on health as those with higher incomes had better access to health care facilities, higher life expectancy, lower infant mortality rate and increased health consciousness.

In the United States occupation is one of the prime factors of social class and is closely linked to an individual's identity. The average work week in the US for those employed full-time was 42.9 hours long with 30% of the population working more than 40 hours a week. It should be noted, however, that many of those in the top two earning quintiles often worked more than 50 hours a week. The Average American worker earned $16.64 an hour in the first two quarters of 2006. Overall Americans worked more than their counterparts in other developed post-industrial nations. While the average worker in Denmark enjoyed 30 days of vacation annually, the average American only had 16 annual vacation days. In 2000 the average American worked 1,978 hours per year, 500 hours more than the average German, yet 100 hours less than the average Czech. Overall the US labor force was the most productive in the world (overall, not by hour worked), largely due to its workers working more than those in any other post-industrial country (excluding South Korea). Americans generally hold working and being productive in high regard; being busy as and working extensively may also serve as the means to obtain esteem.

Race

Race in the United States is based on physical characteristics and skin color and has played an essential part in shaping American society even before the nation's conception. Until the civil rights movement of the 1960s racial minorities in the United States faced discrimination and social as well as economic marginalization(边缘化). Today the US Department of Commerce's Bureau of the Census recognized four races, Native American or American Indian, African American, Asian and White (European American). Hispanic Americans do not technically according to the US Government, constitute a race but rather an ethnic group.

Until the Thirteenth Amendment to the United States Constitution was ratified on December 6th 1865 the United States was a slave society. While the northern states had outlawed slavery in their territory in the late 18th and early 19th century their industrial economies relied on the raw materials produced by slave labor. Following the Reconstruction period in the 1870s, Southern states initialized an apartheid regulated by Jim Crow laws that provided for legal segregation. Lynching occurred throughout the US until the 1930s, continuing well into the civil rights movement in the South. Asian Americans were also marginalized during much of US history. Between 1882 and 1943 the United States government instituted the Chinese Exclusion Act which prohibited Chinese immigrants from entering the nation. During the second world war roughly 120, 000 Japanese Americans, 62% of whom were US citizens, were imprisoned in Japanese internment camps. Hispanic American also faced segregation and other types of discrimination. Despite being considered White in many states such as California, Hispanics were regularly subject to second class citizen status.

Largely as a result of being de jure(根据法律的) or de facto(事实上) excluded and marginalized from so-called mainstream society, racial minorities in the United States developed their own unique sub-cultures. During the 1920s for example, Harlem, New York became home to the Harlem Renaissance. Music styles such as Jazz, Blues and Rap as well as numerous folk-songs such as Blue Tail Fly (Jimmy Crack Corn) originated within the realms of African American culture. Chinatowns can be found in many cities across the nation and Asian cuisine has become a common staple in America. The Hispanic community has also had a dramatic impact on American culture. Today, Catholics are the largest religious denomination in the United States and out-number Protestants in the South-west and California. Mariachi(墨西哥流浪乐队)music and Mexican cuisine are commonly found throughout the Southwest, with some Latin dishes such burritos(墨西哥玉米煎饼)and tacos(玉米面豆卷) found anywhere in the nation. Economic discrepancies and de-facto segregation, however, continue and is a prominent feature of mundane life in the United States. While Asian Americans have prospered and have a median household income and educational attainment far exceeding that of Whites, the same cannot be said for the other racial minorities. African Americans, Hispanics and Native Americans have considerably lower income and education than do White Americans. In 2005 the median household income of Whites was 62.5% higher than that of African American, nearly one-quarter of whom live below the poverty line. Furthermore 46.9% of homicide victims in the United States are African American indicating the many severe socio-economic problems African Americans and minorities in general continue to face in the twenty-first century.

Some aspects of American culture codify racism. For example, the prevailing idea in American culture, perpetuated by the media, has been that black features are less attractive or desirable than white features. The idea that blackness was ugly was highly damaging to the psyche of African Americans, manifesting itself as internalized racism. The Black is beautiful cultural movement sought to dispel this notion.

Group Affiliations

As the United States is a very diverse nation, it is home to numerous organization and social groups and individuals may derive their group affiliated identity from a variety of sources. Many Americans, especially white collar professionals belong to professional organizations such as the APA, ASA or ATFLC, although books like Bowling Alone indicate that Americans affiliate with these sorts of groups less often than they did in the 1950s and 1960s. Today, Americans derive a great deal of their identity through their work and professional affiliation, especially among individuals higher on the economic ladder. Recently professional identification has led to many clerical and low-level employees giving their occupations new, more respectable titles, such as "Sanitation service engineer" instead of "Janitor". Additionally many Americans belong to non-profit organizations and religious establishments and may volunteer their services to such organizations. The Rotary Club, the Knights of Columbus or even the SPCA are examples of such non-profit and mostly volunteer run organizations. Ethnicity plays another important role in providing Americans with group identity, especially among those who recently immigrated. Many American cities are home to ethnic enclaves such as a Chinatown and Little Italies remain in some cities. Local patriotism may be also provide group identity. For example, a person may be particularly proud to be from California or New York City, and may display clothing from local sports team. Political lobbies such as the AARP not only provide individuals with a sentiment of intra-group allegiance (忠诚) but also increase their political representation in the nation's political system. Combined, profession, ethnicity, religious, and other group affiliations have provided Americans with a multitude of options from which to derive their group based identity.

8.2 American Social Life

Technology, Gadgets(小器具), and Automobiles

Americans, by and large, are often fascinated by new technology and new gadgets. There are many within the United States that share the attitude that through technology, many of the evils in the society can be solved. Many of the new technological innovations in the modern world were either first invented in the United States and/or first widely adopted by Americans. Examples include: the light bulb, the airplane, the transistor, nuclear power, the personal computer, video games and online shopping, as well as the development of the Internet. By comparison with Japan, however, only a small fraction of electronic devices make it to sale in the US, and household items such as toilets are rarely festooned with remotes and electronic buttons as they are in some parts of Asia.

Automobiles play a great role in American culture, whether it is in the mundane lives of private individuals or in the areas of arts and entertainment. The rise of suburbs and the need for workers to commute to cities brought about the popularization of automobiles. In 2001, 90% of Americans drove to work in cars. Lower energy and land costs favor the production of relatively large, powerful cars. The culture in the 1950s and 1960s often catered to the automobile with motels and drive-in restaurants. Americans tend to view obtaining a driver's license as a rite of passage. Outside of a relative few urban areas, it is considered a necessity for most Americans to own and drive cars. New York City is the only locality in the United States where more than half of all households do not own a car.

Drugs, Alcohol and Smoking

American attitudes towards drugs and alcoholic beverages have evolved considerably throughout the country's history. In the 19th century, alcohol was readily available and consumed, and no laws restricted the use of other drugs. A movement to ban alcoholic beverages, called the Prohibition movement, emerged in the late 19th century. Several American Protestant religious groups, as well as women's groups such as the Women's Christian Temperance Union, supported the movement. In 1919, Prohibitionists(禁酒主义者) succeeded in amending the Constitution to prohibit the sale of alcohol. Although the Prohibition period did result in lowering alcohol consumption overall, banning alcohol outright proved to be unworkable, as the previously legitimate distillery industry was replaced by criminal gangs which trafficked in alcohol. Prohibition was repealed in 1931. States and localities retained the right to remain "dry", and to this day, a handful still do.

During the Vietnam War era, attitudes swung well away from prohibition. Commentators noted that an 18 year old could be drafted to war but could not buy a beer. Most states lowered the legal drinking age to 18.

Since 1980, the trend has been toward greater restrictions on alcohol and drug use. The focus this time, however, has been to criminalize behaviors associated with alcohol, rather than attempt to prohibit consumption outright. New York was the first state to enact tough drunk-driving laws in 1980; since then all other states have followed suit. A "Just Say No to Drugs" movement replaced the more libertine (放纵者) ethos of the 1960s. Tobacco use, meanwhile, has declined to the point where most Americans consider smoking to be both unseemly and annoying. Virtually all public indoor spaces ban smoking.

Clothing

Apart from professional business attire(服装), clothing in the United States is eclectic and predominantly informal. While Americans' diverse cultural roots are reflected in their clothing, particularly those of recent immigrants, cowboy hats and boots and leather motorcycle jackets are emblematic of specifically American styles. Blue jeans were popularized as work clothes in the 1850s by merchant Levi Strauss, a Jewish-German immigrant in San Francisco, and adopted by many American teenagers a century later. They are now widely worn on every continent by people of all ages and social classes. Along with mass-marketed informal wear in general, blue jeans are arguably US culture's primary contribution to global fashion. The country is also home to the headquarters of many leading designer labels such as Ralph Lauren and Calvin Klein. Labels such as Abercrombie & Fitch and Eckō cater to various niche markets.

Education

In the year 2000, there were 76.6 million students enrolled in schools from kindergarten through graduate schools. Of these, 72 percent aged 12 to 17 were judged academically "on track" for their age (enrolled in school at or above grade level). Of those enrolled in compulsory education, 5.2 million (10.4 percent) were attending private schools. Among the country's adult population, over 85 percent have completed high school and 27 percent have received a bachelor's degree or higher.

Language

The primary, although not official, language of the United States is American English. According to the 2000 US Census, more than 97% of Americans can speak English well, and for 81% it is the only language spoken at home. Nearly 30 million native speakers of Spanish also reside in the US. There are more than 300 languages besides English which can claim native speakers in the United States—some of which are spoken by the indigenous peoples (about 150 living languages) and others which were imported by immigrants. American Sign Language, used mainly by the deaf, is also native to the country. Hawaiian is also a language native to the United States, as it is indigenous nowhere else except in the state of Hawaii. Spanish is the second most common language in the United States, and is one of the official languages, and the most widely spoken, in the US Commonwealth of Puerto Rico.

There are four major regional dialects in the United States: northeastern, south, inland north, and midwestern. The Midwestern accent (considered the "standard accent" in the United States, and analogous in some respects to the received pronunciation elsewhere in the English-speaking world) extends from what were once the "Middle Colonies" across the Midwest to the Pacific states.

Housing

Immediately after World War Ⅱ, Americans began living in increasing numbers in the suburbs, belts around major cities with higher density than rural areas, but much lower than urban areas. This move has been attributed to many factors such as the automobile, the availability of large tracts of land, the convenience of more and longer paved roads, the increasing violence in urban centers, and the cheapness of housing. These new single-family houses were usually one or two stories tall, and often were part of large contracts of homes built by a single developer. The resulting low-density development has been given the pejorative label "urban sprawl". This is changing, however. "White flight" is reversing, with many Yuppies and upper-middle-class, empty nest Baby Boomers returning to urban living, usually in condominiums, such as in New York City's Lower East Side, and Chicago's South Loop. The result has been the displacement of many poorer, inner-city residents. American cities with housing prices near the national median have also been losing the middle income neighborhoods, those with median income between 80% and 120% of the metropolitan area's median household income. Here, the more affluent members of the middle class, who are also often referred to as being professional or upper middle class, have left in search of larger homes in more exclusive suburbs. This trend is largely attributed to the so called "Middle class squeeze," which has caused a starker distinction between the statistical middle class and the more privileged members of the middle class. In more expensive areas such as California, however, another trend has been taking place where an influx of more affluent middle class households has displaced those in the actual middle of society and converted former middle-middle class neighborhoods into upper middle class neighborhoods.

The population of rural areas has been declining over time as more and more people migrate to cities for work and entertainment. The great exodus from the farms came in the 1940s; in recent years fewer than 2% of the population lives on farms (though others live in the countryside and commute to work). Electricity and telephone, and sometimes cable and Internet services are available to all but the most remote regions. As in the cities, children attend school up to and including high school and only help with farming during the summer months or after school.

About half of Americans now live in what is known as the suburbs. The suburban nuclear family has been identified as part of the "American dream": a married couple with children owning a house in the suburbs. This archetype(原型)is reinforced by mass media, religious practices, and government policies and is based on traditions from Anglo-Saxon cultures. One of the biggest differences in suburban living is the housing occupied by the families. The suburbs are filled with single-family homes separated from retail districts, industrial areas, and sometimes even public schools. However, many American suburbs are incorporating these districts on smaller scales, attracting more people to these communities.

Aside from housing, which may include more apartments and semi-attached homes than in the suburbs or small towns, the major difference from suburban living is the density and diversity of many different subcultures, as well as retail and manufacturing buildings mixed with housing. Urban residents are also more likely to travel by mass transit, and children are more likely to walk or bicycle rather than being driven by their parents.

Gender Relations

Courtship(追求期), Cohabitation, and Adolescent Sexuality

Couples often meet through religious institutions, work, school, or friends. "Dating services," services that are geared to assist people in finding partners, are popular both on and offline. The trend over the past few decades has been for more and more couples deciding to cohabit before, or instead of, getting married. The 2000 Census reported 9.7 million different-sex partners living together and about 1.3 million same-sex partners living together. These cohabitation arrangements have not been the subject of many laws regulating them, though some states now have domestic partner statutes and judge-made palimony(供养费) doctrines that confer some legal support for unmarried couples.

Adolescent sex is common; most Americans first have intercourse in their teens. The current data suggests that by the time a person turns 18, slightly more than half of females and nearly two-thirds of males will have had intercourse. More than half of sexually active teens have had sexual partners they are dating. Risky sexual behaviors that involve "anything intercourse related" are "rampant" among teenagers. Teen pregnancies in the United States decreased 28% between 1990 and 2000 from 117 pregnancies per every 1,000 teens to 84 per 1,000. The US is rated, based on 2002 numbers, 84 out of 170 countries based on teenage fertility rate, according to the World Health Organization.

Marriage and Divorce

Marriage laws are established by individual states. Same-sex marriage is currently legal in Massachusetts, Iowa, Vermont, Maine, New Hampshire, and Connecticut. New Jersey, California, Oregon, Washington, D.C., Washington, and Nevada allow same-sex couples access to most state-level marriage benefits with civil unions or domestic partnerships; Hawaii, Maryland and Colorado offer some benefits to couples in domestic partnerships. New York recognizes out-of-state same-sex marriages but does not perform them. In many states, it is illegal to cross state lines to obtain a marriage that would be illegal in the home state. The typical wedding involves a couple proclaiming their commitment to one another in front of their close relatives and friends, often presided over by a religious figure such as a minister, priest, or rabbi, depending upon the faith of the couple. In traditional Christian ceremonies, the bride's father will "give away" (hand off) the bride to the groom. Secular weddings are also common, often presided over by a judge, Justice of the Peace, or other municipal official.

Divorce is the province of state governments, so divorce law varies from state to state. Prior to the 1970s, divorcing spouses had to allege that the other spouse was guilty of a crime or sin like abandonment or adultery; when spouses simply could not get along, lawyers were forced to manufacture "uncontested" divorces. The no-fault divorce revolution began in 1969 in California; South Dakota was the last state to allow no-fault divorce, in 1985. No-fault divorce on the grounds of "irreconcilable differences" is now available in all states. However, many states have recently required separation periods prior to a formal divorce decree. State law provides for child support where children are involved, and sometimes for alimony(赡养费). "Married adults now divorce two-and-a-half times as often as adults did 20 years ago and four times as often as they did 50 years ago... between 40% and 60% of *new* marriages will eventually end in divorce. The probability within ... the first five years is 20%, and the probability of its ending within the first 10 years is 33%... Perhaps 25% of children ages 16 and under live with a stepparent." The median length for a marriage in the US today is 11 years with 90% of all divorces being settled out of court.

Gender Roles

Since the 1970s, traditional gender roles of male and female have been increasingly challenged by both legal and social means. Today, there are far fewer roles that are legally restricted by one's sex. The military remains a notable exception, where women may not be put into direct combat by law. Asymmetrical warfare, however, has put women into situations which are direct combat operations in all but name.

Most social roles are not gender-restricted by law, though there are still cultural inhibitions surrounding certain roles. More and more women have entered the workplace, and in the year 2000 made up 46.6% of the labor force, up from 18.3% in 1900. Most men, however, have not taken up the traditional full-time homemaker role; likewise, few men have taken traditionally feminine jobs such as receptionist or nurse (although nursing was traditionally a male role before the American Civil War).

Death Rituals

It is customary for Americans to hold a wake in a funeral home within a couple days of the death of a loved one. The body of the deceased may be embalmed and dressed in fine clothing if there will be an open-casket viewing. Traditional Jewish and Muslim practice include a ritual bath and no embalming. Friends, relatives and acquaintances gather, often from distant parts of the country, to "pay their last respects" to the deceased. Flowers are brought to the coffin and sometimes eulogies, elegies, personal anecdotes or group prayers are recited. Otherwise, the attendees sit, stand or kneel in quiet contemplation or prayer. Kissing the corpse on the forehead is typical among Italian Americans and others. Condolences are also offered to the widow or widower and other close relatives.

A funeral may be held immediately afterwards or the next day. The funeral ceremony varies according to religion and culture. American Catholics typically hold a funeral mass in a church, which sometimes takes the form of a Requiem mass. Jewish Americans may hold a service in a synagogue or temple. Pallbearers(护柩者) carry the coffin of the deceased to the hearse, which then proceeds in a procession to the place of final repose, usually a cemetery. The unique Jazz funeral of New Orleans features joyous and raucous music and dancing during the procession.

Mount Auburn Cemetery (founded in 1831) is known as "America's first garden cemetery". American cemeteries created since are distinctive for their park-like setting. Rows of graves are covered by lawns and are interspersed with trees and flowers. Headstones, mausoleums, statuary or simple plaques typically mark off the individual graves. Cremation is another common practice in the United States, though it is frowned upon by various religions. The ashes of the deceased are usually placed in an urn, which may be kept in a private house, or they are interred. Sometimes the ashes are released into the atmosphere. The "sprinkling" or "scattering" of the ashes may be part of an informal ceremony, often taking place at a scenic natural feature (a cliff, lake or mountain) that was favored by the deceased.

A so-called death industry has developed in the United States that has replaced earlier, more informal traditions. Before the popularity of funeral homes, a wake would be held in an ordinary, private house. Often the most ELEGANT room was reserved for this purpose.

Household Arrangements

Family arrangements in the US have become more diverse with no particular households arrangement being prevalent enough to be identified as the average.

Today, family arrangements in the United States reflect the diverse and dynamic nature of contemporary American society. Although for a relatively brief period of time in the 20th century most families adhered to the nuclear family concept (two-married adults with a biological child), single-parent families, childless/childfree couples, and fused families now constitute the majority of families. Most Americans will marry and get divorced at least once during their life; thus, most individuals will live in a variety of family arrangements. A person may grow up in a single-parent family, go on to marry and live in childless couple arrangement, then get divorced, live as a single for a couple of years, re-marry, have children and live in a nuclear family arrangement.

> "The nuclear family... is the idealized version of what most people think when they think of family..." The old definition of what a family is... the nuclear family- no longer seems adequate to cover the wide diversity of household arrangements we see today, according to many social scientists (Edwards 1991; Stacey 1996). Thus has arisen the term *postmodern family*, which is meant to describe the great variability in family forms, including single-parent

families and child-free couples. "Brian K. Williams, Stacey C. Sawyer, Carl M. Wahlstrom, *Marriages, Families & Intinamte Relationships*, 2005."

Other changes to the landscape of American family arrangements include dual-income earner households and delayed independence among American youths. Whereas most families in the 1950s and 1960s relied on one income earner, most commonly the husband, the vast majority of family households now have two-income earners. Another change is the ever-increasing age at which young Americans leave their parental home. Traditionally, a person past "college age" who lived with their parent(s) was viewed negatively, but today it is not uncommon for children to live with their parents until their mid-twenties. This trend can be mostly attributed to rising living costs that far exceed those in decades past. Thus, many young adults now remain with their parents well past their mid-20s. This topic was a cover article of TIME magazine in 2005. Exceptions to the custom of leaving home in one's mid-20s can occur especially among Italian and Hispanic Americans, and in expensive urban real estate markets such as New York City California, and Honolulu, where monthly rents commonly exceed $1,000 a month.

Year	Families (69.7%)				Non-families (31.2%)		
	Married couples (52.5%)		Single Parents	Other blood relatives	Singles (25.5%)		Other non-family
	Nuclear family	Without children			Male	Female	
2000	24.1%	28.7%	9.9%	7%	10.7%	14.8%	5.7%
1970	40.3%	30.3%	5.2%	5.5%	5.6%	11.5%	1.7%

Single-parent households are households consisting of a single adult (most often a woman) and one or more children. In the single-parent household, one parent typically raises the children with little to no help from the other. This parent is the sole "breadwinner" of the family and thus these households are particularly vulnerable economically. They have higher rates of poverty, and children of these households are more likely to have educational problems.

Regional Variations

Cultural differences in the various regions of the United States are explored in New England, Mid-Atlantic States, Southern United States, Midwestern United States, Southwest United States, Western United States and Pacific Northwestern United States pages. The western coast of the continental US consisting of California, Oregon, and the state of Washington is also sometimes referred to as the Left Coast, indicating its political orientation and tendency towards liberal norms, folkways (社会习俗) and values. Strong cultural differences have a long history in the US with the southern slave society in the antebellum(战前的)period serving as a prime example. Not only social, but also economic tensions between the Northern and Southern states were so severe that they eventually caused the South to declare itself an independent nation, the Confederate States of America; thus provoking the American civil war. One example of regional variations is the attitude towards the discussion of sex, often sexual discussions would have less restrictions in the Northeastern United States, but yet is seen as taboo in the Southern United States.

Health Care

Health care in the United States is provided by many separate legal entities. Health care facilities are largely owned and operated by the private sector. Health insurance is primarily provided by the private sector, with the exception of programs such as Medicare, Medicaid, the Children's Health Insurance Program and the Veterans Health Administration.

At least 15% of the population is completely uninsured, and a substantial additional portion of the population is "underinsured", or less than fully insured for medical costs they might incur. More money per person is spent on health care in the United States than in any other nation in the world, and a greater percentage of total income in the nation is spent on health care in the US than in any United Nations member state except for East Timor. Despite the fact that not all citizens are covered, the United States has the third highest public healthcare expenditure per capita. Medical debt is the principal cause of personal bankruptcy in the United States.

Active debate about health care reform in the United States concerns questions of a right to health care, access, fairness, efficiency, cost, and quality. Many have argued that the system does not deliver equivalent value for the money spent. The US pays twice as much yet lags behind other wealthy nations in such measures as infant mortality and life expectancy. Currently the US has a higher infant mortality rate than most of the world's industrialized nations. The USA's life expectancy lags 42nd in the world, after most rich nations, lagging last of the G5 (Japan, France, Germany, UK, USA) and just after Chile (35th) and Cuba (37th). The USA's life expectancy is ranked 50th in the world after the European Union (40th). The World Health Organization (WHO), in 2000, ranked the US health care system as the highest in cost, first in responsiveness, 37th in overall performance, and 72nd by overall level of health (among 191 member nations included in the study). A 2008 report by the Commonwealth Fund ranked the United States last in the quality of health care among the 19 compared countries.

According to the Institute of Medicine of the National Academy of Sciences, the United States is the "only wealthy, industrialized nation that does not ensure that all citizens have coverage" (i. e. some kind of insurance). The same Institute of Medicine report notes that "Lack of health insurance causes roughly 18,000 unnecessary deaths every year in the United States." while a 2009 Harvard study published in the American Journal of Public Health found a much higher figure of more than 44,800 excess deaths annually in the United States due to Americans lacking health insurance. More broadly, the total number of people in the United States, whether insured or uninsured, who die because of lack of medical care was estimated in a 1997 analysis to be nearly 100,000 per year.

Health Care Debate

A poll released in March 2008 by the Harvard School of Public Health and Harris Interactive found that Americans are divided in their views of the US health system, and that there are significant differences by political affiliation. When asked whether the US has the best health care system or if other countries have better systems, 45% said that the US system was best and 39% said that other countries' systems are better. Belief that the US system is best was highest among Republicans (68%), lower among independents (40%), and lowest among Democrats (32%). Over half of Democrats (56%) said they would be more likely to support a presidential candidate who advocates making the US system more like those of other countries; 37% of independents and 19% of Republicans said they would be more likely to support such a candidate. 45% of Republicans said that they would be less likely to support such a candidate, compared to 17% of independents and 7% of Democrats.

According to the Institute of Medicine of the National Academy of Sciences, the United States is the only wealthy, industrialized nation that does not ensure universal coverage. There is currently an ongoing political debate centering around questions of access, efficiency, quality, and sustainability. Whether a government-mandated system of universal health care should be implemented in the US remains a hotly debated political topic, with Americans divided along party lines in their views of the US health system and what should be done to improve it. Those in favor of universal health care argue that the large number of uninsured Americans creates direct and hidden costs shared by all, and that extending coverage to all would lower costs and improve quality. Cato Institute Senior Fellow Alan Reynolds argues that people should be free to opt out of health insurance, citing a study by Economists Craig Perry and Harvey Rosen that found "the lack of health insurance among the self-employed does not affect their health. For virtually every subjective and objective measure of their health status, the self-employed and wage-earners are statistically indistinguishable for each other." Both sides of the political spectrum have also looked to more philosophical arguments, debating whether people have a fundamental right to have health care provided to them by their government.

An impediment (妨碍物) to implementing any US healthcare reform that does not benefit insurance companies or the private health care industry is the power of insurance company and health care industry lobbyists Possibly as a consequence of the power of lobbyists, key politicians such as Senator Max Baucus have taken the option of single payer health care off the table entirely. In a June 2009 NBC News/Wall Street Journal survey, 76 percent said it was either "extremely" or "quite" important to "give people a choice of both a public plan administered by the federal government and a private plan for their health insurance."

Advocates for single-payer health care often point to other countries, where national government-funded systems produce better health outcomes at lower cost. Opponents deride this type of system as "socialized medicine", and it has not been one of the favored reform options by Congress or the President in both the Clinton and Obama reform efforts.

As an example of how government intervention has had unintended consequences, in 1973, the federal government passed the Health Maintenance Organization Act, which heavily subsidized the HMO business model — a model that was in decline prior to such legislative intervention. The law was intended to create market incentives that would lower health care costs, but HMOs have never achieved their cost-reduction potential.

Piecemeal (逐段的) market-based reform efforts are complex. One study evaluating current popular market-based reform policy packages concluded that if market-oriented reforms are not implemented on a systematic basis with appropriate safeguards, they have the potential to cause more problems than they solve.

According to economist and former US Secretary of Labor, Robert Reich, only a "big, national, public option" can force insurance companies to cooperate, share information, and reduce costs. Scattered, localized, "insurance cooperatives" are too small to do that and are "designed to fail" by the moneyed forces opposing Democratic health care reform.

8.3 National Holidays

The United States observes holidays and traditions that are derived from significant events in US history, Religious traditions, and National Patriarchs.

As a legacy of colonization, Thanksgiving has become a traditional American holiday which evolved from the will of English pilgrims to "give thanks" for their welfare. Today, Thanksgiving is generally celebrated as a family reunion with a large afternoon feast. European colonization has led to many traditional Christian holidays such as Easter, Lent(大斋节), St. Patrick's Day, and Christmas to be widely observed albeit they are celebrated in a secular manner by many people today.

Independence Day (colloquially known as the Fourth of July) celebrates the anniversary of the country's Declaration of Independence from the Kingdom of Great Britain. It is generally observed by parades throughout the day and the shooting of fireworks at night.

Halloween is thought to have evolved from the ancient celtic festival of Samhain which was introduced in the American colonies by Irish settlers. It has become a holiday that is widely celebrated by children and teens who traditionally dress up in costumes and go door to door saying the words "Trick or Treat" in exchange for candy. It also brings about an emphasis on eerie and frightening urban legends and movies.

Additionally, Mardi Gras, which evolved from the Catholic tradition of Carnival(狂欢节), is observed notably in New Orleans, St. Louis, and Mobile, AL as well as numerous other towns. Texas still observes the anniversary of its Independence Day from Mexico.

Federally recognized holidays are as follows:

Natinal Holidays

Date	Official Name	Remarks
January 1	New Year's Day	Celebrates beginning of the Gregorian calendar year. Festivities include counting down to midnight (12:00 AM) on the preceding night, New Year's Eve. Traditional end of holiday season.
Third Monday in January	Birthday of Martin Luther King, Jr., or Martin Luther King, Jr. Day	Honors Martin Luther King, Jr., Civil Rights leader, who was actually born on January 15, 1929; combined with other holidays in several states.
January 20, the first January 20 following a Presidential election	Inauguration Day	Observed only by federal government employees in Washington, D.C., and the border counties of Maryland and Virginia, in order to relieve congestion that occurs with this major event. Swearing-in of President of the United States and Vice President of the United States. Celebrated every fourth year. *Note*: Takes place on January 21 if the 20th is a Sunday (although the President is still privately inaugurated on the 20th). If Inauguration Day falls on a Saturday or a Sunday, the preceding Friday or following Monday is not a Federal Holiday.
Third Monday in February	Washington's Birthday	Washington's Birthday was first declared a federal holiday by an 1879 act of Congress. The Uniform Holidays Act, 1968, shifted the date of the commemoration of Washington's Birthday from February 22 to the third Monday in February. Many people now refer to this holiday as "Presidents' Day" and consider it a day honoring all American presidents. However, neither the Uniform Holidays Act nor any subsequent law changed the name of the holiday from Washington's Birthday to Presidents' Day.

Continued

Date	Official Name	Remarks
Last Monday in May	Memorial Day	Honors the nation's war dead from the Civil War onwards; marks the unofficial beginning of the summer season. (traditionally May 30, shifted by the Uniform Holidays Act 1968)
July 4	Independence Day	CelebratesDeclaration of Independence, also called the Fourth of July.
First Monday in September	Labor Day	Celebrates the achievements of workers and the labor movement; marks the unofficial end of the summer season.
Second Monday in October	Columbus Day	Honors Christopher Columbus, traditional discoverer of the Americas. In some areas it is also a celebration of Italian culture and heritage. (traditionally October 12); celebrated as American Indian Heritage Day and Fraternal Day in Alabama; celebrated as Native American Day in South Dakota. In Hawaii, it is celebrated as Discoverer's Day, though is not an official state holiday.
November 11	Veterans Day	Honors all veterans of the United States armed forces. A traditional observation is a moment of silence at 11:00 a. m. remembering those killed in war. (Commemorates the 1918 armistice(停战), which began at "the eleventh hour of the eleventh day of the eleventh month.")
Fourth Thursday in November	Thanksgiving Day	Traditionally celebrates the giving of thanks for the autumn harvest. Traditionally includes the consumption of a turkey dinner. Traditional start of the holiday season.

Continued

Date	Official Name	Remarks
December 25	Christmas	Celebrates the Nativity of Jesus. Some people consider aspects of this religious holiday, such as giving gifts and decorating a Christmas tree, to be secular rather than explicitly Christian.

Other Holidays Observed Nationwide

In addition to the official holidays, many religious, ethnic, and other traditional holidays populate the calendar, as well as observances proclaimed by officials and lighter celebrations. These are rarely observed by businesses as holidays; indeed, many are viewed as opportunities for commercial promotion. Because of this commercialization, some critics apply the deprecatory term *Hallmark holiday* to such days, after the Hallmark greeting card company.

Date	Official Name	Remarks
February or March, date varies	Mardi Gras and Ash Wednesday	A festive season (Carnival) leading up to Shrove Tuesday or Mardi Gras. Closes with Ash Wednesday (40 days before Easter, not counting Sundays), which starts the season of Lent in the Christian calendar.
First Sunday in February	Super Bowl Sunday	The day of the National Football League's championship, the Super Bowl, which is the top prize in the sport of American football. Festivities generally include in-home parties and watching the game on television with beverages and snacks.
February 2	Groundhog Day	The day on which the behavior of a groundhog emerging from its burrow is said to predict the onset of Spring.
February 14	Valentine's Day	Traditional celebration of love and romance, including the exchange of cards, candy, flowers, and other gifts.

Continued

Date	Official Name	Remarks
March 17	St. Patrick's Day	A celebration of Irish heritage and culture, based on the Catholic feast of St. Patrick. Primary activity is simply the wearing of green clothing ("wearing o' the green"), although drinking beer dyed green is also popular. Attending St. Patrick's Day parades has historically been more popular in the United States than in Ireland.
April 1	April Fools' Day	A day to play tricks on family, friends, and coworkers, if so inclined. This day used to be the start of the New Year. The tradition started when New Year's Day was moved from April 1 to January 1.
late March or April (Date varies) (March 21 for 2008)	Good Friday	Commemorates the crucifixion of Jesus Christ by Pontius Pilate, believed by Christians to have taken place (traditionally) on April 1, AD 33. Sometimes celebrated as a "*Spring holiday*" for Universities and schools in certain states. Christians traditionally celebrate by abstaining from meat to honoring Christ's death.
Spring Sunday (date varies), first Sunday after the first ecclesiastical full moon after the vernal equinox	Easter	Celebrates the Christian belief in the resurrection of Jesus. For Christians, Easter is a day of religious services and the gathering of family. Many Americans follow old traditions of coloring hard-boiled eggs and giving children baskets of candy. On the next day, Easter Monday, the President of the United States holds an annual Easter egg roll on the White House lawn for young children. The holiday is also often celebrated as a nonsectarian spring holiday. Not generally observed by most businesses as it always falls on a Sunday. Most financial markets and some other businesses close on the Friday prior, Good Friday (which is a state holiday in many states). Roman Catholic and Protestant groups celebrate Easter on a different Sunday (most years) than Orthodox groups.

Continued

Date	Official Name	Remarks
April 22 (varies by location and observance)	Earth Day	A day used to promote environmentalism.
Spring, date varies	Arbor Day	A day for the planting of trees, commonly the last Friday of April but depending on the climate of the state.
May 5	Cinco de Mayo	Primarily a celebration of Mexican culture by Mexican-Americans living in the United States. Although this is the anniversary of the victory of the Mexican Army over the French at the Battle of Puebla in 1862, Cinco de Mayo is far more important in the USA than in México itself. Additionally, this "holiday" is often mistaken by Americans as being Mexican Independence Day, which is actually observed on September 16.
Second Sunday in May	Mother's Day	Honors mothers and motherhood (made a "Federal Holiday" by Presidential order, although most Federal agencies are already closed on Sundays)
June 14	Flag Day	Commemorates the adoption of the flag of the United States.
Third Sunday in June	Father's Day	Honors fathers and fatherhood.
August 26	Women's Equality Day	Celebrates the fight for, and progress towards, equality for women. Established by the United States Congress in 1971 to commemorate two anniversaries: Passage of the Nineteenth Amendment to the United States Constitution ensuring Woman Suffrage in 1920 and a nation-wide demonstration for equal rights, the Women's Strike for Equality, in 1970.

Continued

Date	Official Name	Remarks
September 11	Patriot Day	Discretionary day of remembrance designated in memory of the 2, 993 casualties in the September 11, 2001, attacks.
September 17	Constitution/ Citizenship Day	Commemorates the adoption of the Constitution of the United States.
September or October (depends on Hebrew calendar)	Rosh Hashanah	Traditional beginning of the Jewish High Holidays. It is also celebrates the beginning of a new year on the Hebrew calendar.
September or October (depends on Hebrew calendar)	Yom Kippur	Traditional end of and highest of the Jewish High Holidays.
October 12	Columbus Day	Honors the first European explorer known to have set foot on North America.
October 31	Halloween	Celebrates All Hallow's Eve, decorations include jack o'lanterns, costume wearing parties, and candy such as candy corn are also part of the holiday. Kids go trick-or-treating to neighbors who give away candy. Not generally observed by businesses.
first Tuesday after the first Monday in November	Election Day	Observed by the federal and state governments in applicable years; legal holiday in some states.
Friday after Thanksgiving Day	Black Friday	Kickoff to the Christmas shopping season, known to be the busiest shopping day of the year due to low prices on goods.

Continued

Date	Official Name	Remarks
December (depends on Hebrew calendar)	Hanukkah	an eight-day Jewish holiday commemorating the rededication of the Second Temple in Jerusalem at the time of the Maccabean Revolt of the 2nd century BC.
December 7	Pearl Harbor Remembrance Day	Day to mourn the attack on Pearl Harbor by the Japanese on December 7, 1941
December 21	Winter Solstice	Day to celebrate the sun, because the winter solstice is the day with the least daylight in the Northern Hemisphere.
December 24	Christmas Eve	Day before Christmas Day
December 25	Christmas Day	Celebrates the birth of Jesus of Nazareth. Marks the beginning of the twelve days of Christmas. Has become a major event for many retailers due to heightened economic activity.
December 26 through January 1	Kwanzaa	African American holiday celebration created in 1966 by Dr. Maulana Ron Karenga
December 31	New Year's Eve	Final Day of the Gregorian year. Usually accompanied by much celebration.

8.4 Food and Sport Cultures

Cuisine

The cuisine of the United States is extremely diverse, owing to the vastness of the continent, the relatively large population (1/3 of a billion people) and the number of native and immigrant influences. The types of food served at home vary greatly and depend upon the region of the country and the family's own cultural heritage. Recent immigrants tend to eat food similar to that of their country of origin, and Americanized versions of these cultural foods, such as American Chinese cuisine or Italian-American cuisine often eventually appear; an example is Vietnamese cuisine, Korean cuisine and Thai cuisine. German cuisine has a profound impact on American cuisine, especially mid-western cuisine, with potatoes, noodles, roasts, stews and cakes/pastries being the most iconic ingredients in both cuisines(烹饪). Dishes such as the hamburger, pot roast, baked ham and hot dogs are examples of American dishes derived from German cuisine. Besides Italian, German, Hungarian and Chinese influences, traditional Native American, Caribbean, Mexican and Greek dishes have also diffused into the general American repertoire. It is not uncommon for a 'middle-class' family from 'middle-America' to eat, for example, restaurant pizza, home-made pizza, enchiladas con carne, chicken paprikas(红辣椒), beef strogan of and bratwurst with sauerkraut for dinner throughout a single week.

Mainstream American culinary arts are similar to those in other Western countries. Wheat is the primary cereal grain. Traditional American cuisine uses ingredients such as turkey, white-tailed deer venison, potatoes, sweet potatoes, corn, squash, and maple syrup, indigenous foods employed by American Indians and early European settlers. Slow-cooked pork and beef barbecue, crab cakes, potato chips, and chocolate chip cookies are distinctively American styles. Soul food, developed by African slaves, is popular around the South and among many African Americans elsewhere. Syncretic cuisines such as Louisiana creole, Cajun, and Tex-Mex are regionally important. Iconic American dishes such as apple pie, fried chicken, pizza, hamburgers, and hot dogs derive from the recipes of various immigrants and domestic innovations. So-called French fries, Mexican dishes such as burritos(墨西哥天朱煎饼) and tacos, and pasta dishes freely adapted from Italian sources are widely consumed. Americans generally prefer coffee to tea, with more than half the adult population drinking at least one cup a day. Marketing by US industries is largely responsible for making orange juice and milk (now often fat-reduced) ubiquitous breakfast beverages. During the 1980s and 1990s, Americans' caloric intake rose 24%; frequent dining at fast food outlets is associated with what health officials call the American "obesity epidemic". Highly sweetened soft drinks are widely popular; sugared beverages account for 9% of the average American's daily caloric intake.

Common American Foods

• Traditional Thanksgiving dinner with Turkey, dressing, sweet potatoes, and cranberry sauce.

• Typical American seafood with Fried fish, shrimp, hush puppies(油炸玉米团粉), and fries.

Caesar salad

Hamburger, fries, and a coke

Chicken Fried Steak (alternatively known as Country Fried Steak)

California club pizza with avocados(鳄梨)and tomatoes

Toasted turkey sandwich

American style breakfast with pancakes, maple syrup, sausage links, bacon strips, and fried eggs

Ethnic and Immigrant Influence

The demand for ethnic foods in the United States reflects the nation's changing diversity as well as its development over time. According to the National Restaurant Association,

Restaurant industry sales are expected to reach a record high of $476 billion in 2005, an increase of 4.9 percent over 2004... Driven by consumer demand, the ethnic food market reached record sales in 2002, and has emerged as the fastest growing category in the food and beverage product sector, according to USBX Advisory Services. Minorities in the US spend a combined $142 billion on food and by 2010, America's ethnic population is expected to grow by 40 percent.

A movement began during the 1980s among popular leading chefs to reclaim America's ethnic foods within its regional traditions, where these trends originated. One of the earliest was Paul Prudhomme, who in 1984 began the introduction of his influential cookbook, Paul Prodhomme's Louisiana Kitchen, by describing the over 200 year history of Creole and Cajun cooking; he aims to "preserve and expand the Louisiana tradition." Prodhomme's success quickly inspired other chefs. Norman Van Aken embraced a Floridian type cuisine fused with many ethnic and globalized elements in his Feast of Sunlight cookbook in 1988. The movement finally gained fame around the world when California became swept up in the movement, then seemingly started to lead the trend itself, in, for example, the popular restaurant Chez Panisse in Berkeley. Examples of the Chez Panisse phenomenon, chefs who embraced a new globalized cuisine, were celebrity chefs like Jeremiah Tower and Wolfgang Puck, both former colleagues at the restaurant. Puck went on to describe his belief in contemporary, new style American cuisine in the introduction to The Wolfgang Puck Cookbook:

Another major breakthrough, whose originators were once thought to be crazy, is the mixing of ethnic cuisines. It is not at all uncommon to find raw fish listed next to tortillas(玉米饼)on the same menu. Ethnic crossovers also occur when distinct elements meet in a single recipe. This country is, after all, a huge melting pot. Why should its cooking not illustrate the American transformation of diversity into unity?

Puck's former colleague, Jeremiah Tower became synonymous with California Cuisine and the overall American culinary revolution. Meanwhile, the restaurant that inspired both Puck and Tower became a distinguished establishment, popularizing its so called "mantra" in its book by Paul Bertolli and owner Alice Waters, Chez Panisse Cooking, in 1988. Published well after the restaurants' founding in 1971, this new cookbook from the restaurant seemed to perfect the idea and philosophy that had developed over the years. The book embraced America's natural bounty, specifically that of California, while containing recipes that reflected Bertoli and Waters' appreciation of both northern Italian and French style foods.

Early Ethnic Influences

While the earliest cuisine of the United States was primarily influenced by indigenous Native Americans, the cuisine of the thirteen colonies or the culture of the antebellum American South; the overall culture of the nation, its gastronomy and the growing culinary arts became ever more influenced by its changing ethnic mix and immigrant patterns over the 20th century unto the present. Some of the ethnic groups that continued to influence the cuisine were here in prior years; while others arrived more numerously during "The Great Transatlantic Migration (of 1870 - 1914) or other mass migrations.

Some of the ethnic influences could be found in the nation from after the

American Civil War and into the History of United States continental expansion during most of the 19th century. Ethnic influences already in the nation at that time would include the following groups and their respective cuisines:

- Indigenous Native Americans in the United States (Indians) and Native American cuisine.
- Select nationalities of Europe and the respective developments from early modern European cuisine of the colonial age:
  - British-Americans and on-going developments in New England cuisine, the national traditions founded in cuisine of the thirteen colonies and some aspects of other regional cuisine.
  - Spanish Americans (Hispano Americans) and early modern Spanish cuisine, as well as Basque-Americans and Basque cuisine.
  - Early German-American or Pennsylvania Dutch and Pennsylvania Dutch cuisine.
  - French Americans and their "New World" regional identities such as:
    - Acadian
    - Cajun and Cajun cuisine
- The various ethnicities originating from early social factors of Race in the United States and the gastronomy and cuisines of the "New World", Latin American cuisine and North American cuisine:
  - African-Americans and "Soul Food".
  - Louisiana Creole and Louisiana Creole cuisine. Louisiana Creole (also called French Créole) refers to native born people of various racial descent who are descended from the Colonial French and/or Spanish settlers of Colonial French Louisiana, before it became part of the United States in 1803 with the Louisiana Purchase.
  - Cuisine of Puerto Rico
  - Mexican-Americans and Mexican-American cuisine; as well as related regional cuisines:
    - Tex-Mex (regional Texas and Mexican fusion).
    - Cal-Mex (regional California and Mexican fusion).
    - Some aspects of "Southwestern cuisine".
  - Cuisine of New Mexico

Later Ethnic and Immigrant Influence

Other ethnic groups may have arrived in the United States prior to 20th Century, but they were either not part of the main colonial settlers, indigenous Native Americans, Latin American experience, African-American slave class or Creole people; as likewise, their population numbers were probably not as numerous as the other existing ethnic groups or the subsequent populations of their own respective ethnicities forthcoming during the years unto "The Great Transatlantic Migration" and other mass migrations of the 19th Century. This would also include what is current day United States of America, as every year the population census and US immigration populations change, thus changing the cultural influences of the nation. . The later arrival of many immigrants into the United States seemingly does not discount their profound impact on the national or regional cuisine. Many other ethnic groups have additionally contributed to Cuisine of the United States, some with greater impact and productive success than others; as indeed, some of these more prominent groups include the following (listed alphabetically):

- Polynesian-Americans, and Polynesian cuisine, Hawaiian cuisine, Cuisine of Philippines
- Caribbean-Americans and Caribbean cuisine, Cuban Cuisine, Cuisine of Jamaica
- Chinese-Americans and American Chinese cuisine
- Irish-Americans and Irish cuisine and Irish pub traditions in America
- Italian-Americans and Italian-American cuisine
- German-Americans and German Texans (namely, post-civil war), exemplified in German cuisine other than Pennsylvania Dutch.
- Greek-Americans and Greek cuisine or Cuisine of the Mediterranean
- Japanese-Americans and Japanese cuisine, Asian cuisine, Fusion cuisine, and related influences on the Cuisine of Hawaii
- Jewish-Americans and Jewish Cuisine and Cuisine of the Mediterranean
- Portuguese-Americans, also known as Luso American and Portuguese cuisine

- Polish-Americans and Polish cuisine and Cuisine of the Midwestern United States
- Russian-Americans and Russian cuisine and Cuisine of the Midwestern United States
- Lithuanian-Americans and Lithuanian cuisine and Cuisine of the Midwestern United States

"Italian, Mexican and Chinese (Cantonese) cuisines have indeed joined the mainstream. These three cuisines have become so ingrained in the American culture that they are no longer foreign to the American palate. According to the study, more than nine out of 10 consumers are familiar with and have tried these foods, and about half report eating them frequently. The research also indicates that Italian, Mexican and Chinese (Cantonese) have become so adapted to such an extent that 'authenticity' is no longer a concern to customers."

Contributions from these ethnic foods have become just as common as traditional "American" fares (食物) like hotdogs, hamburgers, beef steaks, cherry pie, Coca-Cola, milkshakes, fried chicken and so on. Nowadays, Americans also have a ubiquitous consumption of foods like pizza and pasta(意大利面食), tacos and burritos to "General Tso's Chicken" and Fortune Cookies. Fascination with these and other ethnic foods may also vary with region.

Sports

Sports in the United States are an important part of the American culture. However, the sporting culture of the US is unique from that of many other countries. Compared to any other nation, American preferences for sports differ from the rest of the world. For example, soccer, the most popular sport in the world, is not nearly as popular in the United States.

Baseball is the oldest of the major American team sports. Professional baseball dates from 1869 and had no close rivals in popularity until the 1960s; though baseball is no longer the most popular sport it is still referred to as the "national pastime". Also unlike the professional levels of the other popular spectator sports in the US, Major League Baseball teams play almost every day from April to October. American football now attracts more television viewers than baseball; however, National Football League teams play only 16 regular-season games each year, so baseball is the runaway leader in ticket sales.

Basketball is another major sport, represented professionally by the National Basketball Association. Invented in Springfield, Massachusetts 1891, by Canadian-born physical education teacher James Naismith, basketball ranks sixth in popularity behind professional football, baseball, college football, auto racing, and hockey.

American football, known in many anglophone countries as gridiron, is widely considered to be the most popular sport in the United States. The 32-team National Football League (NFL) is the most popular and only major professional American football league. Its championship game, the Super Bowl, is the biggest annual sporting event held in the United States. Additional millions also watch college football throughout the autumn months, and some communities, particularly in rural areas, place great emphasis on their local high school team. American football games usually include cheerleaders and marching bands which aim to raise school spirit and entertain the crowd at half-time.

A college football quarterback looking to pass

Most Americans recognize a fourth major sport—Ice hockey. Always a mainstay of Great Lakes and New England-area culture, the sport gained tenuous footholds in regions like the American South in recent years, as the National Hockey League pursued a policy of expansion.

The quickly growing sport of mixed martial arts has taken off in America since its introduction in the early 1990s. Today, the Ultimate Fighting

Championship is one of the most profitable organizations in the country.

Sports and Community Culture

Homecoming is an annual tradition of the United States. People, towns, high schools and colleges come together, usually in late September or early October, to welcome back former residents and alumni. It is built around a central event, such as a banquet, a parade, and most often, a game of American football, or, on occasion, basketball, or ice hockey. When celebrated by schools, the activities vary widely. However, they usually consist of a football game played on the school's home football field, activities for students and alumni, a parade featuring the school's marching band and sports teams, and the coronation of a Homecoming Queen (and at many schools, a Homecoming King).

Questions

1. What do you think of American sport culture?
2. What is the health care debate about in the US?
3. What is special about American people's housing?
4. Introduce the details of the American social class.

Supplementary Reading 1

Baseball: American Pastime, American Fantasy

Posted by Devin Cohen

Every spring, renewed warmth and sun are accompanied by nostalgic aromas and sights that many Americans know all too well: the scent of hotdogs, stale peanuts, overpriced beer and sunscreen reemerge for the summer months. As opening day ceremonies kicked off around the country last Wednesday, I found it appropriate to write a piece (albeit unorthodox) regarding the sport that has maintained the most yearly ticket sales in America since its inception. This fixture of American culture has become so central to the nation's summer activities that is has garnered the title of "America's Pastime", a label engineered exclusively for the purpose of describing baseball's relationship to America. It doesn't seem too farfetched, as millions flood stadiums from Anaheim to Atlanta to catch nine innings of pulse pounding action as up to four hundred pitches unfold over the course of three to five hours.

Although the game has become ingrained in our national psyche and has a plethora of devoted followers, I will never understand how a sport that combines the repetition of NASCAR, the "hit a ball with a piece wood" theme of cricket, and the velocity of a glacier can be enthralling or enjoyable. There's really no point in dancing around it: baseball is inconceivably boring.

Baseball is a sport in which a fan can whip out a copy of Faulkner's As I Lay Dying, read throughout the entire course of the game and still not miss a single thing. The pace of the sport can most accurately be described as golf on cocaine or lacrosse on ambien. However, this tempo is too fast for long-term leisure and too slow to really engage observers and keep them captivated. The limbo that ensues consists of a monotonous cycle of pitch, catch, pitch, hit, pitch, pitch, catch in which the viewer is stuck for an extended period of time. Nine innings isn't just an endurance test for the players, but for the sanity of the crowd.

When watching a game, it doesn't take long to realize that baseball requires the least athleticism out of nearly any popular sport. The fact that David Ortiz couldn't outrun a pack of shihtzu puppies doesn't instill much confidence in that athletic composition of the MLB. If Lebron James stepped onto a baseball field, he would most likely excel with some time and dedication. In contrast, if Tony Gwynne were put on the ice he would most like turn into a piñata, and if Mo Vaughn stepped onto the court he would pass out in the first thirty seconds. This is not to say that all baseball players are out of shape, or that playing baseball does not take talent. Strength and skill are integral components of making it to the big league, but the players must only meet a minimum requirement of athleticism to do so. Pitchers are paid because one of their limbs can perform a function that separates them from the rest of the pack.

In spite of its lack of excitement, Americans love baseball. From the onerous ordeal of sitting through the game to the deified experience of participating, the sport is the truest manifestation of the American spirit that you can find in athletics. The experience of baseball most clearly resembles watching a PG movie with the family: it is non-threatening, non-violent, and the quantity of action is enough to keep a child engrossed (for a while) and an adult sedated. It can even be posited that this "positive" atmosphere for family "bonding" endorses true American family values to a far greater extent than any Republican candidate ever has. This is because watching baseball doesn't even require viewers to pay close, active attention to a television screen.

Some read newspapers, others read magazines. Children lose attention and play with their toys, adults play with their cell phones. The point is that every viewer is at some point absorbed by activities that have nothing to do with the game, because, like a PG movie, it can only entertain us to a certain degree. Some viewers take measures to the point of idiocy: keeping score of the games (balls, strike, and all) on a formatted score sheet rather than looking at the gigantic scoreboard that is present at every stadium, or listening to the home team commentary via radio to contextualize the game even though you're watching it.

These methods only further buttress this new conception of the baseball viewing experience. Baseball games are in fact a space where all fans, including families, can operate under the illusion that they are collectively engaged in something. However, the lack of interesting material or formidable action forces individuals to occupy themselves on their own terms, much like passive television viewing, and the daily activities of suburban America. Why did the originators of baseball implement the seventh inning stretch? For fans to make sure the elderly are breathing, the kids aren't missing, to get up out of that seat for brief second before the latter segment of the show commences—nearly identical to the home viewing experience.

It is also my belief that baseball is uniquely positioned, more than any other sport in America, to encourage fan participation in another American pastime: gratuitous consumption. The connection with over-consumption can at times be displayed quite explicitly, as it is with ballpark cuisine. Certain foods have become so deeply woven into the fabric of the baseball scene that they are as relevant as the game itself. I have never attended a hockey or football game and felt the sharp urge to purchase an item simply because it is integral to the viewing experience. Peanuts, Cracker Jack and hot dogs are foods so closely linked with baseball that huge numbers of fans feel compelled to buy them to complete their viewing experience.

Another item that seems like a logical acquisition during a ball game would be alcohol. The mundane routine and non-existent momentum of the game is very much conducive to individuals wanting to chemically shift their perceptions to augment amusement. Alcohol creates the mirage of accelerated time, and has gotten me through some horrifically exhausting duels. Baseball befriends alcohol, and its structure advocates its use. The fact that many Americans are immune to this subconscious advertising and sit through games stone cold sober reflects another one of our obvious collective qualities as a people: a satisfaction with the static, metamorphic structures we are accustomed to, and a determination to enjoy them.

Another form of consumption is through clothing, specifically the baseball cap. Unlike football jerseys, hockey jerseys, and to an extent basketball jerseys (which have taken off in certain social circles), baseball caps have permeated nearly every level of the fashion industry. From the hip-hop artist to the lacrosse player, the Nantucket vacationer to the surfer, baseball caps are found in every stratum of American society. The game has cultivated one of the largest-grossing businesses in America, making it a true proponent of consumption if there ever was one.

In comparing baseball to the American lifestyle, it becomes clear that the sport represents more of a fantasy than a reality. This is especially true when we examine the logistics of the sport. A home team spends the top half of an inning out on the field, by and large standing around and watching, and adjusting position when there is action. Players spend almost the entire bottom half of the inning sitting on a bench waiting to bat. If a player succeeds three out of ten times in the batter's box, he is considered successful. This is the only sport, the only profession, in which a thirty percent success rate is considered adequate. Can you imagine if Kobe shot thirty percent? Or if Peyton completed thirty percent of his passes?

I am not saying that it is easy to swing a bat and hit a ball, but this serves as an example of how something seemingly subpar (不够标准的) can be conceptualized as superb. And how much do baseball's athletes get paid for their "outstanding" performances? Ask A-Rod while he's in one of his four mansions, K-Rod while he's rejuvenating at his expansive estate or any other player whose name has been irritatingly abbreviated by some imbecile on ESPN. Or don't ask, because most of the time the answer is higher than Americans are taught to count to.

The attributes associated with playing baseball paint a portrait remarkably similar to the modern American dream: little exertion leads to wealth and triumph. Who would not want to be a baseball player? They are exorbitantly paid for playing a game outside all summer. And most of the time, they're just sitting or standing around. Additionally, baseball is the only sport where mediocrity (by all conventional standards) is not only expected, but also awarded. Most Americans would kill for these positions, and I would maintain that spectators watch these games to live vicariously through players' conquests on the field, as well as covet the lifestyles they perpetuate off the field. While they play, we envy the idea they represent: a notion that effort and skill can still be rewarded even if the result is not astonishing or exceptional.

So why do we love baseball as a nation? Because the game is just as American as we are. Baseball viewing is the quintessential American affair, a combination of ADD, consumption and boredom during which one can daydream about a bountiful lifestyle achieved by mediocre performance. It is an escape from the cruel realities of our country, a getaway from the inescapable fact that effort and talent are rarely rewarded absent of a positive outcome. Even though I will never comprehend why folks find the sport interesting, the subconscious reasons for becoming a spectator are numerous. Playing baseball is the American fantasy, and watching baseball is the embodiment of American life.

*http://thecollegevoice.org/*2011/04/04/*baseball-american-pastime-american-fantasy-2/*

Supplementary Reading 2

A Matter of Taste: Europeans on American Food

By Rick Steves

US breakfasts get respect, and McDonald's is tops for fast food in Europe.

People always tell me how lucky I am to be eating my way through Europe. But my appreciation of good food was slow in coming. On my first trip to Europe sans parents, I packed along a big plastic tube filled with a swirl of peanut butter and strawberry jam. Every meal I spread it on bread and washed it down with soda pop.

I'm still on the go in Europe, but I eat much better now. During my guidebook research, I get into a rhythm in the last three hours of my long day — blitzing the restaurants on my list, and then returning to my favorite place at the very end of the evening. I often sit down and let the chef/owner cook me up whatever he wants me to experience. These chefs seem to thoroughly enjoy taking off their apron, washing up, and sitting down to share a glass of wine with their last customer of the day — that's me — eating their favorite dishes.

We usually talk about food, and the conversation sometimes shifts to what I eat back home. It can come as a surprise, but Europeans don't always have a dim view of American cooking. After all, McDonald's is the number one fast-food chain in Europe — the one on the Champs-Elysees is the most profitable in the world.

Over one long Italian meal, Claudia (a Roman tour guide) says she loves American food. Her favorites include the BLT sandwich and "chili soup". She's charmed by our breakfast culture and that we "meet for breakfast." She says you would never see families going out for breakfast in Italy.

But she notes that in the United States, size matters more than quality. She says that the average number of ingredients in an American restaurant salad or pasta is eight or 10, while in Italy the average salad or pasta has only four or five ingredients. And she can't understand our heavily flavored salad dressings. "If your lettuce and tomato are good, why cover it up with a heavy dressing? We use only oil and vinegar," she says. When I try to defend the fancy dishes as complex, she says, "Perhaps 'jumbled' is a better word."

Some of my other Italian friends are less tactful. At dinner with three Tuscan friends — Manfredo, Roberto and Ilaria — I listen to a sharp critique. "I think American pioneers did not know to make a good salami or prosciutto so they could not preserve their meat properly," Manfredo says. "This is why you have the barbecue sauce: to hide this taste of rotting meat."

"Is there no barbecue sauce in Italy?" I ask.

"No," says Manfredo, "but I like very much to make Buffalo wings. Could you kindly send me a package of Frank's Original Red Hot Cayenne Pepper Sauce when you return home?"

We all laugh, and then Roberto adds, "I think, in America, a restaurant is looking not for what is good food. What is good is what sells. Real lasagna is only this thick," he says, sticking his knife through two steamy inches of lasagna on the plate in front of him. "In the United States they make it twice this thick" — flipping another serving on top — "and they fill it with mozzarella. There is no mozzarella in lasagna!" The others cluck in agreement.

Roberto continues, "If you go to an American restaurant and say the food is bad, you get a coupon for a free meal. More bad food. If you say the food is bad in a restaurant in Italy, you get kicked out. To get free food here, it is vice versa — you say, 'This is the best beefsteak I've ever eaten.' Chef will then say, 'You must try the dessert.' You say, 'Oh no.' He says, 'Here. Please. Take it for free.'"

"In a real Italian restaurant when you complain, the chef will tell you, 'I cooked this as a boy the way my grandmother cooked this,'" Manfredo says. "It cannot be wrong."

"In the United States, what is right is what sells." Roberto jumps in. "And the computer tells you what food on the menu makes good business. In America, you eat first with your eyes and second with your mouth."

Raising my glass of wine I offer a toast to Italian food. "To la cucina Italiana."

Manfredo follows that, saying magnanimously, "To bacon and eggs." We all agree that American breakfasts are unbeatable.

"Omelets, hash browns," Roberto reminisces. "On my last visit to New York, I gained four kilos in three weeks."

Raising our glasses, we make another toast. "To American breakfasts."

http://www.msnbc.msn.com/id/42324401/ns/travel-destination_travel/

Chapter 9 Media of the United States

The media of the United States consist of several different types of communications media: television, radio, cinema, newspapers, magazines, and Internet-based Web sites. The US also has a strong music industry.

Many of the media are controlled by large for-profit corporations who reap revenue from advertising, subscriptions, and sale of copyrighted material. American media conglomerates tend to be leading global players, generating large profits as well as large criticism in many parts of the world. Further deregulation and convergence are under way, leading to mega-mergers, further concentration of media ownership, and the emergence of multinational media conglomerates. Critics allege that localism, local news and other content at the community level, media spending and coverage of news, and diversity of ownership and views have suffered as a result of these processes of media concentration.

The organization Reporters Without Borders compiles and publishes an annual ranking of countries based upon the organization's assessment of their press freedom records. In 2007, USA was ranked 48th, which was an improvement from the preceding year.

9.1 Radio

American radio broadcasts in two bands: FM and AM. Some stations are only talk radio — featuring interviews and discussions — while music radio stations broadcast one particular type of music: Top 40, hip-hop, country, etc. Radio broadcast companies have become increasingly consolidated in recent years. National Public Radio is the nation's primary public radio network, but most radio stations are commercial and profit-oriented.

Talk radio as a political medium has also exploded in popularity during the 1990s, due to the 1987 repeal of the Fairness Doctrine, which meant that stations no longer had to "balance" their day by programming alternative points of view.

The FCC has recently approved a transition to digital radio technology which allows both FM and AM stations to "piggyback" digital data on top of their existing analog broadcasts. When the transition is complete at some point in the far future, the analog broadcasts will be replaced with true high-quality digital broadcasts.

A new form of radio that is gaining popularity is satellite radio. The two biggest subscriptions based radio services are Sirius Satellite Radio and XM Satellite Radio, which have recently both merged together to form Sirius XM Radio. Unlike terrestrial radio music channels are commercial free and other channels feature very minimal commercials. Satellite radio also is not regulated by the FCC.

9.2 Newspapers and Magazines

Newspapers have declined in their influence and penetration into American households over the years. The US does not have a national paper. *The New York Times and the Wall Street Journal* are sold in most US cities.

Although the *Times'* primary audience has always been the people of New York City, the *New York Times* has gradually become the dominant national "newspaper of record". Apart from its daily nationwide distribution, the term means that back issues are archived on microfilm by every decent-sized public library in the nation, and the Times' articles are often cited by both historians and judges as evidence that a major historical event occurred on a certain date. *The Los Angeles Times* and the *Wall Street Journal* are also newspapers of record to a lesser extent. Although USA Today has tried to establish itself as a national paper, it has been widely derided by the academic world as the "McPaper" and is not subscribed to (let alone archived) by most libraries.

Apart from the newspapers just mentioned, all major metropolitan areas have their own local newspapers. Typically, a metropolitan area will support at most one or two major newspapers, with many smaller publications targeted towards particular audiences. Although the cost of publishing has increased over the years, the price of newspapers has generally remained low, forcing newspapers to rely more on advertising revenue and on articles provided by a major wire service, such as the Associated Press or Reuters, for their national and world coverage.

With a very few exceptions, all the newspapers in the US are privately owned, either by large chains such as Gannett or McClatchy, which own dozens or even hundreds of newspapers; by small chains that own a handful of papers; or in a situation that is increasingly rare, by individuals or families.

Most general-purpose newspapers are either being printed one time a week, usually on Thursday or Friday, or are printed daily. Weekly newspapers tend to have much smaller circulation and are more prevalent in rural communities or small towns. Major cities often have "alternative weeklies" to complement the mainstream daily paper(s), for example, New York City's Village Voice or Los Angeles' L. A. Weekly, to name two of the most well-known. Major cities may also support a local business journal, trade papers relating to local industries and papers for local ethnic and social groups.

Probably due to competition from other media, the number of daily newspapers in the US has declined over the past half-century, according to Editor & Publisher, the trade journal of American newspapers. In particular, the number of evening newspapers has fallen by almost one-half since 1970, while the number of morning editions and Sunday editions has grown.

For comparison, in 1950, there were 1,772 daily papers (and 1,450 — or about 70 percent — of them were evening papers) while in 2000, there were 1,480 daily papers (and 766—or about half—of them were evening papers.)

Daily newspaper circulation is also slowly declining in America, partly due to the near-demise of two-newspaper towns, as the weaker newspapers in most cities have folded:

The primary source of newspaper income is advertising — in the form of "classifieds" or inserted advertising circulars — rather than circulation income. However, since the late 1990s, this revenue source has been directly challenged by Web sites like eBay (for sales of secondhand items), Monster. com (jobs), and Craigslist (everything).

The largest newspapers (by circulation) in the United States are *USA Today*, the *Wall Street Journal*, the *New York Times* and the *Los Angeles Times*.

Magazines

Thanks to the huge size of the English-speaking North American media market, the United States has a large magazine industry with hundreds of magazines serving almost every interest, as can be determined by glancing at any newsstand in any large American city. Most magazines are owned by one of the large media conglomerates or by one of their smaller regional brethren.

The US has three leading weekly newsmagazines: TIME, Newsweek and US News and World Report. Time and Newsweek are center-left while US News and World Report tends to be center-right, although all three (in theory, at least) strive to provide objective news reporting and limit personal bias to the opinion pages. Time is well-known for naming a "Person of the Year" each year, while US News publishes annual ratings of American colleges and universities.

The US also has over a dozen major political magazines (the exact number is debatable, of course), serving every part of the political spectrum from left to right.

Finally, besides the hundreds of specialized magazines that serve the diverse interests and hobbies of the American people, there are also dozens of magazines published by professional organizations for their members, such as *Communications of the ACM* (for computer science specialists) and the *ABA Journal* (for lawyers).

Internet

The Internet has provided a means for newspapers and other media organizations to deliver news and, significantly, the means to look up old news. Some organizations only make limited amounts of their output available for free, and charge for access to the rest. Other organizations allow their archives to be freely browsed. It is possible that the latter type obtain more influence, as they are true to the spirit of freedom of information by virtue of making it free. Anyone who has followed external links only to be confronted with a pay to view banner, might attest that the reputations of organizations that charge is not enhanced by their charging policy, particularly when the same information is available from sources that don't charge.

The Internet, by means of making available such constantly growing news archives, is, in effect, writing our history as it happens, at a level of detail never before known. While proprietary(私有的)archives are slowly exposed to the public after many decades, organizations that maintain immediately-updating resources have more control over what will be remembered by the general public in the near future.

9.3 Television in the United States

Television is one of the major mass media of the United States. Ninety-nine percent of American households have at least one television and the majority of households have more than one.

Television Channels and Networks

There are three basic types of television in: broadcast, or "over-the-air" television, which is freely available to anyone with a TV in the broadcast area, cable television, and satellite television, both of which require a subscription to receive.

Broadcast Television

The United States has a decentralized, market-oriented television system. Unlike many other countries, the United States has no national broadcast programming services. Instead, local media markets have their own television stations, which may be affiliated or owned and operated by a TV network. Stations may sign affiliation agreements with one of the national networks. Except in very small markets with few stations, affiliation agreements are usually exclusive: If a station is an NBC affiliate, the station would not air programs from ABC, CBS or other networks.

However, to ensure local presences in television broadcasting, federal law restricts the amount of network programming local stations can run. Until the 1970s and 80s, local stations supplemented network programming with a good deal of their own produced shows. Today, however, many stations produce only local news shows. They fill the rest of their schedule with syndicated shows, or material produced independently and sold to individual stations in each local market.

The Three Major Networks

The three in the US are the National Broadcasting Company (NBC) and Columbia Broadcasting System (CBS), which date to the early days of television (in fact, they both began in the 1920s as radio networks), and the American Broadcasting Company (ABC), which began its life as a radio network spun off from NBC in 1943. In big cities, affiliates of these networks were almost always broadcast in the VHF band before the transition to digital television in 2009, which, in the days before cable became widespread, was premium real estate.

Major-network affiliates run very similar schedules. Typically, they begin weekdays with an early-morning locally produced news show, followed by a network morning show, such as NBC's Today, which mixes news, weather, interviews and music. Syndicated programming, especially talk shows, fill the late morning, followed often by local news at noon (Eastern Time). Network run Soap operas dominate the early afternoon, while syndicated talk shows such as *The Oprah Winfrey Show* appear in the late afternoon. Local news comes on again in the early evening, followed by the national network's news program at 6:30 or 5:30 p.m., followed by more news.

More syndication occupies the next hour (or hour in the Central time zone, called prime access slot) before the networks take over for prime time, the most-watched three hours of television. Typically, family-oriented comedy programs led in the early part of prime time, although in recent years, reality television like Dancing with the Stars has largely replaced them. Later in the evening, dramas like CSI: Crime Scene Investigation, House, M. D., and Grey's Anatomy air.

At 10 or 11 p. m., another local news program comes on, usually followed by late-night interview shows, such as Late Show with David Letterman or The Tonight Show with Conan O'Brien. Rather than sign off for the early hours of the morning (as was standard practice until the early 1970s in larger markets and until the mid 1980's in smaller ones), TV stations now fill the time with syndicated programming, reruns of prime time television shows and/or the local 10 or 11 o'clock news, or 30-minute advertisements, known as infomercials.

Saturday mornings usually feature network programming aimed at children (including animated cartoons), while Sunday mornings include public-affairs programs that help fulfill stations' legal obligations to provide public-service programming. Sports and infomercials can be found on weekend afternoons, followed again by the same type of prime-time shows aired during the week.

Other Over-the-air Commercial Television

From 1955 until 1986, all English-language stations not affiliated with the big three networks were independent, airing only locally produced and syndicated programming. Many independent stations still exist in the US, usually historically broadcasting on the UHF band. Syndicated shows, often reruns of old TV series and old movies, take up much of their schedule.

In 1986, however, the Fox Broadcasting Company launched a challenge to the big three networks. Thanks largely to the success of shows like The Simpsons, as well as the network's acquisition of rights to show National Football League games, Fox has established itself as a major player in broadcast television. However, Fox differs from the three older networks in that it does not air a nightly news program, its nightly prime-time schedule is only two hours long, some of its big-city affiliates used to broadcast on UHF before the transition to digital and its flagship stations are WNYW, not WFOX and KTTV, not KFOX (but KFOX-TV is used for El Paso's Fox affiliate). Its only scheduled news program is Fox News Sunday, on Sunday mornings; special news coverage on Fox comes from the staff of cable's Fox News Channel. Most

Fox affiliates now have local newscasts, usually airing an hour earlier competing with network dramas, rather than other local newscasts.

In the 1990s, three new networks—The WB (1995), UPN (1995) and PAX (1998; became "i" in 2005 and ION in 2007)—launched. The fledging WB and UPN merged into The CW in fall 2006, while News Corporation's MyNetworkTV, created to replace UPN programming on Fox's O&Os, debuted in fall 2006 as well.

ION broadcasts 24 hours a day, 7 days a week, making the ION network totally responsible for its affiliates, although it mostly airs infomercials outside its prime time. My Network TV broadcasts 12 hours a week, Monday through Saturday. The CW broadcasts 13 hours a week in prime time, 10 hours in daytime.

Non-commercial Television

Public television has a far smaller role than in most other countries. There is no federal state-owned broadcasting authority. However, a number of states, namely West Virginia, Maryland, Kentucky, and South Carolina, do have state-owned public broadcasting authorities which operate and fund all public television stations in their respective states. The federal government does subsidize non-commercial educational television stations through the Corporation for Public Broadcasting. The income received from the government is insufficient to cover expenses and stations rely on corporate sponsorships and viewer contributions.

American public television stations air programming that commercial stations do not offer, such as educational, including cultural, and public affairs programming. Most public TV stations are affiliates of the Public Broadcasting Service, sharing programs like Sesame Street and Masterpiece Theatre. Unlike the commercial networks, PBS does not produce its own programming; instead, individual PBS stations create programming and provide these to other affiliates. New York City's municipally-owned broadcast service, NYCTV, creates original programming that airs in several markets. Few cities have major municipally-owned stations. Many religious broadcasting stations exist, also surviving on viewer contributions.

Cable and Satellite Television

While pay television systems existed as early as the late 1940s, cable television was used, up until the early 1970s, only to rebroadcast over-the-air TV to areas that had trouble receiving signals. In that decade, national networks dedicated exclusively to cable broadcasting appeared, along with cable-TV systems that provided service to major cities. By the mid 1970's cable-TV was available at least to a limited degree in almost every market that already had some form of free-TV. Today, most American households receive cable TV, and cable networks collectively have greater viewership than broadcast networks.

Unlike broadcast networks, most cable networks air the same programming nationwide. Top cable networks include USA Network (general entertainment), ESPN and Versus (sports), MTV (music), Fox News and CNN (news), Syfy (science fiction), Disney Channel (family), Nick and Cartoon Network (Children's), Discovery Channel and Animal Planet (documentaries), TBS (comedy), TNT (drama) and Lifetime (women's).

Cable-TV subscribers receive these channels through local cable system operators, who receive the programming from the networks and transmit them into homes. Usually, local governments award a monopoly to a system operator to provide cable-TV service in a given area. By law, cable systems must include local over-the-air stations in their offerings to customers.

Today Direct broadcast satellite television services, which became available in the US in the 1990s, offers programming similar to cable TV. Dish Network and DirecTV are the major DBS providers in the country. Satellites were originally launched and used by the Television networks as a method of distributing their programs from headquarters to local affiliates. In the 1970s, individuals in remote locations, without access to terrestrial television broadcasts, found they could get free television by installing large satellite dishes and aiming them at the various satellites owned by the networks. This had the additional benefit of providing channels that others could not receive. This included programs without commercials, live feeds not intended for broadcast, broadcasts from other countries and eventually cable television programming. To prevent people from receiving pay content for free, satellite transmissions are now scrambled. Newer transmission technology enabled satellite dishes to be much smaller and subscription services were developed.

The Business of Television

Over-the-air commercial stations and networks generate the vast majority of their revenue from advertisements. According to a 2001 survey, broadcast stations allocated 16 to 21 minutes per hour to commercials. Most cable networks also generate income from advertisements, although most basic cable networks also receive subscription fees. However, premium cable networks, such as the movie network HBO, do not air commercials. Instead, cable-TV subscribers must pay extra to receive the premium networks.

In the days of broadcast television, networks allocated a portion of commercial time for their shows to the local affilates(分支机构), which allowed the local stations to generate revenue. In the same manner, cable-TV system operators generate some of their revenue by selling local commercial time for each cable network being broadcast. The other main source of revenue for the cable-TV operators is subscription fees.

Programming

American television has had very successful programming that has inspired television networks across the world to make shows of similar types or broadcast these shows in their own country. Some of these shows are still on the air and some are still alive and well in syndication. The opposite is also true; a number of popular American programs were based on shows from other countries, especially the United Kingdom and Canada.

Primetime comedy has included situation comedies such as I Love Lucy, M * A * S * H, All in the Family, The Jeffersons, The Cosby Show, Seinfeld, Friends, George Lopez and Everybody Loves Raymond, as well as sketch comedy/variety series such as Milton Berle's early shows, The Carol Burnett Show and Rowan and Martin's Laugh-In.

Dramatic series have taken many forms over the years. Westerns such as Gunsmoke had their greatest popularity in the '50s and '60s. Medical dramas have endured (Marcus Welby, M. D., St. Elsewhere, ER), as have family dramas (Eight is Enough, The Waltons, Little House on the Prairie) and crime dramas (Dragnet, Hawaii Five-O, Hill Street Blues, Law & Order and CSI: Crime Scene Investigation—the last two of which have spawned multiple spin-offs).

The major networks all offer a morning news program (NBC's The Today Show and ABC's Good Morning America are the standard bearers), as well as an early-evening newscast anchored by the de facto face of the network's news operations (Walter Cronkite and Dan Rather for CBS; NBC's Chet Huntley, David Brinkley and Tom Brokaw; ABC's Peter Jennings). Successful news magazines have included 60 Minutes, 20/20, and Dateline in primetime and Meet the Press (the US's oldest series, having debuted in 1947), Face the Nation and This Week on Sunday mornings.

Reality television has long existed in the United States, both played for laughs (Candid Camera, Real People) and as drama (COPS, The Real World). A new variant—competition series placing ordinary people in unusual circumstances or in talent contests, generally eliminating one participant per week—exploded in popularity in 2000 with the launch of Survivor. Big Brother, America's Next Top Model and So You Think You Can Dance followed; American Idol, based on the UK's Pop Idol, debuted in 2002 and has dominated the ratings consistently as of 2009, while The Amazing Race has won the Emmy for its program category every year since its 2001 debut.

American soap operas have been running for over six decades. Of the seven current daytime soaps, three have been on the air for over forty years: As the World Turns, General Hospital and Days of our Lives. Previous long-running daytime dramas included Search for Tomorrow, Love of Life, The Doctors, Another World and Guiding Light—the latter of which ended a 72-year run (combining TV and radio) in September 2009. Primetime soap operas of note have included Peyton Place, Dallas, Dynasty, Beverly Hills, 90210 and Desperate Housewives.

Daytime has also been home of many popular game shows over the years (particularly during the 1970s), such as The Price is Right, Family Feud, Match Game, The Newlywed Game and Concentration. Wheel of Fortune and Jeopardy! have found their greatest success in the early-evening slot before primetime, while game shows actually aired within primetime had great popularity in the 1950s and 1960s (What's My Line? I've Got a Secret, To Tell the Truth) and again, intermittently, in the 2000s (Who Wants to Be a Millionaire, The Weakest Link, Deal or No Deal). The Price Is Right, which has appeared on CBS since 1972, was the only daytime game show remaining on the broadcast networks for fifteen years (prior to CBS's announcement it would be joined by a remake of Let's Make a Deal in October 2009).

The most successful talk show has been the late-night (after 11:30 p.m. Eastern/Pacific) Tonight Show (particularly during the 29-year run of third host Johnny Carson). Tonight ushered in a multi-decade period of dominance by one network in American late-night programming and paved the way for many similar combinations of comedy and celebrity interviews, such as those hosted by Merv Griffin and David Letterman.

Daytime talk show hits have included The Oprah Winfrey Show, Phil Donahue, The Ellen DeGeneres Show, and Live with Regis and Kelly, and run the gamut from serious to lighthearted; a subset of so-called trash TV talk shows such as The Jerry Springer Show also veered into exploitation and titillation.

Regulation

Broadcast television is regulated by the Federal Communications Commission. The FCC awards licenses to local stations, which stipulate stations' commitments to educational and public-interest programming. The FCC also prohibits the airing of "indecent" material over the air between6 a.m. and 10 p.m. Although broadcast stations can legally air almost anything they want late at night—and cable networks at all hours—nudity and profanity are very rare on American television. Broadcasters fear that airing such material will turn off advertisers and encourage the federal government to strengthen its regulation of television content. Premium cable networks are exceptions, and often air very racy programming at night. Some networks, such as Playboy TV, are devoted exclusively to "adult" content.

Cable television is largely, but not entirely, unregulated. Cable systems must include local over-the-air stations in their offerings and give them low channel numbers. The systems cannot show broadcast-network affiliates from other parts of the country.

History of American television

Television first became commercialized in the US in the early 1940s, initially by RCA (through NBC, which it owned) and CBS. A number of different broadcast systems had been developed through the end of the 1930s. The National Television System Committee (NTSC) standardized on a 525-line broadcast in 1941 that would provide the basis for TV across the country through the end of the century. Television development halted with the onset of World War Ⅱ, but pioneers returned to the airwaves when that conflict ended.

There were only a few dozen stations operating at the end of the decade, concentrated on the East and West coasts. The FCC began handing out broadcasting licenses to communities of all sizes in the early 1950s, spurring an explosion of growth in the medium. A brief debacle over the system to use for color broadcasts occurred at this time, but was soon settled. Half of all US households had TV sets by 1955, though color was a premium feature for many years (most households able to purchase TV sets could only afford black-and-white models, and few programs were broadcast in color until the mid-1960s).

Many of the earliest TV programs were modified versions of well-established radio shows. The '50s saw the first flowering of the genres that would distinguish TV from movies and radio: talk shows like The Jack Paar Show and sitcoms(情景喜剧) like I Love Lucy. Stations across the country also produced their own local programs. Usually carried live, they ranged from simple advertisements to game shows and children's shows that often featured clowns and other offbeat characters. Local shows could often be popular and profitable, but concerns about product promotion and other issues led them to almost completely disappear by the mid-1970s.

Subscription television (such as cable and satellite) became popular in the early 1980s, and has been growing in significance since *then spurring the emergence of multinational conglomerates such as Fox*.

9.4 Cinema of the United States

The cinema of the United States has had a profound effect on cinema across the world since the early 20th century. Its history is sometimes separated into four main periods: the silent film era, classical Hollywood cinema, New Hollywood, and the contemporary period (after 1980). Since the 1920s, the American film industry has grossed more money every year than that of any other country.

In 1878, Eadweard Muybridge demonstrated the power of photography to capture motion. In 1894, the world's first commercial motion picture exhibition was given in New York City, using Thomas Edison's Kinetoscope. The United States was in the forefront of sound film's development in the following decades. Since the early twentieth century, the US film industry has largely been based in and around Hollywood, Los Angeles, California. Picture City, FL was doubtfully also a planned site for a movie picture production center in the 1920s, but due to the 1928 Okeechobee hurricane, the idea collapsed and Picture City was returned back to the original name of Hobe Sound. Director D. W. Griffith was central to the development of film grammar and Orson Welles's Citizen Kane (1941) is frequently cited in critics' polls as the greatest film of all time. American screen actors like John Wayne and Marilyn Monroe have become iconic figures, while producer/entrepreneur Walt Disney was a leader in both animated film and movie merchandising. The major film studios of Hollywood are the primary source of the most commercially successful movies in the world, such as *Star Wars* (1977), *Titanic* (1997), and the contemporaneous *Avatar* (2009), and the products of Hollywood today dominate the global film industry.

History

Origins

The second recorded instance of photographs capturing and reproducing motion was Eadweard Muybridge's series of photographs of a running horse, which he captured in Palo Alto, California, using a set of still cameras placed in a row. Muybridge's accomplishment led inventors everywhere to attempt to make similar devices that would capture such motion. In the United States, Thomas Alva Edison was among the first to produce such a device, the kinetoscope(活动照相机), whose heavy-handed patent enforcement caused early filmmakers to look for alternatives.

In the United States, the first exhibitions of films for large audiences typically followed the intermissions in vaudeville (歌舞杂耍) shows. Entrepreneurs began traveling to exhibit their films, bringing to the world the first forays(尝试)into dramatic film-making.

In the earliest days of the American film industry, New York was the epicenter of film-making. The Kaufman Astoria Studios in Queens, built during the silent film era, was used by the Marx Brothers and W. C. Fields. Chelsea, Manhattan was also frequently used. Mary Pickford, an Academy Award winning actress, shot some of her early films in this area. Other major centers of film production included Chicago, Florida, California and Cuba.

The film patents wars of the early 20th Century led to the spread of film companies across the US. Many worked with equipment for which they did not own the rights, and thus filming in New York could be dangerous; it was close to Edison's Company headquarters, and to agents the company set out to seize cameras. By 1912, most major film companies had set up production facilities because of the location's proximity to Mexico, though the region's optimal year-round weather is generally sited as the primary reason.

Golden Age of Hollywood

Hollywood in L/A

During the so-called Golden Age of Hollywood, which lasted from the end of the silent era in American cinema in the late 1920s to the late 1950s, thousands of movies were issued from the Hollywood studios. The start of the Golden Age was arguably when *The Jazz Singer* was released in 1927, ending the silent era and increasing box-office profits for films as sound was introduced to feature films. Most Hollywood pictures adhered closely to a formula—Western, slapstick comedy, musical, animated cartoon, biopic (biographical picture)—and the same creative teams often worked on films made by the same studio. For example, Cedric Gibbons and Herbert Stothart always worked on MGM films, Alfred Newman worked at 20th Century Fox for twenty years, Cecil B. De Mille's films were almost all made at Paramount, and director Henry King's films were mostly made for 20th Century Fox. At the same time, one could usually guess which studio made which film, largely because of the actors who appeared in it; MGM, for example, claimed it had contracted "more stars than there are in heaven." Each studio had its own style and characteristic touches which made it possible to know this — a trait that does not exist today. Yet each movie was a little different, and, unlike the craftsmen who made cars, many of the people who made movies were artists. For example, To Have and Have Not (1944) is famous not only for the first pairing of actors Humphrey Bogart (1899 – 1957) and Lauren Bacall (1924 –) but also for being written by two future winners of the Nobel Prize in Literature: Ernest Hemingway (1899 – 1961), the author of the novel on which the script was nominally based, and William Faulkner (1897 – 1962), who worked on the screen adaptation.

After The Jazz Singer was released in 1927, Warner Bros. gained huge success and was able to acquire their own string of movie theaters, after purchasing Stanley Theaters and First National Productions in 1928. MGM had also owned the Loews string of theaters since forming in 1924, and the Fox Film Corporation owned the Fox Theatre strings as well. Also, RKO (a 1928 merger between Keith-Orpheum Theaters and the Radio Corporation of America) responded to the Western Electric/ERPI monopoly over sound in films, and developed their own method, known as Photophone, to put sound in films. Paramount, who already acquired Balaban and Katz in 1926, would answer to the success of Warner Bros. and RKO, and buy a number of theaters in the late 1920s as well, and would hold a monopoly on theaters in Detroit, Michigan. By the 1930s, all of America's theaters were owned by the Big Five studios—MGM, Paramount Pictures, RKO, Warner Bros., and Twentieth Century Fox.

Movie-making was still a business however, and motion picture companies made money by operating under the studio system. The major studios kept thousands of people on salary — actors, producers, directors, writers, stunt men, craftspersons, and technicians. And they owned hundreds of theaters in cities and towns across the nation, theaters that showed their films and that were always in need of fresh material. In 1930, MPDAA President Will Hays created the Hays (Production) Code, which followed censorship guidelines and went into effect after government threats of censorship expanded by 1930. However, the code was never enforced until 1934, after the Catholic watchdog organization The Legion of Decency—appalled by Mae West's very successful sexual appearances in She Done Him Wrong and I'm No Angel—threatened a boycott of motion pictures if it didn't go into effect. Those films that didn't obtain a seal of approval from the Production Code Administration had to pay a $25,000,00 fine and could not profit in the theaters, as the MPDDA owned every theater in the country through the Big Five studios.

Throughout the 1930s, as well as most of the golden age, MGM dominated the film screen and had the top stars in Hollywood, and was also credited for creating the Hollywood star system altogether. Some MGM stars included "King of Hollywood" Clark Gable, Lionel Barrymore, Jean Harlow, Norma Shearer, Greta Garbo, Jeanette MacDonald and husband Gene Raymond, Spencer Tracy, Judy Garland, and Gene Kelly. Another great achievement of US cinema during this era came through Walt Disney's animation company. In 1937, Disney created the most successful film of its time, *Snow White and the Seven Dwarfs*. Also in 1939, MGM would create what is still, when adjusted for inflation, the most successful film of all time, *Gone with the Wind*.

Many film historians have remarked upon the many great works of cinema that emerged from this period of highly regimented film-making. One reason this was possible is that, with so many movies being made, not every one had to be a big hit. A studio could gamble on a medium-budget feature with a good script and relatively unknown actors: Citizen Kane, directed by Orson Welles (1915 - 1985) and often regarded as the greatest film of all time, fits that description. In other cases, strong-willed directors like Howard Hawks (1896 - 1977), Alfred Hitchcock (1899 - 1980) and Frank Capra (1897 - 1991) battled the studios in order to achieve their artistic visions. The apogee(最高点)of the studio system may have been the year 1939, which saw the release of such classics as The Wizard of Oz, Gone with the Wind, Stagecoach, Mr. Smith Goes to Washington, Wuthering Heights, Only Angels Have Wings, Ninotchka, and Midnight. Among the other films from the Golden Age period that are now considered to be classics: *Casablanca*, *It's a Wonderful Life*, *It Happened One Night*, the original *King Kong*, *Mutiny on the Bounty*, *City Lights*, *Red River* and *Top Hat*.

Decline of the Studio System

The studio system and the Golden Age of Hollywood succumbed to two forces that developed in the late 1940s:

- a federal antitrust action that separated the production of films from their exhibition; and
- the advent of television.

In 1938, Walt Disney's *Snow White and the Seven Dwarfs* was released during a run of lackluster films from the major studios, and quickly became the highest-grossing film released to that point. Embarrassingly for the studios, it was an independently-produced animated film that did not feature any studio-employed stars. This stoked already widespread frustration at the practice of *block-booking*, in which studios would only sell an entire year's schedule of films at a time to theaters and use the lock-in to cover for releases of mediocre quality. Assistant Attorney General Thurman Arnold—a noted "trust buster"(反托拉斯能手) of the Roosevelt administration — took this opportunity to initiate proceedings against the eight largest Hollywood studios in July 1938 for violations of the Sherman Anti-Trust Act. The federal suit resulted in five of the eight studios (the "Big Five": Warner Bros., MGM, Fox, RKO and Paramount) reaching a compromise with Arnold in October 1940 and signing a consent decree agreeing to, within three years:

- Eliminate the block-booking of short film subjects, in an arrangement known as "one shot", or "full force" block-booking.
- Eliminate the block-booking of any more than five features in their theaters.

- No longer engage in *blind buying* (or the buying of films by theater districts without seeing films beforehand) and instead have *trade-showing*, in which all 31 theater districts in US would see films every two weeks before showing movies in theaters.
- Set up an administration board in each theater district to enforce these requirements.

The "Little Three" (Universal Studios, United Artists, and Columbia Pictures), who did not own any theaters, refused to participate in the consent decree. A number of independent film producers were also unhappy with the compromise and formed a union known as the Society of Independent Motion Picture Producers and sued Paramount for the monopoly they still had over the Detroit Theaters — as Paramount was also gaining dominance through actors like Bob Hope, Paulette Goddard, Veronica Lake, Betty Hutton, crooner Bing Crosby, Alan Ladd, and longtime actor for studio Gary Cooper too- by 1942. The Big Five studios didn't meet the requirements of the Consent of Decree during WWⅡ, without major consequence, but after the war ended they joined Paramount as defendants in the Hollywood anti-trust case, as did the Little Three studios also. The Supreme Court eventually ruled that the major studios ownership of theaters and film distribution was a violation of the Sherman Antitrust Act. As a result, the studios began to release actors and technical staff from their contracts with the studios. This changed the paradigm of film making by the major Hollywood studios, as each could have an entirely different cast and creative team. This resulted in the gradual loss of the characteristics which made MGM, Paramount, Universal, Columbia, RKO, and Fox films immediately identifiable. But certain movie people, such as Cecil B. DeMille, either remained contract artists till the end of their careers or used the same creative teams on their films, so that a DeMille film still looked like one whether it was made in 1932 or 1956. Also, the number of movies being produced annually dropped as the average budget soared, marking a major change in strategy for the industry. Studios now aimed to produce entertainment that could not be offered by television: spectacular, larger-than-life productions. Studios also began to sell portions of their theatrical film libraries to other companies to sell to television. By 1949, all major film studios had given up ownership of their theaters.

Television was also instrumental in the decline of Hollywood's Golden Age as it broke the movie industry's hegemony（霸权主义）in American entertainment. Despite this, the film industry was also able to gain some leverage(影响)for future films as longtime government censorship faded in the 1950s. After the Paramount anti-trust case ended, Hollywood movie studios no longer owned theaters, and thus made it so foreign films could be released in American theaters without censorship. This was complemented with the 1952 Miracle Decision in the Joseph Burstyn Inc. v Wilson case, in which the Supreme Court of the United States reversed its earlier position, from 1915's Mutual Film Corporation v. Industrial Commission of Ohio case, and stated that motion pictures were a form of art and were entitled to the protection of the First amendment; US laws could no longer censor films. By 1968, the Motion Picture Association of America (MPAA) had replaced the Hays Code-which was now greatly violated after the government threat of censorship that justified the origin of the code had ended- with the film rating system.

The "New Hollywood" and Post-classical Cinema

"Post-classical cinema" is a term used to describe the changing methods of storytelling in the New Hollywood. It has been argued that new approaches to drama and characterization played upon audience expectations acquired in the classical period: chronology may be scrambled, story lines may feature "twist endings", and lines between the antagonist and protagonist may be blurred. The roots of post-classical storytelling may be seen in film noir, in Rebel Without a Cause (1955), and in Hitchcock's storyline-shattering Psycho.

"New Hollywood" is a term used to describe the emergence of a new generation of film school-trained directors who had absorbed the techniques developed in Europe in the 1960s; The 1967 film Bonnie and Clyde marked the beginning of American cinema rebounding as well, as a new generation of films would afterwards gain success at the box offices as well. Filmmakers like Francis Ford Coppola, George Lucas, Brian de Palma, Martin Scorsese, William Friedkin and Steven Spielberg came to produce fare that paid homage to the history of film, and developed upon existing genres and techniques. In the early 1970s, their films were often both critically acclaimed and commercially successful. While the early New Hollywood films like Bonnie and Clyde and Easy Rider had been relatively low-budget affairs with amoral heroes and increased sexuality and violence, the enormous success enjoyed by Coppola, Spielberg and Lucas with The Godfather, Jaws, and Star Wars, respectively helped to give rise to the modern "blockbuster", and induced studios to focus ever more heavily on trying to produce enormous hits.

The increasing indulgence of these young directors didn't help. Often, they'd go overschedule, and overbudget, thus bankrupting themselves or the studio. The two most famous examples of this are Francis Coppola's *One From The Heart* and particularly Michael Cimino's *Heaven's Gate*, which single-handedly bankrupted United Artists.

Blockbusters(大片)

The drive to produce a spectacle on the movie screen has largely shaped American cinema ever since. Spectacular epics which took advantage of new wide screen processes had been increasingly popular from the 1950s onwards. Since then, American films have become increasingly divided into two categories: Blockbusters and independent films. Studios have focused on relying on a handful of extremely expensive releases every year in order to remain profitable. Such blockbusters emphasize spectacle, star power, and high production value, all of which entail an enormous budget. Blockbusters typically rely upon star power and massive advertising to attract a huge audience. A successful blockbuster will attract an audience large enough to offset production costs and reap considerable profits. Such productions carry a substantial risk of failure, and most studios release blockbusters that both over- and underperform in a year.

Independent Film

Studios supplement these movies with independent productions, made with small budgets and often independently of the studio corporation. Movies made in this manner typically emphasize high professional quality in terms of acting, directing, screenwriting, and other elements associated with production, and also upon creativity and innovation. These movies usually rely upon critical praise or niche marketing to garner an audience. Because of an independent film's low budgets, a successful independent film can have a high profit-to-cost ratio, while a failure will incur minimal losses, allowing for studios to sponsor dozens of such productions in addition to their high-stakes releases.

American independent cinema was revitalized in the late 1980s and early 1990s when another new generation of moviemakers, including Spike Lee, Steven Soderbergh, Kevin Smith, and Quentin Tarantino made movies like, respectively: Do the Right Thing; Sex, Lies, and Videotape; Clerks; and Reservoir Dogs. In terms of directing, screenwriting, editing, and other elements, these movies were innovative and often irreverent, playing with and contradicting the conventions of Hollywood movies. Furthermore, their considerable financial successes and crossover into popular culture reestablished the commercial viability of independent film. Since then, the independent film industry has become more clearly defined and more influential in American cinema. Many of the major studios have capitalised on this by developing subsidiaries to produce similar films; for example Fox Searchlight Pictures.

To a lesser degree in the 2000s, film types that were previously considered to have only a minor presence in the mainstream movie market began to arise as more potent American box office draws. These include foreign-language films such as Crouching Tiger, Hidden Dragon and Hero and documentary films such as Super Size Me, March of the Penguins, and Michael Moore's Bowling *for Columbine* and *Fahrenheit* 9/11.

Rise of the Home Video Market

The 1980s and 1990s saw another significant development. The full acceptance of home video by studios opened a vast new business to exploit. Films such as *The Secret of NIMH* and *The Shawshank Redemption*, which performed poorly in their theatrical run, were now able to find success in the video market. It also saw the first generation of film makers with access to video tapes emerge. Directors such as Quentin Tarantino and P. T. Anderson had been able to view thousands of films and produced films with vast numbers of references and connections to previous works. This, along with the explosion of independent film and ever-decreasing costs for filmmaking, changed the landscape of American movie-making once again, and led a renaissance of filmmaking among Hollywood's lower and middle-classes—those without access to studio financial resources.

With the rise of the DVD in the 21st century, DVDs have quickly become even more profitable to studios and have led to an explosion of packaging extra scenes, extended versions, and commentary tracks with the films.

The Relation between Hollywood and the Politicians

Hollywood is also an endless pool of money for any presidential candidate. The relation between Hollywood and Washington began with a need for Hollywood to acquire a status of power by being seen with politicians and that relation is today reversed with Washington's need for Hollywood's money.

It all started in the beginnings of Hollywood, mostly during the moguls'(巨头) era, the founders of the studios. Douglas Fairbanks, Charlie Chaplin and Mary Pickford were used to sell war bonds for World War 1 and their image worked to attract crowds. It wasn't so long until the moguls began looking for something else than fame and money from their successful businesses. Most of the moguls and power figures of Hollywood in the 1920s were Jews. Being a Jew in this era was seen as negative, in a time when Jews were not welcomed in America. Despite their success, the moguls did not have the respect or the social status that they wanted. By being seen with powerful politicians, they would raise their social status and assure the respect they wanted. MGM's powerful executive Louis B. Mayer accomplished this desire by being a good friend with candidate Herbert Hoover. The role of Hollywood in national politics began with this friendship between Mayer and Hoover. From this friendship, Hoover gained the support of Mayer's friend William Randolph Hearst, press lord and producer, in his cause. Mayer was a strong supporter of Hoover who eventually became the 31st President of the United States, and Mayer succeeded in being well respected and became an even more powerful figure in Hollywood.

In the 1930s the Democrats and the Republicans saw a huge pool of money in Hollywood. President Franklin Roosevelt saw a huge partnership with Hollywood. He used the first real potential of Hollywood's stars in a national campaign. Melvyn Douglas toured Washington in 1939 and met the key New Dealers. Endorsements letters from leading actors were signed, radio appearances and printed advertising were made. The use of a star was to draw a large audience into the political view of the party. By the 1960s John F. Kennedy and Frank Sinatra had a strong friendship in this glamour era when young Kennedy was a new face for Washington. The last moguls of Hollywood were gone and young new executives and producers began generating more liberal ideas. The celebrity and the money attracted the politicians into the high-class glittering Hollywood life-style. As Ronald Brownstein wrote in his book "The Power and the Glitter", the television in the 1970s and 1980s was an enormously important new media into the politics and Hollywood helped in that media with actors making speeches on their political beliefs, like Jane Fonda against the Vietnam War. In this era we saw former actor Ronald Reagan became Governor of California and then President of the United States. It continued with Arnold Schwarzenegger as California's Governor in 2003.

Today Washington's interest is in Hollywood being a money provider, with its huge pool of money. On February 20, 2007, for example, Senator Barack Obama had a $2300-a-plate Hollywood gala (盛会), being hosted by David Geffen, Jeffrey Katzenberg and Steven Spielberg at the Beverly Hilton. Hollywood is a huge donator for presidential campaigns and this money is attracting politicians into Hollywood. Not only is Hollywood influencing Washington with its glamour and money but Washington is also influencing Hollywood. With the help of the Pentagon and, based on Jean-Michel Valantin analysis in "Hollywood, le Pentagone et Washington", Capitol Hill and the White House influence most notably the War films of Hollywood with their politics and ideologies.

In the 20th century, the motion picture industry rose to become one of the most successful and powerful industries in the US Along with other intellectual property industries, its relative importance to the American economy has strengthened as the importance of manufacturing and agriculture have decreased (due to globalization).

Questions

1. Please introduce three TV networks in the US .
2. Introduce the most popular American newspapers.

3. When was the Golden Age of Hollywood? What was the cinema like at that time?

4. As a new medium, how is Internet influencing the US?

Supplementary Reading 1

New Rules for the Ways We Watch

By David Carr

For the last year, media pundits like me have been running around screaming our heads off about falling skies and collapsing paradigms, and yet as 2011 comes to an end, the sky is still there.

Yes, competition is storming out of every device and connection, and consumers have choices and leverage they never dreamed of. But network television continues to waltz along, attracting advertisers in big numbers. Cable had a great year, and media octopuses like Time Warner and News Corporation continue to find plenty of profits. Big media companies still rely on huge, well-entrenched assets that include brands, distribution and capital.

But even if the sky is still aloft, there are visible, portentous cracks appearing. The inertia that has kept consumers from bolting from traditional content providers is beginning to erode as a new generation remakes media in its own image. Device companies and search outfits are intent on manufacturing their own content. And the migration of movies, music and video to the cloud could change the weather in a hurry.

Even as some of the old truisms in media still obtain — content wears the crown and strong brands break through clutter — a few new rules are taking shape.

A SCREEN IS A SCREEN Steve Jobs taught us a bunch before he exited, but one of his most current lessons could be the one with the most far-reaching implications. Content has a price tag, which is reassuring, but the old dividing lines between television, radio, Web and print disappear within the four corners of a tablet. That means, for instance, that CNBC and The Wall Street Journal are not in different businesses anymore, and in fact The Journal is adding hours of live video with each passing month. The BBC and Al Jazeera are no longer regional curios, they're here. Every cable channel with two nickels and more than a few digital enterprises is financing the kind of narrative television that used to be available only at a certain time on a certain network.

NEW NETWORKS EVERY DAY On Christmas Day, a lot of people took the ribbon off a Web-enabled flat-screen television, and now the fight for real estate on all those enhanced television screens will be fast and furious. Cable providers will try to keep people from downloading the products of insurgent Web "broadcasters," but they can't stop what's coming. They will have to win by providing value that trumps the now-infinite channel universe of the Web.

The $27 billion that traditional media just paid to the National Football League is a hedge, not an answer. So-called virtual operators — Netflix, Hulu, Amazon, Google and Apple — have none of the legacy or infrastructure costs. Google has unleashed $100 million to seed new programming on YouTube, and Netflix is financing a series by the director David Fincher. That gaming device your children are playing with? That too is a network in the making. Traditional networks and cable providers have the content, but if they hold on too tight, they will miss out on vast new avenues of distribution and revenue.

THE REMOTE AS BRICK The iPad is a screen on your lap that makes it easy to navigate toward a completely personal experience. That screen on your living room wall is going to have to perform the same way to remain relevant. As it has in many other areas of technology, the smartphone will point the way. Our phones — and now tablets — are always on and poised for action.

When I switched from the first iPad, which took a few seconds to boot, to the iPad2, which stands ready for duty every time I lift its cover, my use more than doubled. I expect that other devices will greet me in similar fashion. Navigating is as easy as a swipe of the finger or, in the case of the new iPhone, a verbal request to Siri.

As for your remote control, well, using it is a little like hitting your television with a stick until it finally delivers what you want. If things go as they should, we will spend less time looking under the couch for the remote and more time telling our television to get us the seventh episode of the second season of "Boardwalk Empire." (Beginning in December, Xbox 360 owners were already able to search TV shows by voice.) And our media identity is becoming ubiquitous, and transportable: someday, I should be able to walk into a hotel in Kansas, tell the television who I am and find everything I have bought and paid for, there for the consuming.

CELEBRITY AS COMMODITY The multiplatform and infinite-channel universe can manufacture its own celebrities. Is Scott Pelley a more important asset than Kim Kardashian? You may not know who Rebecca Black is, but more than 14 million YouTube users do and have spun her ridiculous music video "Friday" to laugh at or with her. Oprah Winfrey, the celebrity with the golden touch, got clobbered when she started her own network. Anderson Cooper felt compelled to do a daytime show to diversify his bets. Keith Olbermann and Charlie Sheen thought their audiences were a movable feast, but big chunks of their followers stayed put to watch Rachel Maddow and Ashton Kutcher in their slots.

THE FUTURE WILL BE HACKED I happened to be at dinner with Howard Stringer back in June when Sony and its PlayStation network were under attack by hackers. Mr. Stringer, an even-keeled executive who has lived through all kinds of challenges, looked as if he had stumbled onto a beehive. It's nice that NBC News has a Twitter account for breaking news; but when the hacked version started spitting out alarmist messages about an attack during the run-up to the Sept. 11 anniversary? Not so great. In November, the digital wrenches of Anonymous wreaked similar havoc on Fox News. As more vital content is distributed from the cloud and not cables, security breaches will not be something media companies report about, but something they live through.

THE CONSUMER WILL DECIDE Yes, consumers are programming their own mediated universe, but they can snap healthy companies in two while they are at it. Last year I wrote a story about Netflix's deft understanding of consumer preferences, but in September the company decided to split its DVD and streaming options into two services, and that, in addition to a price increase, cost the company almost a million customers. The Daily, an iPad-only newspaper started by The Wall Street Journal, came out to a herald of trumpets and now hears only the sound of crickets. Research in Motion decided people wanted a cheaper tablet. Turns out they wanted one that worked, as well.

MASH-UPS AND HYBRIDS WILL RULE Everything that can be mashed together will be. The Tea Party will do a debate with CNN, and the Showtime series "Homeland" will be a cable series, an on-demand product, an app and a community. That informational crawl at the bottom of your television set? It could come from the broadcaster or it might come from Twitter. Soon the Oscars award show could be accompanied by comments from your wisecracking friends, not on your phone but on the bottom of your flat-screen. Huge world events will first appear on social media platforms and then leap to mainstream media and back again. The books you read to your children will take over when you are tired and read themselves, or they might turn into a game when the joys of unadorned narrative begin to bore.

SOCIAL MEDIA AS ITS OWN FRIEND Facebook wants to be your cultural operating system, providing recommendations and serving as a platform for music, movies and news. Twitter has taken its initial lightweight design and begun to offer more windows of content, hoping to keep you tuned in for more than 140 characters. If these services are capable of fomenting revolutions against repressive regimes, they can do plenty of world-changing right here. Occupy Wall Street drew enough notice with D. I. Y. media to command a national stage and reorder the discussion.

What else will we be watching for in the coming year? The fates of Julian Assange and Rupert Murdoch, two men who changed the world in very different ways and are now both being pursued, will probably be decided. We'll find out whether the 38 or so Republican debates will give the party's nominee an advantage against the president. And everyone, especially the people at Apple, knows that the consumer response to its next big thing — iTV anyone? — will be a referendum on whether the company can prosper absent its visionary in chief.

http://www.nytimes.com/2011/12/26/business/media/rules-for-the-new-ways-of-watching-david-carr.html? src=me&ref=business

Supplementary Reading 2

Why Google Isn't the New Microsoft

By Harry McCracken

The European Commission, which is investigating whether Google's search engine violates European antitrust law, received a formal letter of complaint last week from an interested party. The complainant charged Google with "a broadening pattern of conduct aimed at stopping anyone else from creating a competitive alternative." It accused the company of hurting consumers by refusing to open up services like YouTube to other search engines, said its practices were "disconcerting" and "troubling", and called on European officials to step in and clamp down.

The outfit lobbying the EC wasn't some strident consumer-affairs group. It was Microsoft, the proprietor of Bing, the second biggest search engine — and a company that knows thing or two about anticompetitive behavior and its legal repercussions. (See pictures of work and life at Google.)

After all, in 1998, the US Department of Justice sued Microsoft over its bundling of Internet Explorer with Windows, saying that gave it an unreasonable advantage over other browser makers like Netscape. A judge initially ruled that the software behemoth should be split into two companies; it eventually avoided that fate but agreed to operate under restrictions designed to give its rivals a fighting chance.

Seeing Microsoft play the role of 97-pound weakling shows how things have changed since the '90s, when it was a muscle-bound terror that kicked sand in the faces of other tech companies at will. But it's far from the only player questioning Google's recent behavior. For example, Google Books suffered a massive setback last month when a federal judge rejected a settlement Google had reached with publishers to permit the selling of 12 million scanned e-books as anticompetitive. Three states are reportedly poised to launch antitrust probes. Rumor even has it that the federal government may launch an investigation as soon as it can figure out whether the Justice Department or the Federal Trade Commission should be doing the investigating.

It's true that certain things about Google's position on the Web are reminiscent of the clout Microsoft wielded back when the computing universe revolved around desktop PCs. Google's share of the US search market stands at a daunting 65 percent; most of the rest is taken up by Bing and by Bing-powered results at Yahoo. (In Europe, Google's share is estimated at 85% or more, which may help explain why officials there have a head start on their US counterparts in probing the company.) (See the top 10 Google Earth finds.)

If Google weren't absurdly flush with cash from search-engine ads, it couldn't enter new fields willy-nilly — from office suites to next-generation broadband to self-driving cars — without fretting over their immediate profit potential. That's similar to the way that Microsoft's twin cash cows, Windows and Office, have long funded the company's battles on other fronts against less prosperous competitors.

And some of the recent scuttlebutt about Google does involve tactics that sound a tad Microsoftian. Bloomberg Businessweek, for instance, recently reported that the company was obstructing Verizon's plans for phones that run Google's Android operating system but swap out Google's search engine for Bing. If true, that's curious considering that Google reminds the world at every possible opportunity that Android is open-source software that hardware makers can — presumably — customize as they see fit.

Overall, though, Google's current dominance has little of the reign-of-terror feel I associate with Microsoft's, um, heyday. When I did an audit of my Google usage, I found that I use 10 of the company's services every day, and nine others multiple times a week. But I use them because I like them. (Gmail is an occasional exception.) More important, I don't feel trapped. In every instance, solid alternatives from other companies are just a few clicks away — usually at no charge. (See "The E. U. Probe: Is Google Rigging Its Search Results?")

That's nothing like the bad old days of Microsoft's monopoly over PC operating systems, browsers and office suites. Back then, important applications ran only on Windows, major sites required IE, and the documents that your pals created in Office might or might not open up properly in suites such as WordPerfect and StarOffice. All of that made it tough to opt out of Bill Gates' world even if you preferred not to be part of it.

Again and again, Google has proven that it's not very good at turning its commanding position in search into success elsewhere. It said a service called Wave was the future of communications; so few people bought that idea that Wave died within months. Buzz, its answer to Twitter, hasn't amounted to much. And for all of Google's might, it's clearly been rattled by the rise of Facebook, a site that already matters at least as much to millions of people as any search engine. (Its latest stab at Facebook-style social networking, +1, is too new to judge.)

How things have played out with Microsoft in recent years also gives me hope: its fading power has had less to do with government intervention than with consumer preference. When Mozilla came up with a better browser in Firefox, millions of people dumped Internet Explorer. The arrival of Apple's iPhone led to the collapse of the market for the suddenly antiquated Windows Mobile. Similarly, the iPad was an instant blockbuster even though Microsoft had spent a decade failing to convince the masses that Tablet PCs were the computers of the future. (See "Search-Engine Wars: Can Bing (or Blekko) Beat Google?")

Consumers, in other words, tend to be pretty good at figuring out what's good for consumers. I trust their take on Google and its competitors more than that of any government agency. And the great democratizing power of the Internet puts them in an excellent position to call the shots.

http://www.time.com/time/business/article/*0,8599,2063693,00.*html

Chapter 10 American Literature

American literature is the written or literary work produced in the area of the United States and Colonial America. During its early history, America was a series of British colonies on the eastern coast of the present-day United States. Therefore, its literary tradition begins as linked to the broader tradition of English literature. However, unique American characteristics and the breadth of its production usually now cause it to be considered a separate path and tradition.

10.1 Colonial Literature

Some of the earliest forms of American literature were pamphlets and writings extolling the benefits of the colonies to both a European and colonist audience. Captain John Smith could be considered the first American author with his works: A True Relation of ... Virginia ... (1608) and The General Historie of Virginia, New England, and the Summer Isles (1624). Other writers of this manner included Daniel Denton, Thomas Ashe, William Penn, George Percy, William Strachey, Daniel Coxe, Gabriel Thomas, and John Lawson.

The religious disputes that prompted settlement in America were also topics of early writing. A journal written by John Winthrop discussed the religious foundations of the Massachusetts Bay Colony. Edward Winslow also recorded a diary of the first years after the Mayflower's arrival. Other religiously influenced writers included Increase Mather and William Bradford, author of the journal published as a History of Plymouth Plantation, 1620 – 1647. Others like Roger Williams and Nathaniel Ward more fiercely argued state and church separation.

Some poetry also existed. Anne Bradstreet and Edward Taylor are especially noted. Michael Wigglesworth wrote a best-selling poem, The Day of Doom, describing the time of judgment. Nicholas Noyes was also known for his doggerel (打油诗)verse.

Other late writings described conflicts and interaction with the Indians, as seen in writings by Daniel Gookin, Alexander Whitaker, John Mason, Benjamin Church, and Mary Rowlandson. John Eliot translated the Bible into the Algonquin language.

Jonathan Edwards and George Whitefield represented the Great Awakening, a religious revival in the early 18th century that asserted strict Calvinism(加尔文主义). Other Puritan and religious writers include Thomas Hooker, Thomas Shepard, John Wise, and Samuel Willard. Less strict and serious writers included Samuel Sewall, Sarah Kemble Knight, and William Byrd.

The revolutionary period also contained political writings, including those by colonists Samuel Adams, Josiah Quincy, John Dickinson, and Joseph Galloway, a loyalist to the crown. Two key figures were Benjamin Franklin and Thomas Paine. Franklin's Poor Richard's Almanac and The Autobiography of Benjamin Franklin are esteemed works with their wit and influence toward the formation of a budding American identity. Paine's pamphlet Common Sense and The American Crisis writings are seen as playing a key role in influencing the political tone of the period.

During the revolution itself, poems and songs such as "Yankee Doodle" and "Nathan Hale" were popular. Major satirists included John Trumbull and Francis Hopkinson. Philip Morin Freneau also wrote poems about the war's course.

Post-independence

In the post-war period, The Federalist essays by Alexander Hamilton, James Madison, and John Jay presented a significant historical discussion of American government organization and republican values. Thomas Jefferson's United States Declaration of Independence, his influence on the American Constitution, his autobiography, the Notes on the State of Virginia, and his many letters solidify his spot as one of the most talented early American writers. Fisher Ames, James Otis, and Patrick Henry are also valued for their political writings and orations.

Much of the early literature of the new nation struggled to find a uniquely

American voice in existing literary genre, and this tendency was also reflected in novels. European forms and styles were often transferred to new locales and critics often saw them as inferior.

Unique American Style

With the War of 1812 and an increasing desire to produce uniquely American literature and culture, a number of key new literary figures emerged, perhaps most prominently Washington Irving, William Cullen Bryant, James Fenimore Cooper, and Edgar Allan Poe. Irving, often considered the first writer to develop a unique American style (although this has been debated) wrote humorous works in *Salmagundi* and the well-known satire *A History of New York*, by Diedrich Knickerbocker (1809). Bryant wrote early romantic and nature-inspired poetry, which evolved away from their European origins. In 1832, Poe began writing short stories—including "The Masque of the Red Death", "The Pit and the Pendulum", "The Fall of the House of Usher", and "The Murders in the Rue Morgue"—that explore previously hidden levels of human psychology and push the boundaries of fiction toward mystery and fantasy. Cooper's Leatherstocking Tales about Natty Bumppo (which includes The Last of the Mohicans) were popular both in the new country and abroad.

Humorous writers were also popular and included Seba Smith and Benjamin P. Shillaber in New England and Davy Crockett, Augustus Baldwin Longstreet, Johnson J. Hooper, Thomas Bangs Thorpe, and George Washington Harris writing about the American frontier.

The New England Brahmins were a group of writers connected to Harvard University and its seat in Cambridge, Massachusetts. The core included James Russell Lowell, Henry Wadsworth Longfellow, and Oliver Wendell Holmes, Sr.

In 1836, Ralph Waldo Emerson (1803 - 1882), an ex-minister, published a startling nonfiction work called Nature, in which he claimed it was possible to dispense with organized religion and reach a lofty spiritual state by studying and responding to the natural world. His work influenced not only the writers who gathered around him, forming a movement known as Transcendentalism(超验主义), but also the public, who heard him lecture.

Emerson's most gifted fellow-thinker was perhaps Henry David Thoreau (1817 – 1862), a resolute nonconformist. After living mostly by himself for two years in a cabin by a wooded pond, Thoreau wrote Walden, a book-length memoir that urges resistance to the meddlesome(爱干涉的)dictates of organized society. His radical writings express a deep-rooted tendency toward individualism in the American character. Other writers influenced by Transcendentalism were Bronson Alcott, Margaret Fuller, George Ripley, Orestes Brownson, and Jones Very.

Ralph Waldo Emerson
(1803 – 1882)

The political conflict surrounding Abolitionism inspired the writings of William Lloyd Garrison and his paper The Liberator, along with poet John Greenleaf Whittier and Harriet Beecher Stowe in her world-famous *Uncle Tom's Cabin*.

In 1837, the young Nathaniel Hawthorne (1804 – 1864) collected some of his stories as Twice-Told Tales, a volume rich in symbolism and occult incidents. Hawthorne went on to write full-length "romances", quasi-allegorical (类似寓言的) novels that explore such themes as guilt, pride, and emotional repression in his native New England. His masterpiece, *The Scarlet Letter*, is the stark drama of a woman cast out of her community for committing adultery.

Nathaniel Hawthorne
(1804 – 1864)

Hawthorne's fiction had a profound impact on his friend Herman Melville (1819 – 1891), who first made a name for himself by turning material from his seafaring days into exotic and sensational sea narrative novels. Inspired by Hawthorne's focus on allegories and dark psychology, Melville went on to write romances replete with philosophical speculation. In Moby-Dick, an adventurous whaling voyage becomes the vehicle for examining such themes as obsession, the nature of evil, and human struggle against the elements. In another fine work, the short novel Billy Budd,

Melville dramatizes the conflicting claims of duty and compassion on board a ship in time of war. His more profound books sold poorly, and he had been long forgotten by the time of his death. He was rediscovered in the early decades of the 20th century.

Anti-transcendental works from Melville, Hawthorne, and Poe all comprise the Dark Romanticism subgenre of literature popular during this time.

10.2 American Poetry

America's two greatest 19th-century poets could hardly have been more different in temperament and style. Walt Whitman (1819 - 1892) was a working man, a traveler, a self-appointed nurse during the American Civil War (1861 - 1865), and a poetic innovator. His magnum opus(巨著)was *Leaves of Grass*, in which he uses a free-flowing verse and lines of irregular length to depict the all-inclusiveness of American democracy. Taking that motif one step further, the poet equates the vast range of American experience with himself without being egotistical. For example, in *Song of Myself*, the long, central poem in *Leaves of Grass*, Whitman writes: "These are really the thoughts of all men in all ages and lands, they are not original with me ..."

Whitman was also a poet of the body—"the body electric," as he called it. In *Studies in Classic American Literature*, the English novelist D. H. Lawrence wrote that Whitman "was the first to smash the old moral conception that the soul of man is something 'superior' and 'above' the flesh."

Walt Whitman
(1819 - 1892)

Emily Dickinson (1830 - 1886), on the other hand, lived the sheltered life of a genteel unmarried woman in small-townAmherst, Massachusetts. Within its formal structure, her poetry is ingenious, witty, exquisitely wrought, and psychologically penetrating. Her work was unconventional for its day, and little of it was published during her lifetime.

Many of her poems dwell on death, often with a mischievous twist. One, "Because I could not stop for Death," begins, "He kindly stopped for me." The opening of another Dickinson poem toys with her position as a woman in a male-dominated society and an unrecognized poet: "I'm nobody! Who are you? / Are you nobody too?"

American poetry arguably reached its peak in the early to mid 20th century, with such noted writers as Wallace Stevens, Sylvia Plath, Anne Sexton, Ezra Pound, T. S. Eliot, William Carlos Williams, Stephen Vincent Benet, Robert Frost, Carl Sandburg, Robinson Jeffers, Hart Crane, E. E. Cummings, John Berryman, Allen Ginsberg, Robert Lowell, Edna St. Vincent Millay, and many others.

10.3 Realism, Post-World War Ⅱ

Realism, Twain and James

Mark Twain (the pen name of Samuel Langhorne Clemens, 1835 - 1910) was the first major American writer to be born away from the East Coast—in the border state of Missouri. His regional masterpieces were the memoir *Life on the Mississippi* and the novel *Adventures of Huckleberry Finn*. Twain's style—influenced by journalism, wedded to the vernacular(本国语), direct and unadorned but also highly evocative (唤起感情的) and irreverently humorous-changed the way Americans write their language. His characters speak like real people and sound distinctively American, using local dialects, newly invented words, and regional accents. Other writers interested in regional differences and dialect were George W. Cable, Thomas Nelson Page, Joel

Mark Twain
(1835 - 1910)

Chandler Harris, Mary Noailles Murfree (Charles Egbert Craddock), Sarah Orne Jewett, Mary E. Wilkins Freeman, Henry Cuyler Bunner, and William Sydney Porter (O. Henry).

William Dean Howells also represented the realist tradition through his novels, including The Rise of Silas Lapham and his work as editor of the Atlantic Monthly.

Henry James (1843 - 1916) confronted the Old World-New World dilemma by writing directly about it. Although born in New York City, he spent most of his adult years in England. Many of his novels center on Americans who live in or travel to Europe. With its intricate, highly qualified sentences and dissection of emotional and psychological nuance (细微差别), James's fiction can be daunting. Among his more accessible works are the novellas *Daisy Miller*, about an enchanting American girl in Europe, and *The Turn of the Screw*, an enigmatic ghost story.

Turn of the Century

At the beginning of the 20th century, American novelists were expanding fiction's social spectrum to encompass both high and low life and sometimes connected to the naturalist school of realism. In her stories and novels, Edith Wharton (1862 - 1937) scrutinized the upper-class, Eastern-seaboard society in which she had grown up. One of her finest books, *The Age of Innocence*, centers on a man who chooses to marry a conventional, socially acceptable woman rather than a fascinating outsider. At about the same time, Stephen Crane (1871 - 1900), best known for his Civil War novel *The Red Badge of Courage*, depicted the life of New York City prostitutes in Maggie: A Girl of the Streets. And in Sister Carrie, Theodore Dreiser (1871 - 1945) portrayed a country girl who moves to Chicago and becomes a kept woman. Hamlin Garland and Frank Norris wrote about the problems of American farmers and other social issues from a naturalist perspective.

More directly political writings discussed social issues and power of corporations. Some like Edward Bellamy in Looking Backward outlined other possible political and social frameworks. Upton Sinclair, most famous for his meat-packing novel The Jungle, advocated socialism. Other political writers of the period included Edwin Markham, William Vaughn Moody. Journalistic critics, including Ida M. Tarbell and Lincoln Steffens were labeled The Muckrakers. Henry Brooks Adams' literate autobiography, The Education of Henry Adams also depicted a stinging description of the education system and modern life.

Experimentation in style and form soon joined the new freedom in subject matter. In 1909, Gertrude Stein (1874 - 1946), by then an expatriate in Paris, published Three Lives, an innovative work of fiction influenced by her familiarity with cubism, jazz, and other movements in contemporary art and music. Stein labeled a group of American literary notables who lived in Paris in the 1920s and 1930s as the "Lost Generation."

The poet Ezra Pound (1885 - 1972) was born in Idaho but spent much of his adult life in Europe. His work is complex, sometimes obscure, with multiple references to other art forms and to a vast range of literature, both Western and Eastern. He influenced many other poets, notably T. S. Eliot (1888 - 1965), another expatriate. Eliot wrote spare, cerebral poetry, carried by a dense structure of symbols. In The Waste Land, he embodied a jaundiced vision of post-World War I society in fragmented, haunted images. Like Pound's, Eliot's poetry could be highly allusive, and some editions of The Waste Land come with footnotes supplied by the poet. In 1948, Eliot won the Nobel Prize in Literature.

American writers also expressed the disillusionment following upon the war. The stories and novels of F. Scott Fitzgerald (1896 - 1940) capture the restless, pleasure-hungry, defiant mood of the 1920s. Fitzgerald's characteristic theme, expressed poignantly in The Great Gatsby, is the tendency of youth's golden dreams to dissolve in failure and disappointment. Fitzgerald also elucidates the collapse of some key American Ideals, set out in the Declaration of Independence, such as liberty, social unity, good governance and peace, features which were severely threatened by the pressures of modern early 20th century society. Sinclair Lewis and Sherwood Anderson also wrote novels with critical depictions of American life. John Dos Passos wrote about the war and also the USA. trilogy which extended into the Depression.

Ernest Hemingway (1899 - 1961) saw violence and death first-hand as an ambulance driver in World War I, and the carnage persuaded him that abstract language was mostly empty and misleading. He cut out unnecessary words from his writing, simplified the sentence structure, and concentrated on concrete objects and actions. He adhered to a moral code that emphasized grace under pressure, and his protagonists were strong, silent men who often dealt awkwardly with women. *The Sun Also Rises* and *A Farewell to Arms* are generally considered his best novels; in 1954, he won the Nobel Prize in Literature.

Francis Scott Fitzgerald
(1896 - 1940)

Five years before Hemingway, another American novelist had won the Nobel Prize: William Faulkner (1897 - 1962). Faulkner managed to encompass an enormous range of humanity in Yoknapatawpha County, a Mississippian region of his own invention. He recorded his characters' seemingly unedited ramblings in order to represent their inner states, a technique called "stream of consciousness." (In fact, these passages are carefully crafted, and their seemingly chaotic structure conceals multiple layers of meaning.) He also jumbled time sequences to show how the past—especially the slave-holding era of the Deep South—endures in the present. Among his great works are *The Sound and the Fury*, *Absalom, Absalom!*, *Go Down, Moses*, and *The Unvanquished*.(未经修饰的)

Ernest Hemingway in World War I uniform
(1899 - 1961)

Depression-era Literature

Depression era literature was blunt and direct in its social criticism. John Steinbeck (1902 - 1968) was born in Salinas, California, where he set many of his stories. His style was simple and evocative, winning him the favor of the readers but not of the critics. Steinbeck often wrote about poor, working-class people and their struggle to lead a decent and honest life. The Grapes of Wrath, considered his masterpiece, is a strong, socially-oriented novel that tells the story of the Joads, a poor family from Oklahoma and their journey to California in search of a better life. Other popular novels include Tortilla Flat, Of Mice and Men, Cannery Row, and East of Eden. He was awarded the Nobel Prize in Literature in 1962. Other writers sometimes considered part of the proletarian school include Nathanael West, Olive Tilford Dargan, Tom Kromer, Robert Cantwell, and Edward Anderson.

Henry Miller assumed a unique place in American Literature in the 1930s when his semi-autobiographical novels, written and published in Paris, were banned from the US. Although his major works, which include *Tropic of Cancer* and *Black Spring*, would not be cleared for American sale and publication until 1962, their themes and stylistic innovations had already exerted a major influence on succeeding generations of American writers.

Post-World War Ⅱ

The period in time from the end of World War Ⅱ up until, roughly, the late 1960s and early 1970s saw the publication of some of the most popular works in American history. The last few of the more realistic modernists along with the wildly Romantic beatniks largely dominated the period, while the direct respondents to America's involvement in World War Ⅱ contributed in their notable influence.

Though born in Canada, Chicago-raised Saul Bellow would become one of the most influential novelists in America in the decades directly following World War Ⅱ. In works like The Adventures of Augie March and Herzog, Bellow painted vivid portraits of the American city and the distinctive characters that peopled it. Bellow went on to win the Nobel Prize for Literature in 1976.

From J. D. Salinger's Nine Stories and The Catcher in the Rye to Sylvia Plath's The Bell Jar, the perceived madness of the state of affairs in America was brought to the forefront of the nation's literary expression. Émigré(流亡者)

authors such as Vladimir Nabokov, with Lolita, forged on with the theme, and, at almost the same time, the beatniks took a concerted step away from their Lost Generation predecessors, developing a style and tone of their own by drawing on Eastern theology and experimenting with recreational drugs.

The poetry and fiction of the "Beat Generation", largely born of a circle of intellects formed in New York City around Columbia University and established more officially some time later in San Francisco, came of age. The term Beat referred, all at the same time, to the countercultural rhythm of the Jazz scene, to a sense of rebellion regarding the conservative stress of post-war society, and to an interest in new forms of spiritual experience through drugs, alcohol, philosophy, and religion, and specifically through Zen Buddhism. Allen Ginsberg set the tone of the movement in his poem Howl, a Whitmanesque work that began: "I saw the best minds of my generation destroyed by madness ..." At the same time, his good friend Jack Kerouac (1922 - 1969) celebrated the Beats' rollicking(无忧无虑), spontaneous, and vagrant life-style in, among many other works, his masterful and most popular novel *On the Road*.

Regarding the war novel specifically, there was a literary explosion in America during the post-World War Ⅱ era. Some of the best known of the works produced included Norman Mailer's *The Naked and the Dead* (1948), Joseph Heller's *Catch-22* (1961) and Kurt Vonnegut Jr.'s *Slaughterhouse-Five* (1969). *MacBird*, written by Barbara Garson, was another well-received work exposing the absurdity of war. *The Moviegoer* (1962), by Southern author Walker Percy, winner of the National Book Award, was his attempt at exploring "the dislocation of man in the modern age".

Writer Jack Kerouac(1922 - 1969), one of the best-known figures of the Beat Generation

In contrast, John Updike approached American life from a more reflective but no less subversive perspective. His 1960 novel *Rabbit, Run*, the first of four chronicling the rising and falling fortunes of Harry "Rabbit" Angstrom over the course of four decades against the backdrop of the major events of the second half of the twentieth century, broke new ground on its release in its characterization and detail of the American middle class and frank discussion of taboo topics such as adultery. Notable among Updike's characteristic innovations was his use of present-tense narration, his rich, stylized language, and his attention to sensual detail. His work is also deeply imbued with Christian themes. The two final installments of the Rabbit series, *Rabbit is Rich* (1981) and *Rabbit at Rest* (1990), were both awarded the Pulitzer Prize for Fiction. Other notable works include the Henry Bech novels (1970 – 1998), *The Witches of Eastwick* (1984), *Roger's Version* (1986) and *In the Beauty of the Lilies* (1996), which literary critic Michiko Kakutani called "arguably his finest."

Norman Mailer(1923 – 2007)

Frequently linked with Updike is the novelist Philip Roth. Roth vigorously explores Jewish identity in American society, especially in the postwar era and the early 21st century. Frequently set in Newark, New Jersey, Roth's work is known to be highly autobiographical, and many of Roth's main characters, most famously the Jewish novelist Nathan Zuckerman, are thought to be alter egos of Roth. With these techniques, and armed with his articulate and fast-paced style, Roth explores the distinction between reality and fiction in literature while provocatively examining American culture. His most famous work includes the Zuckerman novels, the controversial Portnoy's Complaint (1969), and Goodbye, Columbus (1959). Among the most decorated American writers of his generation, he has won every major American literary award, including the Pulitzer Prize for his major novel

John Updike(1931 – 2009)

American Pastoral (1997).

Ralph Ellison's 1953 novel Invisible Man was instantly recognized as among the most powerful and sensational works of the immediate post-war years. The story of a black man in the urban north, the novel laid bare the often repressed racial tension still prevailing in the nation while also succeeding as an existential character study.

Flannery O'Connor (b. March 25, 1925 in Georgia—d. August 3, 1964 in Georgia) also explored and developed the theme of 'the South' in American literature that was dear to Mark Twain and other leading authors of American literary history (*Wise Blood* 1952; *The Violent Bear It Away* 1960; *Everything That Rises Must Converge*, her best-known short story, and an eponymous collection published posthumously in 1965).

10.4 Contemporary American Literature

Comtemporary American Literature(1970 - 2000)

Though its exact parameters remain debatable, from the early 1970s to the present day the most salient literary movement has been postmodernism. Thomas Pynchon, a seminal practitioner of the postmodern style, drawing on modernist fixtures such as temporal distortion, unreliable narrators and internal monologue and coupling them with distinctly postmodern techniques such as metafiction, absurdist humor and a subversive commingling(混合)of high and low culture, in 1973 published one of the seminal (开创性的) works of postmodernism, Gravity's Rainbow. His other important works include The Crying of Lot 49 (1966) and Mason & Dixon (1997).

Toni Morrison, the most recent American recipient of the Nobel Prize for Literature, writing in the realist tradition in a distinctive poetic and deeply evocative prose style, published her controversial debut novel, The Bluest Eye, to widespread critical acclaim in 1970. Coming on the heels of the signing of the Civil Rights Act of 1965, the novel includes a description of incestuous rape and explores the conventions of beauty established by a historically racist society, painting a portrait of a self-immolating black family in search of beauty in whiteness. Among her best-known novels are *Sula* (1974), *Song of Solomon* (1977), and *Beloved* (1987). The latter was chosen in a 2006 survey conducted by the *New York Times* as the most important work of fiction of the last 25 years.

Toni Morrison(1931 -)

Writing in a lyrical, flowing style that eschews excessive use of the comma and semicolon and recalls William Faulkner and Ernest Hemingway in equal measure, rich with metaphor and polysyndeton, Cormac McCarthy is an author whose oeuvre(艺术作品)seizes on the literary traditions of several regions in the United States and spans multiple genres. He writes in the Southern Gothic aesthetic in his distinctly Faulknerian 1965 debut, *The Orchard Keeper*; in the western tradition in *Blo*od Meridian (1985), which critic Harold Bloom likened to Moby-Dick; in a much more pastoral tone in his celebrated Border Trilogy (1992 - 1998), including All the Pretty Horses (1992), winner of the National Book Award; and in the post-apocalyptic genre in the Pulitzer Prize-winning The Road (2007). His novels are noted for achieving both commercial and literary success, several of his works having been adapted to film.

Don DeLillo, who rose to literary prominence with the publication of his 1985 novel, White Noise, a work broaching the subjects of death and consumerism and doubling as a piece of social criticism, began his writing career in 1971 with Americana. He is listed by Harold Bloom as being among the preeminent contemporary American writers, in the company of such giants as Philip Roth, Cormac McCarthy, and Thomas Pynchon. His 1997 novel Underworld, a gargantuan work chronicling American life through and immediately after the Cold War and examining with equal depth subjects as various as baseball and nuclear weapons, is generally agreed upon to be his masterpiece and was the runner-up in a survey asking writers to identify the most important work of fiction of the last 25 years. Among his other important novels are Libra (1988), Mao Ⅱ (1991) and Falling Man (2007).

Among the younger generation of contemporary American writers, Paul Auster, like Thomas Pynchon an acolyte(随从)of postmodernism, stands out. Known for his experimentation with fragmented narratives, unreliable narrators, metafiction(超小说), intertextuality(互文)and multiple points of view, Auster marries absurdism with elements of crime fiction. A former translator of French literature, he brings to American letters a distinct pool of influences, among them those of Albert Camus, Jacques Derrida and Jean-Paul Sartre on the one hand and pulp fiction writer Dashiell Hammett on the other. Among his most critically successful works are The New York Trilogy (1987), Moon Palace (1989), Leviathan (1992) and Oracle Night (2004). Richard Ford, writing in a much more realist style reminiscent of John Updike and Walker Percy, rose to literary prominence in 1986 with the publication of the acclaimed The Sportswriter, the first of a trio of novels to feature his memorable everyman character Frank Bascombe. The second, Independence Day (1995), would win Ford the Pulitzer Prize for Fiction, and the third, *The Lay of the Land*, was published to critical acclaim in 2006.

Millennial and Immigrant Literature

At the turn of the twenty-first century, several new writers surfaced, drawing on immigrant experiences in an ever more culturally diverse American landscape. Indian-American author Jhumpa Lahiri won the Pulitzer Prize for Fiction for her debut collection of short stories, *Interprete*r of Maladies (1999), and went on to write a well-received novel, The Namesake (2003), which was shortly adapted to film in 2007. In her second collection of stories, Unaccustomed Earth, released to widespread commercial and critical success, Lahiri shifts focus and treats the experiences of the second and third generation.

Chinese-American author Ha Jin in 1999 won the National Book Award for his second novel, Waiting, about a Chinese soldier in the Revolutionary Army who has to wait 18 years to divorce his wife for another woman, all the while having to worry about persecution for his protracted affair, and twice won the PEN/Faulkner Award, in 2000 for Waiting and in 2005 for War Trash. Other notable Asian-American novelists include Amy Tan, best known for her novel, The Joy Luck Club (1989), tracing the lives of four immigrant families brought together by the game of Mahjong; and Maxine Hong Kingston, best known for her memoir, The Woman Warrior (1976), and debut novel, China Men (1980). Dominican-American author Junot Díaz, spurred to writing by Mexican-American author Sandra Cisneros, an icon of an emerging Chicano(墨裔美国人) literature whose 1984 bildungsroman(教育小说) *The House on Mango Street* is taught in schools across the United States, was awarded the Pulitzer Prize for Fiction for his 2007 novel *The Brief Wondrous Life of Oscar Wao*, which tells the story of an overweight Dominican boy growing up as a social outcast in Paterson, New Jersey. Both authors are members of a growing community of Latin American writers and artists.

Other notable writers of the turn of the century include David Foster Wallace, whose 1996 novel Infinite Jest(妙语), a futuristic portrait of America and a withering critique of the media-saturated nature of American existence, has been consistently ranked among the most important works of the twentieth century; Michael Chabon, whose Pulitzer Prize-winning The Amazing Adventures of Kavalier & Clay (2000) tells the story of two friends, Joe Kavalier and Sam Clay, as they rise through the ranks of the comics industry in its heyday; Jonathan Franzen, whose 2001 novel The Corrections, a tragicomedy about the disintegrating Lambert family, won the National Book Award; Richard Russo, author of the Pulitzer Prize-winning Empire Falls (2002), a novel laying bare the mysteries and legacies of the flagging logging and textile industries in the fictional Maine town of Empire Falls; and Marilynne Robinson, whose 2004 novel *Gilead*, a family saga centered around religion and set during the Civil War, was awarded the Pulitzer Prize for Fiction.

Questions

1. Can you introduce some American poets?
2. What is Transcendentalism? Introduce some writers of this movement.
3. What is the poetry and fiction of "Beat Generation"? Introduce some writers who represented it.
4. What is postmodernism? Introduce some writers or works of this

movement.

5. Please introduce American Immigrant literature.

Supplementary Reading 1

Bonds That Seem Cruel Can Be Kind

By Michiko Kakutani

A horrifying act stood at the center of Toni Morrison's 1987 masterwork, "Beloved": a runaway slave, caught in her effort to escape, cuts the throat of her baby daughter with a handsaw, determined to spare the girl the fate she herself has suffered as a slave. A similarly indelible act stands at the center of Ms. Morrison's remarkable new novella, "A Mercy", a small, plangent gem of a story that is, at once, a kind of prelude to "Beloved" and a variation on that earlier book's exploration of the personal costs of slavery — a system that moves men and women and children around "like checkers" and casts a looming shadow over both parental and romantic love.

Set some 200 years before "Beloved", "A Mercy" conjures up the beautiful, untamed, lawless world that was America in the 17th century with the same sort of lyrical, verdant prose that distinguished that earlier novel. Gone are the didactic language and schematic architecture that hobbled the author's 1998 novel, "Paradise"; gone are the cartoonish characters that marred her 2003 novel, "Love". Instead Ms. Morrison has rediscovered an urgent, poetic voice that enables her to move back and forth with immediacy and ease between the worlds of history and myth, between ordinary daily life and the realm of fable.

All the central characters in this story are orphans, cast off by their parents or swept away from their families by acts of God or nature or human cruelty — literal or figurative exiles susceptible to the centrifugal forces of history. There is Jacob, an Anglo-Dutch trader, whose memories of his own parentless years on the streets "stealing food and cadging gratuities for errands" have left him with a "pulse of pity for orphans and strays." There is his wife, Rebekka, who as a girl of 16 was sent abroad to America by her father, who, happy to have one less mouth to feed, readily accepted Jacob's offer of "'reimbursement' for clothing, expenses and a few supplies" in exchange for a "healthy, chaste wife willing to travel abroad." And there is Florens, whose mother sees the kindness in Jacob's heart and begs him to take her young daughter (as payment for a debt owed by their domineering owner) in the hopes that the trader will give her a better life and the possibility of a future as a free woman, not a slave.

But what is "a mercy" to Florens's mother is experienced by the girl as an act of abandonment, and it will leave her with a hole in her heart and an abiding need for love and approval. For a time Florens finds a sense of belonging on Jacob's farm — the illusion, even, of family. Jacob is often away from home doing business, and Rebekka and Lina, the American Indian slave who helped Jacob get the farm started, find the daily hardships of frontier life bringing them together in an alliance of survival that slowly turns into friendship.

Both are wary of the first waif Jacob brings home: a strange, daft girl named Sorrow, who was found half-drowned in a river. Rebekka regards Sorrow as useless around the farm, while Lina, who has survived the devastation of her own tribe by a plague, sees the stranger as "bad luck in the flesh" and blames her for the early deaths of Rebekka's children.

Florens, in contrast, awakens a maternal instinct in Lina, and she embraces the girl as if she were long-lost kin: "A frightened, long-necked child who did not speak for weeks but when she did, her light, singsong voice was lovely to hear. Some how, some way, the child assuaged the tiny yet eternal yearning for the home Lina once knew, where everyone had anything, and no one had everything."

Years later Florens falls passionately in love with a visiting blacksmith, a free black man who has come to work on a fancy gate for Jacob's new house, and who miraculously cures Sorrow of a deathly illness. Lina warns her of the perils of giving away her heart — "You are one leaf on his tree," she says — but Florens insists she is "his tree".

When his work is done, however, the blacksmith leaves without even troubling to say goodbye, and like so many earlier Morrison characters, Florens learns the perils of caring too much — and the legacy of loss and leaving bequeathed to her by her mother.

As long as Jacob is alive, Ms. Morrison writes, "it was easy to veil the truth: that they were not a family — not even a like-minded group." But when he suddenly dies of the pox, and Rebekka, too, falls gravely ill, Lina, Florens and Sorrow realize their precarious position.

"Three unmastered women," alone, "belonging to no one, became wild game for anyone": "Female and illegal, they would be interlopers, squatters, if they stayed on after Mistress died, subject to purchase, hire, assault, abduction, exile." Their one hope is to find the blacksmith and persuade him to return to work his magic on Rebekka. It is Florens who is sent on this quest, her passion for the man both a spur and a hazard to her mission.

The main storyteller in this volume is Florens, who, abandoned by the blacksmith, feels herself "an ice floecut away from the riverbank." But her voice is just one in this choral tale — a tale that not only emerges as a heartbreaking account of lost innocence and fractured dreams, but also stands, with "Beloved," as one of Ms. Morrison's most haunting works yet.

http://www.nytimes.com/2008/11/04/*books*/04*kaku.html*? *ref* = *tonimorrison*

Supplementary Reading 2

Underestimate Poe's Legacy Nevermore

By Michael Frank

Reviewing the life and career of Edgar Allan Poe can be a hall-of-mirrors-like experience. There are as many Poes, it seems, as there are people to make, calumniate and rehabilitate his reputation, with some observers doing double duty as both foe and friend.

There is Poe the hybrid of genius and charlatan whose literary criticism was "the most complete and exquisite specimen of provincialism ever prepared for the edification of men" (Henry James). There is Poe who possesses "the intellect of a highly gifted young person before puberty" yet whose "variety and ardor" of curiosity nevertheless "delight and dazzle" (T. S. Eliot). There is Poe who "endows imagination with Godlike power" and "anticipates the special hell of modern man" (Allen Tate by way of Daniel Hoffman).

There is Poe the poet, Poe the pauper, Poe the mourner, Poe the alcoholic. There is Poe the working writer (less generously referred to as hack) and frequent magazine contributor, and there is Poe the inventor of the detective story and the science-fiction tale and tales of ratiocination. There is the Poe who applied himself to graphology, ciphers, cryptograms, puzzles, labyrinths and mesmerism. There is Poe who quarreled with editors and colleagues, made friends of his enemies and enemies of his friends.

Bringing up the actual man from the erosive, turbulent sea that has been Poe's particularly ill-fated mixture of life and legend is no easy task, but it is one that, in a modest way, the Pierpont Morgan Library has set about doing with "Poe: The Ardent Imagination," an exhibition mounted in commemoration of the 150th anniversary of his death.

Dispelling the Gloom

Edgar Allan Poe had one of the most unfortunate executorial experiences in the history of American letters. He entrusted his posthumous opus to the Rev. Rufus W. Griswold, whose blackening of Poe demonstrated "a sustained hatred," as Auden once put it. Auden characterized Griswold's treatment of Poe as subtle, but it's hard to see much that is subtle in a man who, albeit after praising Poe as a skilled writer of faultless taste, maligned him as erratic, unprincipled and immoral; portrayed him flailing his arms and speaking to spirits; falsified letters to "prove" his treachery to his friends; alleged that he had deserted the Army and had been expelled from a university, and intimated that he was the lover of his mother-in-law, who was also, as it happens, his aunt.

It is little wonder that upon Poe's death a representative obituary (in The New York Daily Tribune) described him as "pale even to ghastliness" and reported that his heart was "gnawed with anguish" and his face "shrouded in gloom," thereby helping to inaugurate the mythic, tortured Poe whom Christine

Nelson, the curator of the exhibition, seeks to rein in with her presentation of manuscripts and memorabilia drawn entirely from the Morgan's collection.

Ms. Nelson follows in the path of other rescuers of Poe, notably Arthur Hobson Quinn, who exposed Griswold's libel; Kenneth Silverman, who is the author of a superb recent biography, "Edgar A. Poe: Mournful and Never-Ending Remembrance," and the poet Daniel Hoffman, whose eccentric "Poe Poe Poe Poe Poe Poe" joins in a jazzed, delirious dance with the man and his work. Ms. Nelson's goal, she said, was "to look at Poe's importance in his own time, when he was a vibrant critic, a vocal magazine writer and a beloved teller of tales." She was less interested in Poe the tragic hero.

This Poe, it turns out, is not substantially represented in the Morgan holdings, which helps Ms. Nelson emphasize the productive over the pained Poe, but the latter does makes an appearance here nonetheless, in sections titled "Love and Death" and "Personal Suffering."

Loss is one of the great unavoidable themes of Poe's life and work. Both of his parents were actors; his father, who drank, abandoned the family, while his mother died of consumption when Poe was a small boy. Separated from his brother and sister, Poe was raised by a foster mother, who also died of consumption, and a foster father, who cruelly rejected the emerging young writer. Loss came again with the early death of Poe's wife, Virginia, who was Poe's first cousin and 13 years old when he married her. At 25 she, too, died of consumption.

"Of all melancholy topics, what, according to the universal understanding of mankind, is the most melancholy?" Poe once famously asked himself. Death was the reply. And when is this most melancholy of topics most poetical? "When it most closely allies itself to Beauty: the death, then, of a beautiful woman is, unquestionably, the most poetical topic in the world."

Declining Explanation

In support of this "most poetical" topic, we see an autograph manuscript of "Tamerlane," the title poem in Poe's first book, which presents the Tartar conqueror's deathbed recollections of young love. Nearby are fair copies of "Ulalume" and "Annabel Lee," two further examples of Poe's death-of-a-beautiful-woman poems. "Ulalume" is accompanied by an interesting letter to

Susan Ingram, who had heard Poe recite the poem in Virginia in September 1849, a month before his death. She asked him to interpret the obtuse verse; he replied with a handsomely penned copy of the poem and a letter gently refusing the task: "I remember Dr. Johnson's bitter and rather just remarks about the folly of explaining what, if worth explanation, should explain itself."

Early in this century, in her advanced old age, Ingram visited J. P. Morgan, who had bought the manuscript from her in 1906, and asked to see it one more time before she died. Thus at least one woman, though no longer young and perhaps not still beautiful, survived to remember Poe and remain attached to him long after he himself had turned to dust.

The living Poe had some palpably hard times, to be sure. He was a "victim of melancholy," says a letter from his employer at The Southern Literary Messenger, where Poe was an editor. He drank, as his father did, but frequently renounced alcohol. In this sad letter to George Eveleth, a medical student admirer, Poe wrote in February 1848: "The causes which maddened me to the drinking point are no more, and I am done drinking, forever." Alas he was not. Later that spring he was observed there by another editor "in a debauch." "No influence was adequate to keep him from the damnable propensity to drink," that editor remarks in a Morgan letter. "He spoke of himself as the victim of a preordained damnation, as lame perdue."

Crackling With Invention

But there were many periods in his life when Poe's soul was found and redeemed and, more than that, when his mind crackled with invention and rigorous (if occasionally loopy) thinking, as case after case at the Morgan attests. A career as fertile and varied as Poe's time and again vanquishes the damnable propensity to (actually, of course, the illness of) drink.

Consider his notes, for example, for a proposed book about the American literary scene. With many deletions and corrections Poe works up "some honest opinions" on the subject. He comes out against the kind of cliquerie represented by the Transcendentalists ("perhaps the worst feature we have") and in favor of establishing international copyright law. He rails against the depreciation of Southern and Western talent, "which upon the whole is greater, more vivid, fresher, than that of the North."

Attuned to the "proverbial sensitiveness of authors," he recognizes the difficulty of writing about his contemporaries, and he considers it a false notion that American writing, good and bad, merits automatic praise. The latter was a principle Poe lived by. He accused Longfellow, a frequent recipient of Poe's lashings, of "affectation and imitation—an imitation sometimes verging on downright theft."

Inventor of Genres

Poe was not all prickles and burrs and barbs. He was the author of the wildly popular "Raven," which, interestingly, made an early appearance on the back page of a newspaper, embedded among ads for pens, Turkish pipe bowls and Southern Balm, "The Great American Remedy." More reverential treatment came in time: translations by Mallarme (who, along with Baudelaire, was among the French writers greatly influenced by Poe); illustrations by Manet, Gustave Dore and even Matisse; bindings tooled and gilded like jewels.

Poe was also of course a pioneer of the short story, in which he believed a certain unique or single effect should be wrought out—and was, by him, in several genres that he virtually created, detective and science fiction among them. The Morgan displays a rare pamphlet copy of "The Murders in the Rue Morgue," stained with brown spots like drops of blood. Nearby is "The Tell-Tale Heart," which first appeared in James Russell Lowell's short-lived magazine The Pioneer.

Hanging by itself, like a hallowed scroll, is "A Tale of the Ragged Mountains," one of several exceedingly curious autograph manuscripts Poe produced for reasons unknown to Ms. Nelson. In his clearest and most crisp adult hand, he wrote out the story on narrow sheets of paper, then joined them together with sealing wax into a long roll that resembles a mummy's bandage or toilet paper.

Poe was a vigorous, disciplined, driven fellow, hard-working, not above taking mundane jobs for money, a tale spinner and sentence weaver to the marrow. He loved, lost, drank, ached and mourned and struggled with a psyche of much complexity. These two Poes, two of dozens to be sure, hover like specters over the glass cases on East 36th Street. But, perhaps ineluctably, none is as haunting as the daguerreotyped(银板照相的) Poe, whose likeness was taken in Providence in 1848, four days after he attempted suicide the year before his death.

Beneath the finely scored surface, a baggy-eyed, heavy-browed, marble-skinned Poe shimmers in silvery enigmatic silence. He had come to Providence to persuade a woman, a fellow writer, Sarah Helen Whitman, to marry him. He had promised to abstain from drink but had broken his pledge and lost his love. Whitman "bade him farewell," she wrote, "with feelings of profound commiseration for his fate."

Ending a visit to the Morgan on this note would affirm the turbulent, troubled Poe. But this man, intricate in courtship as in his other human relations, remains his fierce, slippery, paradoxical self. "From this day forth I shun the pestilential society of literary women," he wrote a friend. "They are a heartless, unnatural, venomous, dishonorable set." He added, "How great a burden is taken off my heart by my rupture with Mrs. W."

Edgar Allan Poe died on Oct. 7, 1849. "Lord help my poor soul" were the last words he spoke.

An Ardent Riddle

"Poe: The Ardent Imagination" is at the Pierpont Morgan Library, 29 East 36th Street, Manhattan, through May 9. Hours: Tuesdays through Thursdays, 10:30 a.m. to 5 p.m.; Fridays, 10:30 a.m. to 8 p.m.; Saturdays, 10:30 a.m. to 6 p.m.; Sundays, noon to 6 p.m.

Admission: $7; $5 for students and the elderly. Information: (212) 685-0008.

Photo: An illustration by Manet for Mallarme's 1875 French translation of "The Raven" is on view in the Poe exhibition at the Pierpont Morgan Library. (The Morgan Library)

*http://www.nytimes.com/*1999/03/19/*books/underestimate-poe-s-legacy-nevermore.html*

Bibliography

[1] http://www.time.com

[2] http://www.npr.org

[3] http://www.nytimes.com

[4] http://www.latimes.com

[5] http://www.economist.com

[6] http://en.wikipedia.org/wiki/Culture_of_the_United_States

[7] http://en.wikipedia.org/wiki/History_of_immigration_to_the_United_States

[8] http://en.wikipedia.org/wiki/Religion_in_the_United_States

[9] http://en.wikipedia.org/wiki/American_politics

[10] http://en.wikipedia.org/wiki/American_society

[11] http://en.wikipedia.org/wiki/History_of_the_United_States

[12] http://en.wikipedia.org/wiki/United_States

[13] http://en.wikipedia.org/wiki/Television_of_the_United_States

[14] http://en.wikipedia.org/wiki/Public_holidays_in_the_United_States

[15] http://en.wikipedia.org/wiki/Education_in_the_United_States

[16] http://en.wikipedia.org/wiki/Media_of_the_United_States

[17] http://en.wikipedia.org/wiki/Ethnic_groups_in_the_United_States

[18] http://en.wikipedia.org/wiki/Cuisine_of_the_United_States

[19] http://en.wikipedia.org/wiki/Cinema_of_the_United_States

[20] http://en.wikipedia.org/wiki/Geography_of_the_United_States

[21] http://oregonstate.edu/instruct/ed416/module1.html

[22] http://www.internationalstudentguidetotheusa.com/articles/american_education_system.php

[23] http://www.pbs.org/kcet/publicschool/

[24] http://www.hermes-press.com/education_index.htm

[25] http://articles. cnn. com/2009-03-09/living/us. religion. less. christian_1_american-religious-identification-survey-christian-nation-evangelical? _s=PM:LIVING

[26] http://newsjunkiepost. com/2011/04/05/us-politics-a-pseudo-two-party-system-where-the-left-has-no-voice/

[27] http://www. nytimes. com/2011/04/08/us/08florida. html? ref=politics

[28] http://www. koreatimes. co. kr/www/news/opinon/2011/04/137_84302. html

[29] http://www. bbc. co. uk/news/world-us-canada-12925299

[30] http://www. economist. com/node/18488452

[31] http://online. wsj. com/article/SB10001424052748703806304576245030067903412. html

[32] http://www. csmonitor. com/The-Culture/Arts/2011/0406/The-war-that-made-us-we

[33] http://www. time. com/time/business/article/0,8599,2063693,00. html

[34] http://www. time. com/time/specials/packages/0, 28757, 2012721, 00. html

[35] Aguirre, Adalberto Jr. et al. *American Ethnicity*. New York: McGraw-Hill, Inc. , 1995

[36] Binder, Frederick M. , ed. *The Way We Lived*, 2 *vols.*, 2*nd edition*. D. C. Health And Company, 1992

[37] Burns, James MacGregor et al. *Government by the People*, 14*th edition*. New Jersey: Prentice Hall, 1990

[38] Cantor, Norman F. *The American Century: Varieties of Culture in Modern Times*. New York: Harper Collins Publisher, 1997

[39] Doyle, Roger. *The Atlas of Contemporary America: Portrait of a Nation*. New York: Facts on File, Inc. , 1994

[40] Luedtke, Luther S. ed. *Making America: The Society and Culture of the United States*. Washington D. C. : United States Information Agency, 1992

[41] McElroy, John Harmon. *American Beliefs: What Keeps a Big Country and a Diverse People United*, Chicago: Ivan R. Dee, 1999

[42] Stewart, Edward C. et al. *American Cultural Patterns: A Cross-Cultural*

Perspective, *revised edition*, Yarmouth, Maine: Intercultural Press, Inc., 1991

[43] Takaki, Ronald. *A Different Mirror*: *A History of Multicultural America*. Boston: Little, Brown & Company, 1993

[44] Stevenson, DK. *American Life and Institutions*. United States Information Agency, 1989

[45] 王恩铭. *American Culture and Society*. 上海:上海外语教育出版社,2009

[46] 朱永涛. 英美文化基础教程. 北京:外语教学与研究出版社,1991

[47] 刘春伟. 英语国家人文知识概况. 北京:机械工业出版社,2006

[48] 周书麟. 新编英美概况教程. 北京:北京大学出版社,2004

[49] 袁明著. 美国文化与社会. 北京:北京大学出版社,2003

[50] 狄艳华. 美国文化. 长春:吉林科学技术出版社,2002

[51] 周静琼. 当代美国概况. 上海:上海教育出版社,2003

[52] 王九萍. 英美概况. 西安:西安交通大学出版社,2009

[53] 来安方. 英美文化与国家概况. 上海:复旦大学出版社,2008

[54] 常耀信. 美国文学简史. 天津:南开大学出版社,1990

[55] 李延年. 英美概况. 长沙:国防科技大学出版社,2004